GOODBYE, GUNS N' ROSES

GOODBYE, GUNS N' ROSES

THE CRIME, BEAUTY, AND AMPLIFIED CHAOS OF AMERICA'S MOST POLARIZING BAND

ART TAVANA

Copyright © Art Tavana, 2021

Published by ECW Press
665 Gerrard Street East
Toronto, Ontario, Canada M4M 1Y2
416-694-3348 / info@ecwpress.com

Editor for the Press: Michael Holmes
Cover design: Made by Emblem
Cover illustration by Matt Mahurin

PRINTED AND BOUND IN CANADA

LIBRARY AND ARCHIVES CANADA CATALOGUING IN PUBLICATION

Title: Goodbye, Guns N' Roses : the crime, beauty, and
amplified chaos of America's most polarizing band /
Art Tavana.

Names: Tavana, Art, author.

Identifiers: Canadiana (print) 2020038578X | Canadiana
(ebook) 20200385968

ISBN 978-1-77041-511-9 (HARDCOVER)
ISBN 978-1-77305-726-2 (EPUB)
ISBN 978-1-77305-727-9 (PDF)
ISBN 978-1-77305-728-6 (KINDLE)

Subjects: LCSH: Guns n' Roses (Musical group) | LCSH:
Guns n' Roses (Musical group)—Influence. | LCSH: Rock
musicians—United States—Biography. | LCSH: Popular
culture—United States. | LCGFT: Biographies.

Classification: LCC ML421.G976 T231 2021 | DDC
782.42166092/2—dc23

PRINTING: FRIESENS 5 4 3 2 1

"We have a theory that crime enhances one's beauty."

—*Female Trouble* (1974)

TABLE OF CONTENTS

PROLOGUE   IX

1: FAILURE TO COMMUNICATE   1

2: FACES OF DEATH   35

3: RUNNIN' WITH THE DEVIL   48

4: NOT A GLAM BAND   72

5: SWEET CHILD O'DIE   116

6: DAYS OF THUNDER   140

7: ONE IN A MILLION   163

8: STAR-SPANGLED DANGER   192

9: PUMP UP THE VOLUME   204

10: BETTER OFF DEAD   238

PROLOGUE

The following is not a traditional rock bio. This book won't fit neatly among the oft-romanticized canon of exposés and coffee-table books. While I've produced a sweeping history on the subject, that was not my initial quest. This book began as a self-interrogation of taste; to wrestle with whether Guns N' Roses is or is not art. It would evolve into a deconstruction of myth that melds popular culture with my second-generation MTV eyes.

Its title, *Goodbye, Guns N' Roses*, has no purpose beyond a fitting substitute for an epilogue. I have chosen it for that reason.

1

FAILURE TO COMMUNICATE

"All I could think of was getting back into the jungle," Willard says to himself, with the sun bleeding through the venetian blinds of his Saigon hotel. What we see are the illuminated eyes of a caged animal. We hear Jim Morrison's poetry echoing through the rotating blades of a ceiling fan. Willard looks at himself in a mirror and caresses himself like Axl Rose under the gaze of Herb Ritts. When he sees himself "getting softer," he punches his reflection with his naked fist, shattering the glass, as the blood trickles into his palms—making a beast of himself to kill the pain, as Samuel Johnson may have described it. Willard smears the blood over his face. He does martial arts poses in his underwear. He's forgotten how to live outside the theater of war. He's transformed into the beast.

Actor Martin Sheen (Willard) wasn't merely acting; he was showing us what it felt like as the walls began to close in on his stressed heart. Sheen was so deep in the method that he had begun to go mad. He was drinking himself blind, chain-smoking Camel cigarettes, and inching closer to his breaking point. One day on the set, he would feel a sharp pain in his elbow. The feeling slithered into his chest like the venom from a poisonous snake. It was 1976, and Martin Sheen would experience a nearly fatal heart attack

1

on the set of Francis Ford Coppola's *Apocalypse Now* (1979). He was read his last rites by a Catholic priest. Sheen was 36 years old, which is roughly the same age Guns N' Roses guitarist Slash was when doctors discovered that his heart was swollen, giving him weeks to live before installing a defibrillator to keep his heart from going limp. In 2001, Slash, 36, nearly experienced a heart attack while playing with Michael Jackson in Madison Square Garden.

"Once I get up onstage my heart rate skyrockets," Slash told a British reporter in 2009. "When I took the stage with Michael and got into it, I was suddenly hit in the chest by a shock and my vision flooded with electric blue light." It was the first concert since his operation. The stage was Slash's theater of war. Willard was lost without the theater of war. For Slash, an arena filled with roaring fans was his mission. "If I don't play, I'll be a junkie," he told *Kerrang!* in 1996.

"I'll stress over anything that slows me down," Slash told *Rolling Stone* in 1991, referring to the end of their tour in 1988, and the bone-freezing anxiety of being a junkie without a distraction. Imagine, for a moment, Slash walking out of the shower with a white towel wrapped around his mane, like one of Helmut Newton's models, with his wet curls dripping onto his brown skin. Picture him grabbing a rumpled pack of cigarettes and lighting one up like a crackling Marlboro ad, as he would often do, crossing his hairless legs like a painter studying the brushstrokes on his canvas. Slash would pinch the cigarette between his thick lips and use both hands to pull his hair into a ponytail. This is how I imagine Slash being interviewed by *Rolling Stone* in his hotel room. "All of a sudden we got off the road," he told the reporter, "and it was like wind and fucking tumbleweed."

During the doldrums following a series of concerts with the Rolling Stones in 1989, Slash would check into a luxurious bungalow in Arizona (on an exclusive golf resort), and professionally, as if he were a hitman unpacking his silencer, begin to shoot himself up with a speedball. "I could think of no better therapy than shooting coke and smack all night to soothe my soul," he wrote in his 2008 autobiography. Slash would inject so much of it into his body that the shadows inside his bungalow began to animate across the walls. "I started shadowboxing with monsters . . . I was bobbing and weaving." In the morning, Slash would take a hot shower and try to forget his hallucinogenic self-persecution. The curtains extinguished sunlight from illuminating his air-conditioned dungeon. As Slash showered, the steam triggered more hallucinations, as tiny shadows formed behind the thick fog of his glass shower door. "I wasn't going to let them get me, so I punched them as hard as I could, sending the entire pane of glass into pieces all over the floor." With his guitar-playing hands sliced and bleeding all over the floor, Slash once again began to see small creatures, who were now holding machine guns at the doorway. He was tripping on his own demons, like Willard in Saigon. "I decided to flee," Slash wrote. "I broke through the sliding-glass door, cutting myself further and spraying debris all over the room." He would run out of the bungalow and sprint into another bungalow, naked, grabbing an aghast hotel maid and using her as a shield. Sweating profusely, Slash would dash past the monsters and shelter himself inside a shed on a fairway, where he'd hide behind a lawnmower and wait for the creatures to disappear. Sweating, waiting, and wondering what was real, and was not, Slash's Vietnam would become the purgatory between sober reality and druggified illusion (i.e., the jungle).

Apocalypse Now screenwriter John Milius once described Vietnam as a "psychedelic war." The film uses tribal drums and saturated colors to create a surrealistic nightmare. For Slash, his "psychedelic war" was filled inside a needle. The film is introduced with colorful smoke that lulls the viewer into the narcotic and slithering guitar on The Doors' "The End," which trickles over the mustard-colored smoke rising towards the lush palm trees of Vietnam. This is the first scene, as a thrumming helicopter transforms into a musical instrument that accompanies Morrison as he reminds us that this is, in fact, the end, which was the lyrical progenitor of Axl Rose inviting us into his jungle, baby, and informing us that we were about to die. Axl once said that Paul McCartney's "Live and Let Die" shared a bloodline with "Welcome to the Jungle"; separated by two decades, "The End" could be viewed as the more Eastern-sounding prequel to "Welcome to the

Jungle." Though DNA evidence doesn't directly link Coppola's *Apocalypse Now* to Guns N' Roses, it is a film that showed a side of Vietnam that was foreign to most Americans. "Welcome to the Jungle" showed a side of an urban jungle that was foreign to outsiders. It's a song that doesn't offer a shamanic voyage through Williams Blake's doors of perception (later psychedelicized by Aldous Huxley). "Welcome to the Jungle" is a concrete death sentence in a suffocating dystopia. Los Angeles in 1985 was a hedonistic version of the sweaty Midwestern city in John Huston's heist film *The Asphalt Jungle* (1950), where a professional safecracker informs us, "If you want fresh air, don't look for it in this town."

There was no fresh air in the polluted landscape of Los Angeles circa 1985. By 1987, lung autopsies showed that an estimated 27 percent of Angelenos would die with "severely damaged" lungs. "Welcome to the Jungle" is a song that fills your lungs like pollution in the city, or napalm in the jungle, as Slash's guitar stabs your senses with a series of intense daggers. The opening riff is melted down by Axl Rose's scorching yell. It's a machine gun–like screech that sounds terrifying at close range, like the sound of a subway car whizzing past your nose. But Axl's youthful falsetto was detached from any form of modern transit; it felt wobbly, with rivets popping off, as the windows exploded off the frames. He was using his voice to assert control over his uncontrollable moods—turning himself into a beast in the process. Axl wailing would boil his years of internalized trauma. If Jim Morrison was rewriting his childhood through French poetry and sloshed interpretations of the blues, 20 years later Axl Rose was hurling death threats at his audience. For Axl Rose, it began with a need to obliterate, not self-identify, or explore a childlike desire for adventure, like Morrison had. Axl Rose was Jim Morrison as an ex-con warning the cops, teachers, and priests that "no one here gets out alive." He was Rorschach impolitely screaming at other prisoners that he wasn't locked up with them, but that they were locked up with *him*. Morrison wanted us to find some kind of meaning in the melancholy. What Axl wanted was never entirely clear. His philosophy was nihilism as a moving target. He was collateral damage for Vietnam and America's gun-toting military industrial complex. On "Welcome to the

Jungle," the transition from Axl's flamethrower vocals is met with Steven Adler's exploding drums, followed by Slash's guitar rumbling like an army jeep bouncing around a charred war zone. "'Welcome to the Jungle' is an introduction to Guns N' Roses," Slash told a crowd at the Troubadour on July 20, 1985. Like Willard, Slash is a blunt instrument that burns through the jungle to reveal its hidden layers.

The tension in the opening scene of *Apocalypse Now* is transitioned by raining napalm that transforms a verdure jungle into a skin-melting succession of fireballs. The deeper we go into the jungle with Willard, the closer we get to accepting the lunacy of a lieutenant colonel who slaughters civilians to clear a beach for surfing. In the most exhilarating high spot of the film, we find ourselves hypnotized at the barrel of a machine gun being unleashed on a village of innocent schoolchildren, which is scored by Wagner's "Ride of the Valkyries." The nihilism is found in the safe distance between the celluloid experience and the reality of Vietnam as a homicidal playground. In the same way that a suspension of morality is required to digest the orgy of indecency included in *Appetite for Destruction*, there's almost no way to savor the cinematic madness of *Apocalypse Now* without abandoning logical reasoning and simply allowing the blood to wash over you like a crimson ocean wave. *Appetite for Destruction* asks us not to "turn on, tune in, drop out" like Timothy Leary on LSD, but to disconnect from morality like a numb GI who's submitted himself to General Westmoreland's credo to "search and destroy." Guns N' Roses were completely devoid of psychedelia or any of its brain-altering benefits. They were more fascist than hippie (though they don't fit neatly into either category).

To be able to appreciate this band, you have to be drunk; not literally drunk, but drunk like Baudelaire or the New Hollywood filmmaker who did not allow morality to inhibit their senses. You have to relinquish any sense of obligation you may have for the causalities and collateral damage found in the tracks on *Appetite for Destruction*, which include unsimulated sex on the bridge of "Rocket Queen," the junky nightmare of "Mr. Brownstone," and sexual sadism of "It's So Easy," which is a song Axl Rose would described as "art," which bassist Duff McKagan co-wrote, along with both friend West Arkeen and Slash. Duff's bumblebee bass, the most memorable instrument on the track, sounds like rounds being pumped out of an M60 machine gun. You want to dance along to it. It also feels wrong. It feels forbidden. You have to be drunk, as Baudelaire put it, so you don't break your back under the weight of obscenity that reads like D.H. Lawrence without the camouflage of pipe-burning tobacco smoke rising over the winged tips of a Chesterfield chair. There's no brandy snifter in the Guns N' Roses drawing room; it offers only high camp, violence, exploding canons of cum, and the frustrated desk carvings of a juvenile delinquent still incapable of verbalizing his angst. It is a rejection of the puritanism of the religious right, which comes through in Colonel Kurtz (Marlon Brando) in *Apocalypse Now* criticizing the US Army's hypocrisy: "We train young men to drop fire on people, but their commanders won't allow them to write 'fuck' on their airplanes because it's obscene."

He sounds almost like a rock star protesting the military industrial complex. Bear in mind that while Guns N' Roses are art, like *Apocalypse Now*, they're a tawdry and exploitive form of art, like a lowbrow John Carpenter that should never be consumed with high-minded expectations. Guns N' Roses produce adrenaline and a "time bomb of insanity," which ticks through their canon, which is how Tom Snyder described Charles Manson in 1981. The lyrics of *Appetite for Destruction* are appalling in their view of women, as they practically promote sexual assault and general unlawfulness with the titillating insensitivity of an Andrew Dice Clay nursery rhyme. Prepare yourself for shock. In order to digest the fact that most of their lyrics are derived from a medieval view of the opposite sex, you have to translate it as absurdism or black humor, like Paul Verhoeven's sociopathic criminal Clarence Boddicker walking into a room in *RoboCop* (1987) and saying, "Bitches, leave." If you do not suspend your moral judgment when listening to *Appetite for Destruction*, at least temporarily, you simply cannot listen to Guns N' Roses with any sense of authentic pleasure. To really dig their oeuvre, you have to put ethics in a subordinate position to guiltless pleasure, hyper-masculinity, and campy debauchery. It's not an easy thing to do if you're under the age of 40. But you must try to relinquish your sense of righteousness when consuming Guns N' Roses. The reasons are myriad. Take for instance bassist Duff McKagan, who once described a night on the town with Guns N' Roses as a hard-partying take on Westmoreland's sickening motto: "Rape, pillage, *search*, destroy," he told *Music Connection* reporter Karen Burch in 1986, which could have been a nod to the Stooges' "Search and Destroy," in which Iggy expresses his frustration with the system. *Appetite for Destruction* expresses disgust with the establishment while reveling in its collateral damage. It offers an apolitical and almost meaningless reaction to yuppies with gold cards, which had become a cliché in 1987 with the slicked-back ambition of *Wall Street*. Guns N' Roses were the anti-Talking Heads. They were corporate America's aborted fetus talking back to its target demographic the brutal satire of a Verhoeven film. "You're all alone," says an unemployed person in *RoboCop*. "It's the law of the jungle."

Appetite for Destruction is a morally bankrupt reaction to the intelligentsia, like the milkaholic "droogs" from *A Clockwork Orange* (1971) breaking into the home of an author and sexually assaulting his wife. To really listen to Guns N' Roses, you have to accept them as lowbrow art in the lurid tradition of libidinous American cartoonist Robert Crumb and the sexist tropes found in 20th century pulp art. *Appetite for Destruction* is probably more nihilistic than the Stooges' *Raw Power*, which was released on February 7, 1973. A few weeks earlier, President Richard Nixon had spoken to the American people from behind the Resolute desk, as the camera zoomed in on his face as he told us that he was bringing our boys home. In 1973, when combat units began to withdraw from Vietnam, Axl Rose was an 11-year-old product of the Pentecostal Church in Lafayette, a small town in Indiana that has gained mythological importance in the Guns N' Roses story. Before going deeper into the jungle, it's important that we retrace Axl's path from Middle Indiana to the asphalt jungle of Los Angeles.

Lafayette is a dusty small town located in the corn belt of Middle Indiana, where the Wabash River separates the lower-middle-class east with the west. The west is the property of professionals and college students attending Purdue University. Axl Rose grew up in the east, which is littered with corn syrup plants and working-class white men working on greasy engine parts on their driveways. The Ku Klux Klan has old roots in Middle Indiana.

Gathering dust somewhere is a remarkable photo of Axl obediently reading the Bible in church. In the photo, Axl Rose is wearing a striped T-shirt, with ginger hair styled into a thick bowl cut. He's probably 10 years old. When he was a teenager, Axl grew his red hair below his shoulders, which made him a target of intense bigotry. Axl was called both a "faggot" and a "punk" for looking the way he did (slender, green-eyed, feral, possessing a feminine allure) and for believing that the prog-tinged and majestic *Queen II* was the best album in history. When a fearlessly androgynous Mick Jagger tongued Ronnie Wood's lips on *Saturday Night Live* in 1978, teens who listened to the Stones became victims of homophobic bullying. Axl Rose listened to the Stones. Middle Indiana was too small for an ambitious artist like Axl Rose. He felt unwelcome in his conservative village, like the gay men and women who'd walk into the West Hollywood Barney's Beanery and notice a wooden sign hanging under a row of beer bottles: "Faggots—Stay Out." (After years of protests, that sign was finally removed in 1985, right when Guns N' Roses began to play clubs in Hollywood.)

This was the intolerant "Mayberry," where Bill Bailey was born and raised. This was where he became the longhair backpacking through a small town, like John Rambo, who found himself handcuffed by a lawman who viewed him, and those like him, as the reason why America failed in Vietnam. To exorcise his internal rage, Axl would get wasted and throw trash cans through windows on Main Street, Lafayette. Tippecanoe County Court records show him spending 10 days in county jail between July 1980 and September 1982. Originally shared by John Jeremiah Sullivan in *The Paris Review*, there are two infamous mug shots of Axl Rose from those years: one shows him in a flannel shirt from July 1980, where he looks like David Cassidy as a gas station attendant, and another from 1982, where his hair is long and wavy and he's wearing a denim jacket over a nude chest. In the second photo, he looks more like a stoned Leif Garrett. Axl Rose would be charged with battery, public drunkenness, and trespassing. He was arrested four times before his 18th birthday. In 2008, Larry Getlen at the *New York Post* reported that at 16, Axl got drunk and threw a beer bottle at a cop. Then he punched a guy so hard that his teeth fell down his throat. When he was around 18, according to his ex-girlfriend Gina Siler in a *Spin* interview from 1991, Axl showed up to her 17th birthday party wearing a long trench coat and black sunglasses, with his collar popped like Michael Douglas on the VHS cover of *Black Rain* (1989). Axl was trying to evade arrest.

In 1982, when he was 20, Axl would skip town and head west in an effort to dodge arrest warrants and overwhelming amounts of Middle American prejudice. It wasn't the first time. "It's not a whole lot to do there," Axl told reporter Steve Harris during a phone interview in 1987. "And I don't get along with the law there. I get thrown in jail all the time and usually it's for something I didn't do, so then I had to pay lawyer fees to get my way out of court."

Baudelaire famously wrote that genius is childhood recalled at will. For Axl Rose, genius was childhood *trauma* being loaded into a grenade and tossed into a crowd of people he viewed as either elitists or puritans. He was rebelling with fistfuls of childhood trauma.

Fame, Father Time, and trauma would transform the youthful Axl Rose mug shot into a redneck eccentric on February 10, 1998. In terms of Axl mug shots, the most notorious is probably from 1998, when Axl, with slightly thinning hair and more poundage hanging over his cheeks, was arrested in Phoenix's Sky Harbor Airport for disorderly conduct that included, of all things, angrily threatening a security guard for mishandling a glass object. "I'll punch your lights out right here and right now," he told security, as reported in *Rolling Stone* in May 2000 (with Sarah Michelle Gellar on the cover). He was wearing jeans, a red sweatshirt, and a gray beanie. "I don't give a fuck who you are. You are all little people on a power trip."

Axl was booked for a few hours before getting on a flight from Phoenix to Los Angeles. While he was in the air, his team worked diligently to suppress the mug shot from landing in the tabloids. When they failed to prevent the photo from metastasizing, they resorted to more clandestine tactics to prevent Axl Rose from discovering how far it had spread. "He was worried that people would notice his hair was thinning, but he was wearing a hat. It was hat hair," said Kim Estlund, the publicist who worked closely with Axl at the time. It seems Axl was concerned that the unflattering mug shot would be the first image the mainstream public would see of him in at least four years. It was, but there were two jobs on the line to make sure Axl didn't erupt into an apoplectic rage: Geffen publicist Kim Estlund and Axl's manager, Elizabeth "Beta" Lebeis, the former nanny of Axl's ex-girlfriend Stephanie Seymour. Estlund and Lebeis decided to coordinate a plan where they would enter Axl's Malibu mansion, change his satellite dish codes, and then hope that Axl wouldn't be able to see himself on the nightly news. If he did, he would have unraveled like Judy Garland reading her ruinous newspaper headlines. The plan worked. "By the time he figured out the codes were changed, the whole thing would have blown over and he wouldn't have cared. We just needed to make sure he didn't lose it right when he got home," said Estlund.

The peculiar object Axl was so possessive over is said to have been a blown-glass plate or spherical object of some kind—a spiritual birthday present from the whispering canyons of Sedona, Arizona, where Axl was visiting his guru, Sharon Maynard, who was nicknamed "Yoda" by those in his inner circle. Yoda's been described as both a psychic and a New Age charlatan who drained Axl's fortune into the energy vortexes of Sedona's red-rock canyons. Yoda is said to have sold Axl a large quantity of herbal wraps, skin treatments, mud baths, and a $72,000 exorcism, or as Axl described it, "work on my skin," which was reported in *Rolling Stone* on May 11, 2000. She also claimed to have mystical powers that included inspecting photographs of people in order to analyze "their essence, their auras, whatever, it doesn't matter; if Yoda didn't approve, you didn't get to be part of Axl's inner circle," former Geffen A&R rep Tom Zutaut told me. Their relationship dated back to the early '90s, when Axl began to practice past-life regression with his therapist, Suzy London, which included intense sessions of regression therapy (which is different from past-life regression) that would reveal to him that he was sodomized at the age of two by his biological father. Yoda, according to one source, received as much as $35,000 per month for her additional services. "I met with Yoda in Sedona," said Zutaut, who attended one of Yoda's retreats. "I believe she was trying to navigate Axl through his mental illness, and I believe she had a gift." Former manager Doug Goldstein claims Axl Rose spent "millions" on Yoda. Sharon Maynard is thanked in the liner notes of *Chinese Democracy* *("In Memory of Sharon Maynard")*. The only available photo of her depicts a short woman with her hair up in a bun. She is not the micro-celebrity who Suzy London would become, as London would immortalize herself as Axl's therapist in real life and in the music video for "Don't Cry."

Today, the only evidence we have to verify whether Axl was molested by his biological father is through the unsound methods of regression therapy and the questionable work of Suzy London, Yoda, and Axl Rose's eccentric views regarding reincarnation and past lives. While past-life regression is based on the reincarnation hypothesis—which Axl seems to have believed in—age regression therapy is the likely method he used to uncover childhood memories of abuse. One reporter has questioned Axl's *experience*. In a *Musician* interview from June 1992, interviewer Bill Flanagan pressed Axl to explain how uncovering memories in the subconscious could be considered confirmation of actual molestation or rape. To be clear, I'm skeptical of regression therapy and hypnosis, but I'm also a believer: something did happen to Axl when he was a child, but what that was, exactly, depends on your trust in the methodology Axl used to recover those childhood memories.

"I have a lot of corroboration from people who knew something horrible happened," Axl told Flanagan. "Even now I could talk about it with my grandmother and she'd nod her head, yes, but would not talk about it." Flanagan described Axl's therapist as a "phony medium." I choose to view Axl through the lens of Sinéad O'Connor, who said Axl seemed like someone she would, "bring him home and give him a bowl of soup." To others he was a vulnerable millionaire who had been hypnotized to believe that he could leap between lifetimes. Taken from a deposition recorded in

1994, Erin Everly, Axl Rose's ex-wife who alleged the singer had battered and sexually assaulted her, claimed that Axl believed in the existence of past lives. "Axl had told me that in a past life we were Indians and that I killed our children and that's why he was so mean to me in this life." Erin Everly revealed that Axl believed his body was possessed by John Bonham, the deceased drummer of Led Zeppelin. She also claimed that when their dogs died, Axl said that he had their souls transferred into new puppies.

Axl Rose has purposefully evaded publicly talking about his spiritual views. Like Tom Cruise in the early '90s, I believe Axl is shrewdly aware that some of his peculiar beliefs could hurt his box-office appeal among his "rockist" fans. The lack of transparency has forced fans to formulate bizarre conspiracy theories. Some of them are worth retelling for their sheer imagination. In February 2001, former Geffen A&R executive Tom Zutaut was asked by Interscope-Geffen head Jimmy Iovine to fly to Los Angeles to help Axl complete an album that had been in the works for seven years (i.e., *Chinese Democracy*).

By this point, Axl had been estranged from Slash for five years. He had also issued an informal edict that Slash's name was never to be said in his presence. According to Tom Zutuat, Axl Rose once believed that Saul Hudson [Slash] had died, and that a demon had taken over his body. Axl Rose is said to have believed that even a phone call from Slash could infiltrate his aura and "possess his soul." One day, circa 2001, at his recording studio, Zutaut's phone began to ring. It was Slash. Axl is rumored to have grabbed the phone and thrown it out of the room, believing that Slash would infiltrate his body through the cellular device. A similar account appears in *Rolling Stone*, where a confidant told the reporter that Axl believed people were trying to find ways to "control his energy." This story is obviously apocryphal, but the source is reliable, and more importantly—and this is *really* important to understanding Guns N' Roses—there are a lot of people who know it, retell it at Guns N' Roses' gigs, and want to believe it's true. Additional conspiracy theories include Zutaut's claim that Axl Rose believes that Saul Hudson's soul escaped his body when he experienced cardiac arrest for eight minutes, which was replaced with a sinister imposter. Zutaut's also suggested that Axl believes that Slash's soul now inhabits the body of a crow. While all of this sounds like a really distorted interpretation of *The Crow* (1994), it's actually consistent with Erin Everly's sworn deposition, in which she claimed that Axl once insisted that he had transferred the souls of their dead puppies into new ones. This is a portion of the deposition, which appeared in *Spin* in 1999:

"Axl's beliefs were different than mine . . . . [After my dogs died] Axl believed that he had the dogs' souls transferred [into new dogs] . . . . He said I wasn't appreciative that he had given me the opportunity to have [our dogs] Torque and Geneva back, and that I should call [the new dogs] Torque and Geneva."

Axl's fictile-minded receptiveness to what *Rolling Stone* described as the "New Age fringe," and his refusal to elaborate on his own beliefs, has created a vacuum that's often filled with stories that depict Axl as a detached Malibu eccentric. He wasn't always this way. In his 1976 junior high yearbook photo, Axl Rose looked like the adorable little demon from the *Twilight Zone*'s "It's a Good Life" episode. In other childhood photos, he's dressed like Raggedy Andy. In a few others, he looks like the incorrigible redhead from 1990's *Problem Child*. As a he grew up, Axl would become the personification of the tagline on the movie poster for *Problem Child*: "Attila the Hun. Ivan the Terrible. Al Capone. They were all seven once."

Axl would mature to become his band's Ayatollah, which is a nickname he earned following the emergence of the Ayatollah Khomeini in Iran, who had engineered the overthrow of the Shah (Iran's King) in 1979. The Ayatollah would institute an Islamic autocracy where he was given the title of "Supreme Leader." The Ayatollah was *Time*'s "Man of the Year" in 1979. By the mid-1980s, his thick arching eyebrows and ancient beard had become the avatar of evil in the Reagan era. In American popular culture, the Ayatollah had become omnipresent. In *Back to the Future Part II*, he appears as a digital waiter in a retro '80s café. For Slash and Izzy Stradlin, Ayatollah was a synonym for "dictator," which is what Axl Rose had become by the late-80s.

"Axel is just another version of the Ayatollah," Slash said in a 1986

Music Connection interview (where the spelling of Axl Rose's first name appeared as "Axel.").

Doing press for the Monsters of Rock Festival in England in 1988, Axl told a reporter that a band is a "political thing" and that an album is a band's "political stance." That's what made him different from the rest of his bandmates, who viewed Guns N' Roses as an entirely apolitical band. Keep this in mind as we travel through the biography of a band that consistently failed to form a cohesive political agenda.

We have to investigate the small-town roots of their co-founder in order to understand how their contradictory identities were forged. Here is guitarist Izzy Stradlin describing what it was like growing up in Lafayette, which evokes the eerie vacantness of Peter Bogdanovich's *The Last Picture Show* (1971). "It was cool growing up there. There's a courthouse and a college, a river and railroad tracks. It's a small town, so there wasn't much to do. We rode bikes, smoked pot, got into trouble—it was pretty *Beavis and Butt-Head*, actually." This is the America that was left behind in a dustbin of Bibles, flags, guns, and abandoned factories. It was where Izzy would slack off in skintight T-shirts, with shoulder-length hair and bell-bottom jeans, ordering slices of pizza at Arni's and smoking joints at Columbian Park like a Midwestern Spicoli. Lafayette adolescents would often congregate in the parking lot of a frozen custard shop located behind Axl's grandmother's house. According to John Jeremiah Sullivan in *The Paris Review*, Axl was arrested in the same parking lot after striking a woman with a splint on his arm (hitting her with the splint).

Though some have suggested that Izzy was born in Florida, all the available evidence indicates that he was born in Lafayette, Indiana, on April 8, 1962, east of the Wabash River at a time when train tracks ran through the city's downtown. His full name is Jeffrey Dean Isbell. His father was an Alcoa plant worker, his mother a telephone operator. They filed for a marriage license in Tippecanoe County on August 10, 1961. Public records show that Izzy's great-great-great-great-great-grandfather was Captain Godfrey Isbell, a North Carolina militiaman who fought in the Revolutionary War.

Izzy would provide his first impression of William "Bill" Bailey, which happened on their first day of their ninth grade at Jefferson High, or "Jeff," as the students called it. "I hear this noise going on in front and then I see these fucking books fling past," Stradlin told *Musician's* Mark Rowland in 1988. "And I hear yelling and cursing, and then a scuffle, and then I see him, Axl (Bill Bailey), and this teacher's bouncing off the fuckin' door jamb. And then he was gone, tear-assing down the hall with a whole bunch of teachers running after him." In a high school yearbook photo from 1978, a junior named Jeff Isbell (Izzy Stradlin) is seen riding along a 12-foot wall with his skateboard, while another student gestures with a peace sign. Izzy would evolve into a dreadlocked surfer who would study reggae and strum his flat-top Gibson SJ-200 acoustic in his Malibu abode. Axl Rose, for the record, does not surf.

Over the years, the maturation of Bill Bailey from problem child into what *Spin* described as a "rust belt punk" was reminiscent of Paul Newman in 1967's *Cool Hand Luke*, who drunkenly unscrews the heads off parking meters in a quaint small town, which gains him a stint in a Southern chain gang. Axl Rose's chain gang was post-Vietnam malaise and conservatism. Bill Bailey was "Cool Hand" Luke with long hair and a temper as testy as gunpowder.

Cool Hand Luke was released at the height of Vietnam War protests, which culminated in a scene at the Pentagon on October 21, 1967, when a young hippie in a turtleneck inserted a carnation into the barrel of an M14 rifle. Luke represented the disobedience of the protestors at the Pentagon, who refused to assimilate for "the man," the same wide-brim-hat-wearing Captain in the film whose voice is a blend of chain-smoker and gravelly plantation owner (the distinctive voice of actor Strother Martin). His sweltering speech provides a stern reminder of authority and the oppressiveness of America's prison industrial complex: "What we've got here is . . . *failure to communicate*. Some men you just can't reach, so you get what we had here last week, which is the way he *wants* it. Well, he *gets* it."

"Failure to communicate" was a metaphor for the failure of diplomacy that dragged Vietnam into a quagmire, as well as the growing divide between America's youth and Nixon's policies. The post-Vietnam culture—the movies, cynicism, tragic Hollywood endings, outlawishness, and burnouts, often viewed as unpatriotic—had a severe psychological effect on the members of Guns N' Roses. Vietnam is the first war mentioned in the Guns N' Roses canon, which appears in the third verse of "Civil War," their only "protest song," which was recorded in the summer of 1990, when the drums of war were echoing through the Persian Gulf. "Not another Vietnam," President Bush would promise the nation. Guns N' Roses began recording the follow-up to *Appetite* (i.e., *Use Your Illusion*) in January 1990, which was eight months before Iraqi forces invaded Kuwait.

"I wanted Axl to become a sonic statesman, equal to Lennon," former Guns N' Roses manager Alan Niven said. "I believed 'Civil War' showed that to be his path." Niven says that Axl initially wanted to use footage from the Gulf War to record a video for "Civil War." But like Axl's drug-mule horror story pitch for the video for "Sweet Child O' Mine," and his exploding Space Shuttle Challenger cover for *Appetite*, it was visually too risqué for Geffen.

The Captain's speech from *Cool Hand Luke* is used in the introduction of "Civil War," where Axl whistles a version of "When Johnny Comes Marching Home," a Civil War–era tune popular with both Northerners and Southerners. Slash's acoustic guitar gives "Civil War" the flavor of a Western. "Failure to communicate" was not only the most memorable sample ever used in a Guns N' Roses song (which is reused on the glitchy bridge of *Chinese Democracy*'s "Madagascar"), it was also an indication that "civil war" was indirectly a protest of Vietnam, which is lost in the anthemic chorus and moral ambiguity of its authors.

At the time, *Cool Hand Luke*'s connection to Vietnam was mostly undetectable (Axl Rose didn't draw the connection). Most teenagers in the '90s had not seen or heard of *Cool Hand Luke*. "Failure to communicate" could have easily been an allusion to the fact that *Use Your Illusion* was their version of the Beatles (i.e., *White Album*), as the band had been fighting an internal *civil war* during a recording process that produced 30 wildly different songs. It was a process that pulled the band apart with laborious piano ballads and endless studio tinkering. Axl Rose would threaten to quit the band several times a week, according to a number of sources. They were in a state of creative duress that involved writing music over the phone, forcing their drummer to sign a sobriety contract, and the lifting of a giant wall between founders Izzy Stradlin and Axl Rose, and bizarre creative decisions, like recording "Don't Cry" twice, including it on both *Use Your Illusion I* and *II*, once with alternative lyrics. *Use Your Illusion* was an overly ambitious eruption of everything that made Guns N' Roses so overcomplicated and surreal.

The *Cool Hand Luke* sample could have been a history lesson about the failures of compromise that lead to war. The possibilities were endless, but because Axl Rose didn't explain it, we had to draw our own conclusions. The lyrics of "Civil War" paint a portrait of anti-war activism using the moody brushstrokes of Gen-X disillusionment. Axl screams that his hands are tied, that his first memories are of a Kennedy assassination (i.e., Bobby Kennedy, as Axl was born a year before JFK's assassination). It declares that politicians are profiting off dead soldiers produced in human grocery stores. It also does nothing to pull the listener away from the maelstrom of disparate things that are simultaneously happening in the song, including a sample that recalls the American South, a series of incredibly melodramatic guitar solos by Slash, and a Southern boogie coda that sounds like a honky-tonk breakdown from Elton John's *Tumbleweed Connection*.

What makes "Civil War" such a confusing example of a "protest song" is that it doesn't mention a domestic or foreign conflict of any particular interest in the '90s. Metallica's *Metallica* (aka *The Black Album*), for example, seemed more contemporaneous in its grappling with the Gulf War, while "Civil War" offered a mostly vintage protest. Of the three blockbuster rock albums of 1991 (including *Nevermind*), each of which dropped between August and September, *Use Your Illusion* sounds the most fragmented. It lacks a clear and decisive artistic voice and political message. It feels detached and toothless. It bypasses confronting Islamic fundamentalism in Iran (like Billy Joel's "We Didn't Start the Fire"), Saddam Hussein, President Bush, or the invasion of Panama. The framework of the song was written as early as 1988. Like the songs that later appeared on Axl Rose's long overdue release of *Chinese Democracy*, it had gathered dust, and yet, because of its lyric about Vietnam, it was serendipitously newsworthy.

These were some of the headlines in 1990: the *Chicago Tribune*: "Why the Gulf Won't Be 'Another Vietnam'" and the *Washington Post*: "Dealing with the Saddam in the Shadow of Vietnam." Guns N' Roses sounded like a '70s rock band macheting through the jungle, when the rest of America was in the desert watching oil fields burn like million-dollar pyrotechnic displays.

Apologists will argue that Axl Rose was keenly aware that the Persian Gulf War was being orchestrated under the shadow of Vietnam. They'll argue that the song isn't a protest song at all, but a song about how men like to kill each other for conquest, religion, and nationalism. Perhaps so, but then again, nobody could take Guns N' Roses seriously as a band with a message. *Appetite for Destruction* had established them as nihilists, not activists. They were a throwback to the "cock rock" of the '70s, not the floral activism of the '60s. Because of their inability to escape their own overwhelming image, "Civil War" felt more like a fable, or myth, than a righteous anthem. Such a lack of lyrical urgency would become a pattern for Axl Rose over the years. A protest song should produce a "call to action" or provocative fodder for newspaper headlines in the tradition of John Lennon declaring that woman is the "nigger" of the world. "Civil War" put its anti-war message in a subordinate position to its Old West pastiche. Until he began using Twitter to protest the Trump administration, Axl Rose has never been able to connect with the intellectuals or activists of his generation. On 2008's *Chinese Democracy*, Axl suggested he was writing about human rights abuses in China, and yet he would produce a mostly solipsistic record that seemed like a labyrinthian breakup album about former lovers and ex-bandmates. His protest of mainland China was obfuscated by his need to address everything from Slash, to Mark David Chapman's murder of John Lennon, to a mysterious international arms dealer (i.e., "Riad"), and, of course, every "outspoken" Guns N' Roses fan who wrongly blamed him for dissolving the band.

In an interview with *Rolling Stone* in 2000, Axl Rose expressed a desire to have Stephanie Seymour's son hear *Chinese Democracy*, whom he allegedly desired to adopt as his own son. "I hope he'll hear it when he [Dylan] grows up, if he ever wants to know the story, to hear the truth," he told writer David Wild. The "truth" was lost in the album's seemingly endless desire to confuse its audience. *Chinese Democracy* was further complicated by 10 guitar solos by guitarist Buckethead (who wore a Michael Myers mask and recorded inside a chicken coop), no compression on the recording (which made it sound unorthodox in an age of "loudness wars"), and industrial productions that incorporated an endless array of samples and futuristic beats. It felt more like NIN's *Year Zero* than a contemporary hard-rock record. Its history is stained with artistic impenetrability and sheer madness, like Buckethead masturbating in his chicken coop and arriving at the studio in a minivan that had a bloodied female mannequin in the passenger seat. Any sense of empathy for the people of Hong Kong and mainland China (and their religious freedom) is erased when you picture Buckethead watching pornography in the studio. "Buckethead was an absolutely emotionless person," Zutaut told me. "The only thing that allowed him to feel emotion was having things cut up and bleeding around him, so he'd cut the heads off rubber chickens and hang them around the studio."

With the sort of lack of self-awareness that creates either masterpiece or farce (or both), *Chinese Democracy* tried to stay focused by including a 1,200-word letter to fans titled "Fear N' Freedom: The Future of China and Western Society," which was included in a limited-release version of *Chinese Democracy*. Here's a snippet of Axl Rose's protest of autocracy: "Our song, 'Chinese Democracy,' in its irreverence, is for positive purposes and communication with all segments of society; music fans (Guns N' Roses fans in particular) and, especially, the western media, to open a dialogue in areas not necessarily focused on both current events and global social responsibilities . . . I feel that the prejudice and closed mindedness of at least many outspoken Guns N' Roses fans seems to warrant an awareness of the realities of a constantly evolving and ever-growing world where China continues to play an ever-increasing role . . . Why would a government want their people to be under such a level of fear, stress, and emotional bondage?"

This was the political manifesto of someone who was nicknamed "Ayatollah" by his bandmates.

It was not published with the commercial release or revealed in any periodical or magazine. Why was it suppressed? There's also no tangible form of activism in the collection of lyrics that design *Chinese Democracy*, which was produced during the height of the Bush administration's "War on Terror," which the album ignores, completely, while Radiohead's *Hail to the Thief* and so many important records from that period, including NIN's *Year Zero*, either directly or indirectly addressed—while Axl Rose ignored the post-9/11 dystopia that was becoming normalized in American culture. "I really thought about what was at the forefront of my concern," NIN's Trent Reznor said in 2007. "And, at the state I'm at right now, at the age I'm at, just the state of being an American citizen, a lot of concern I have about the direction the country's headed in, and uh, kind of the erosion of freedoms that seems like we're experiencing. . . ."

Chinese Democracy was advertised as a concept album about China's human rights abuses, but aside from its tenuous connection to the Tibetan resistance movement and a Scorsese film about the 14th Dalai Lama, it was allergic to earnest activism and felt synthetic. As a political argument against China's authoritarianism, Axl Rose sounded like an undergrad struggling to find his thesis.

With most Americans focused on a recession, invasions of privacy (i.e., The Patriot Act), and a modern Vietnam in the Middle East, *Chinese Democracy*, like "Civil War" and most of *Use Your Illusion I* and *II*, felt like a moving target with no center of gravity. Axl Rose would include the following message in the liner notes for *Chinese Democracy*: "My apologies to anyone I have unintentionally confused and those I have mistakenly offended." He was talking to his audience. *Chinese Democracy* remains conceptually inaccessible for most rock music fans, for a variety reasons, including Axl's refusal to explain it or define his own politics, in any detail beyond a manifesto that most people never read. China's Ministry of Culture seemed to be the only audience to view *Chinese Democracy* as a legitimate protest, as they banned the sales of the album in China. It remains an unfinished and slightly dissatisfying masterpiece. Like J.D. Salinger, who spent 10 years writing *The Catcher in the Rye*, and the rest of his life grappling with its legacy, Axl Rose spent 14 years in total control of his creative process, only to spend the rest of his life watching his creation slip away from his bejeweled clutches.

Its message might become illuminated once we have it as a complete boxset or visual album. But *Chinese Democracy*, and Axl Rose, no matter how much he elucidates his political ideology, at nearly 60 years old, is simply no longer someone America's youth cares to listen to.

John Lennon's "Give Peace a Chance" resonated because it translated into song the youth's frustration with Vietnam. He was their spokesperson (Axl Rose is allergic to the idea of speaking for anyone except himself). It was a musical version of what John Lennon was telling reporters, while sitting naked in a bed with Yoko Ono. Lennon presented himself as a populist revolutionary who was under constant FBI surveillance for his art and comments in the press. He even looked like the hippies he was advocating on behalf of. Axl drove a Ferrari and dressed himself like a heavy-metal Elvis dripping in bling and designer leather. He had a bodyguard who separated him from his supporters. He refused interviews and seemed to detest a large segment of his most outspoken fan base. He failed to connect with the people, which, for a brief moment in 1992, as he pontificated about his childhood abuse, he almost managed to do.

Pacing back and forth on the stage of the Rosemont Horizon in Chicago, Axl began to unload onto a world that was crumbling around him:

"If we're gonna make it for another 50 years on this planet, we gotta fuckin' change our shit now! And there's a lot of motherfuckers that don't want that shit changed . . . fuck that shit."

Before performing "Chinese Democracy" in Las Vegas in 2001, Axl Rose addressed its meaning: "It's not necessarily pro or con about China. It's just that right now China symbolizes one of the strongest, yet most oppressive countries and governments in the world. And we are fortunate to live in a free country. And so, in thinking about that, it just kind of upset me, and so we wrote this little song."

The title track is the only song on *Chinese Democracy* that directly talks about China. The rest of the album's 13 tracks are abstract reflections of Axl's inner turmoil. One of the more compelling tracks on the album is "Catcher in the Rye," a song about groupthink, John Lennon, and Axl's position that *The Catcher in the Rye* should be "discontinued" from high school reading curriculums. The track had originally featured a dazzling guitar solo by Queen's Brian May (which was cut after May allegedly disagreed with the editing of his solo). Had Brian May's solo remained on the track, it would certainly have connected with a broader audience. It seemed like everything Axl Rose wanted people to pay attention to, he would then camouflage with endless indecisiveness and studio experimentation.

The only things Axl protested on *Chinese Democracy* were minimalism, his former band, his own record label, and the trauma of being naturally selected for extinction by grunge, which seemed to have installed a pathological need in him to create something that felt like a prediction of the future, instead of a product of the past. The ballooning cost, at least $14 million, and equally baffling 14-year recording process was cursed with interruptions, intrusions, and Axl Rose's anxiety of appearing anachronistic. It was delayed by what manager Doug Goldstein described to me as an irrational fear of failure. His desire to create a cyber punk-tinged masterpiece would transform Axl Rose into the visual personification of John Travolta's dreadlocked alien from *Battlefield Earth* (2000). There's a leaked audio recording from June 2014 in which Axl Rose explained his reason for burying *Chinese Democracy* as if it was a disastrous flop (when it was a moderate success). "Listen, listen, you gotta understand," he said. "When you see the real artwork from my album, not what you see [inaudible], there's a reason I didn't promote it, because the real artwork is what I will promote."

Chinese Democracy was intended to be released with three avant-garde covers: a green grenade with a "Good Morning America" pin; a computerized red hand; and a photograph of a bicycle positioned against a wall covered in Guns N' Roses graffiti. Only the sepia-toned photo of a bicycle made it into mass production, which allowed it to permeate through the aesthetic sphere. It is the only cover anyone associates with *Chinese Democracy*. Axl Rose was appalled by the label's unwillingness to complete his experimental vision. His preference was no longer incontrovertible.

He would wage a much colder war by refusing to promote *Chinese Democracy* or even talk about it beyond frenzied fan forum discussions under the moniker of "Dexter," after Dexter Morgan, the TV serial killer. If Axl Rose had truly cared about the oppression of the Chinese people, why wouldn't he amplify his message? To this day, very few people know that "Shackler's Revenge" was written as a response to "senseless school shootings," a message that was lost by the garishness of having it released as a track on a video game, *Rock Band 2*. You can't really be taken seriously when your message is inserted into the PR strategy of a mass-marketed toy. But *Chinese Democracy*'s untidy release wasn't entirely Axl Rose's fault.

"They [Geffen] ripped it [*Chinese Democracy*] away from him," said Tommy Stinson, the former bassist of both the Replacements and Guns N' Roses. "Right at the last second, when he wasn't ready." Stinson refers to the fact that Geffen may have forced the album to be pressed prior to final art approval. For this reason, *Chinese Democracy* remains artistically incomplete. Then again, Axl may have refused to promote *Chinese Democracy* out of fear that if had promoted it, and the album flopped, then it would have definitely proved that his fan base had dwindled to hard-core fans and nostalgists. Aesthetically speaking, he had transformed Guns N' Roses into a confusing melange of cyberpunk and classic rock.

Between 2000 and 2015, during the *Chinese Democracy* era, the Guns N' Roses aesthetic would reflect a rockist take on Chinese propaganda art. Their logo was designed using three red stars and "GN'R" decorated with Chinese font. Axl's motif for *Chinese Democracy* would blend Beijing street fashion with NIN-inspired cyberpunk. One would think a protest of Chinese oppression wouldn't embrace the aesthetic of Chinese propaganda art. Then again, this was the art direction of an insulated figure who once protested war by wearing a Confederate flag jacket with skintight bicycle shorts á la Princess Diana. Though "Civil War" may have seduced the MTV generation into borrowing library books on the Kennedy assassination and American Civil War, it is as believable as Charles Manson's environmentalism, or the Southern historian's propaganda that the Confederacy didn't secede to preserve slavery, but to fight for the noble cause of "states' rights"—a "solution to slavery," as historian Shelby Foote once claimed.

Any sense of progressivism in "Civil War" was bombed into oblivion when Axl performed the song as a jingoistic opera during the Use Your Illusion Tour. One such performance occurred on June 6, 1992, at the Hippodrome in Paris, France; a concert that was available to order on pay-per-view, which aired in 25 countries. There's almost nothing like it, as a bearded Axl Rose whistles in cycling shorts and an oversized Confederate flag jacket. Axl's puffy jacket was part of an uneasy relationship that rock and roll has always had with racist iconography. The flag appears as the backdrop at countless Lynyrd Skynyrd shows, which would influence Southern pro wrestlers to wear it as ring gear. Ted Nugent, Pantera, Tom Petty, and David Lee Roth have all given the Confederate flag more cultural currency than it deserves. Because of 1988's "One in a Million," Axl Rose's Confederate flag would turn him into his generation's version of Ted Nugent.

By the third verse, Axl slipped on a white wide-brimmed cowboy hat and a stars-and-stripes jacket, which made him look like a country singer performing at the Super Bowl. There's a magnificent photo of a bearded Axl in this same jacket, screaming into a white foam-tipped microphone. It's by Robert John. During the coda, he performed a third costume change that included a long-sleeved camo shirt that made him look like Chuck Norris attending an aerobics class. This all happens within the first four minutes of an eight-minute performance, which featured Axl Rose as an off-Broadway Rambo: a cartoonish symbol of America's desire to reestablish its manhood after the emasculation of Vietnam. Axl is Rambo looking into the eyes of his commanding officer in 1985, as he accepts an assignment to go back into Vietnam to rescue prisoners of war: "Sir . . . do we get to win this time?" He had evolved from John Rambo backpacking through a small town in *First Blood* (Axl Rose in 1980), into the steroidal action star in *First Blood Part II*. This is what Axl Rose looked like while performing an anti-war song.

Another thing you need to accept in any study of Guns N' Roses is that, by 1990, Axl was "probably not legally insane, but crazy nonetheless," which is how Los Angeles District Attorney Vincent Bugliosi described Manson Family member Susan Atkins. When it comes to psychoanalyzing Axl Rose during the *Use Your Illusion* era (1990–1994), when he had begun to drift as far away from reality as Willard in *Apocalypse Now*, it's appropriate to use the Bugliosi definition of Atkins. This will make more sense when we talk about Axl's fascination with Charles Manson. While his manager may have wanted him to be a hard-rock John Lennon, Axl was behaving like a blend of cult leader and macho Reagan-era action star. Axl was singing "Civil War" with as much sensitivity as Chuck Norris on the poster of *Missing in Action* (1984), where he brandishes a giant M60 machine gun in a comically masculine attempt to prove America had a bigger dick than Vietnam.

Axl was crooning about human rights in the aftermath of using "nigger" in "One in a Million," refusing to apologize for it, and proceeding to justify it in an astonishingly presumptuous *Rolling Stone* interview where he evokes Jim Morrison. "I don't like boundaries of any kind. I don't like being told what I can and what I can't say. I used the word 'nigger' because it's a word to describe somebody that is basically a pain in your life, a problem. The word 'nigger' doesn't necessarily mean black." Axl would continue to dig himself into a rhetorical swamp: "Why can black people go up to each other and say 'nigger,' but when a white guy does it all of a sudden it's a big putdown?"

One wonders if "Civil War" and its reference to the assassination of Martin Luther King Jr. weren't just a really indirect form of damage control by bassist Duff McKagan, who wrote that particular lyric, or perhaps Axl's own symbolic apology that went beyond the irreverent one included in the original booklet for their 1988 EP *G N' R Lies*: "This song is very simple and extremely generic or generalized, my apologies to those who may take offense."

The negative publicity associated with "One in a Million" inspired Axl to read books about Martin Luther King, Jr. and Malcolm X (a self-imposed "sensitivity training"). It was an education that would have served his career well had it been conducted prior to the composition of "One in a Million."

At the height of tensions between the United States and the Middle East, Axl had proceeded to draw crosshairs around Iranian refugees in metropolitan cities like Los Angeles and New York. On "One in a Million," Axl described immigrants and "faggots" that made no sense to him, who would immigrate to the United States, refuse to assimilate, and spread diseases like AIDS.

Axl tried to illuminate his twisted bigotry in a 1989 *Rolling Stone* interview:

> When I use the word immigrants, what I'm talking about is going to a 7-Eleven or Village Pantries – a lot of people from countries like Iran, Pakistan, China, Japan, et cetera, get jobs in these convenience stores and gas stations. Then they treat you like you don't belong here. I've been chased out of a store with Slash by a six-foot-tall Iranian with a butcher knife because he didn't like the way we were dressed. Scared me to death . . . Maybe I should have been more specific and said, "Joe Schmoladoo at the 7-Eleven and faggots make no sense to me." That's ridiculous! I summed it up simply and said, "Immigrants."

Axl Rose in 1989 sounded like a white nationalist in the Trump era. When you listen to "Civil War" with the backdrop being the Middle East, you have to ask yourself a few questions, like, for example: "What did Axl Rose know about Iran? Did he know anything about it? Did the nickname 'Ayatollah' have something to do with his distorted view of Iranians?"

Axl never expounded on his views. "One a Million" blockaded Axl from becoming a "sonic statesman" in the league of John Lennon.

When Lennon wrote "Woman is the Nigger of the World," which initially drew harsh criticism, he did with the pen of a feminist at his side. He used the shock value to grab headlines for the cause of women's rights. John Lennon was playing chess with the media to get Yoko Ono's second-wave feminism into the papers. Axl wrote "One in a Million" with the logic of Archie Bunker pontificating from his chair about "Blacks" and "Polacks." "One in a Million" was a shock-jock distortion of the steel-mill sentimentality found in John Cougar Mellencamp's *Scarecrow*, whereby Axl Rose isn't being sentimental about the fading American dream, he is unloading his frustration on people of color, gay people, and Iranians who were, in his mind, ripping the dream away from people like him. In 1976, writer Tom Wolfe described the '70s as the "Me" decade. As a product of "Me," Axl wrote a hyper-selfish song that seemed to only connect with a militant strain of the white working class, which put the rest of Guns N' Roses, especially Slash, in a very awkward position. "One in a Million" produced another colossal *failure to communicate*. Releasing an anti-war song in its aftermath—even if it was done for George Harrison's Romanian relief album on July 23, 1990—seemed a bit presumptuous. The fact that the track was included on a charity album is practically dismissed from the historical record, as a year later, it was released as the B-side of "You Could Be Mine," which was the theme of *Terminator 2: Judgment Day* (1991). Any hint of a protest is nuked by the thermonuclear energy of *T2*.

The optics were as broken as Slash's shower door. No matter what Axl was trying to say on "Civil War," the fireworks on the epic chorus, the jangling Western-tinged piano notes, and his well-publicized contempt for Iranian liquor store clerks had turned "Civil War" into a sentimental anthem for America's white working class. By the early '90s, Axl Rose had morphed into a "right-wing hippie," which is how Charles Manson's attorney had described his client.

Axl Rose once said that he had studied Southern rock in the writing process of "Sweet Child O' Mine." It's mostly undetectable in the final mix. "Civil War" includes one of their most Southern rock–tinged arrangements. This is part of why "Civil War" feels like it's romanticizing the Civil War through a novelistic, Old West fantasy. In 2006, reporting for *GQ*, writer John Jeremiah Sullivan visited Lafayette and discovered a memorial for "the sons of Lafayette," which included the names of dead soldiers who served in the war, including the name "William Rose," which Sullivan said was probably Axl's "great-great-great-grandpa" who perished in the Civil War; though it remains unclear if he fought for the Union. The fact that "Civil War" was performed while Axl wore a Confederate flag muted any progressivism it may have tried to project. Its marketing was culturally and aesthetically mishandled, the way Springsteen's blue jeans and American flag transformed "Born in the U.S.A." into an unintentionally patriotic anthem, when, in fact, it was a working-class rejection of the hangover from Vietnam.

Like Axl Rose on pay-per-view, or the political appropriations of "Born in the U.S.A.," *Apocalypse Now* pulls the viewer between the polarities of disgust and exaltation; like the flickering image of Axl gnashing down on his teeth in the video for "Welcome to the Jungle," his first major screen test, where he'd tell his audience that they must learn to live like animals, before reminding them that he would like nothing more than to watch them bleed (which is not, as some have suggested, a metaphor for menstrual bleeding). Such gory references appear through the history of masculine rock. In 1978, AC/DC's Bon Scott threatened his audience with carnage in the streets on "If You Want Blood (You've Got It)."

Like the politician who guises their militarism with phony messages about human rights and freedom, the history of Guns N' Roses is covered in too much blood to ever take their "humanitarianism" seriously.

"Watch you bleed" is one of the more barbaric lyrics from the Guns N' Roses canon, which could be a reference to Axl Rose's tendency to solve his problems with pugilism, as he did in St. Louis on July 2, 1991, when he dove off the stage into a crowd of bikers because one of them was carrying a flash camera (which were banned from the venue). In the process, Axl would slap a security guard across the face, lose a contact lens, and storm off stage in a complete blur of incandescent white heat. At that point in the Use Your Illusion Tour, Axl Rose was like Henry Rollins during Black Flag tours when he'd pummel fans for reaching for his microphone. Like Rollins, Axl was working through his internalized rage by projecting it towards any perceived threat. The key difference between the two was education: Rollins was a skeptic who read Nietzsche, Dostoevsky, Poe, Ellroy, and Kafka, while Axl spent "millions" on New Age mumbo jumbo and read Stephen King paperbacks, James Dean biographies, and Mary Shelley's *Frankenstein*.

"I was told that my mental circuitry was all twisted," Axl told an *L.A Times* reporter in 1991. He was the hard-rock answer to Rollins throwing punches at unruly fans. In his published tour diaries, Rollins wrote, "When they spit at me, when they grab at me, they aren't hurting me. When I push out and mangle the flesh of another, it's falling so short of what I really want to do to them." Both Rollins and Axl Rose hardened their bodies as a way of overcompensating for feelings of abandonment and abuse. Strength and control were their defense mechanisms against the predators they perceived to be hunting them. Violence was their way of working through their trauma; like the soldier who works through his grief behind the unloading rounds of machine-gun fire; or the war-mad surfer who mows down an entire village to find a chill surf spot. The Use Your Illusion Tour was Axl Rose's theater of war—his Vietnam.

The surf-crazed lieutenant colonel in *Apocalypse Now* is played disturbingly well by Robert Duvall, who is so preoccupied with surf conditions that he's willing to risk the lives of an entire platoon to scout beaches, while he calmly sips from a cup of coffee. Rewind to the image of Axl backstage in Montreal in 1992, sipping on champagne and smoking a cigarette as fans tore the arena apart and flipped police cars over because Axl refused to finish his set—putting the entire platoon in jeopardy. Axl would later say that he was suffering from injured vocals cords, but between 1986 and 1993, Axl would abandon concerts for reasons as mundane as a stray lighter colliding with his groin at Giants Stadium in 1992. Axl would regularly exit concerts due to everything from fans trying to bottle him to "technical difficulties" stemming from his tendency to miss sound-checks. He had begun to believe he was a target. At one point, Axl began wearing a baseball catcher's chest protector. No rock star has ever styled himself into a persecution complex the way Axl Rose had on the Use Your Illusion Tour. None of it seems real today. It's like a mockumentary on an arena-rock star who believed he was a head of state. In the summer of 2015, internet trolls manufactured a rumor that Axl Rose was late to a show because he refused to press pause on his VCR. The story alleges that Axl was backstage before a concert in St. Petersburg, Florida, on December 28, 1991, fixated on watching *Teenage Mutant Ninja Turtles II: The Secret of the Ooze* (1991). Guns N' Roses were 80 minutes late for their performance that night, and while the story probably isn't true, as sources close to the band have claimed, the fact that it was so believable further illustrates just how mental Axl Rose was in 1991, which was similar to Duvall's napalm-sniffing surf Nazi. "Charlie don't surf," he tells his terrified troops. "Charlie" is how American soldiers would describe the Viet Cong. Between 1991 and 1993, Axl Rose would wear a slogan T-shirt with "Charlie Don't Surf" printed on the back. On the front side was a portrait of Charles Manson, who once carved a swastika between his eyes and brainwashed his followers with copious amounts of LSD. Axl wore a Charles Manson T-shirt just as he was reconditioning himself with malefic gurus, psychics, therapists, "high-tuned vitamins," expensive New Age treatments, and a victim complex that had started to push him further away from the people.

Under the shadow of Vietnam and the Manson murders, Axl Rose would embrace his image as a right-wing hippie. Axl was promoting Manson, while he evoked civil rights in his music. He did this while Geffen PR was in damage control mode following the 1988 release of "One in a Million." I cannot think of a job as emotionally draining as being a member of Geffen's PR team between 1988 and 1993, where *failure to communicate* could have been its own press release. Axl would wear the Charles Manson T-shirt in the video for "Estranged," broadcasting his fetish to millions across MTV. Unlike Cradle of Filth's "Jesus is a Cunt" T-shirt, which portrayed a masturbating nun, the Manson T-shirt was never a popular item with fans. It was too much, even for Guns N' Roses. Charles Manson was also out of vogue in the '90s, and without the internet, purchasing the Manson T-shirt became too difficult (most of them were only available in alternative clothing shops in Southern California). While *Rolling Stone* described Cradle of Filth's T-shirt as being the "most controversial in rock history," it never caused the kind of damage the Manson T-shirt did, which wounded Axl Rose's image and forced the public to question his sanity. It also secured Charles Manson's place in the Gen X wardrobe. No T-shirt in rock and roll has caused as much legitimate duress as the Charles Manson T-shirt, which was printed using a mug shot of Manson taken on April 22, 1968, which appears under a newspaper headline that's read by soldiers on the naval patrol boat in *Apocalypse Now*, as the article describes the killings as a "protest," which was Coppola's critique of the counterculture movement. For Axl, the image of Charles Manson was his criticism of the mass media, his critics, and America's obsession with celebrity, which he would again comment on when he wore a "Kill Your Idols" T-shirt featuring the face of Christ.

"From Jesse James to Charles Manson," Marilyn Manson told *Rolling Stone* in 1999, "the media, since their inception, have turned criminals into folk heroes."

Axl would go on to regularly wear the Manson shirt during the Use Your Illusion Tour, alternately modeling it in black, white, and red: the color palette of fascism, or the "devil's palette," as philosopher and historian Michel Pastoureau described it. It's a look Axl would embellish by dressing up in stars-and-stripes leggings, a Marlboro cigarette T-shirt (which he'd wear on stage at Willie Nelson's Farm Aid), and oversized cowboy hats. It had been 24 years since actress Sharon Tate had been slaughtered by the Manson Family in her Cielo Drive home, and Patti Tate, her sister, was now on NBC's *Today* accusing Axl of transforming Charles Manson into a cult hero, as Axl didn't simply wear a T-shirt with Manson's face on it, he covered one of his songs as a hidden track on 1993's *The Spaghetti Incident?*

"He's (Axl Rose) made Charles Manson out to be a cult hero to these young kids," Tate told *Today*. "The young kids don't know the details. They don't what Charles Manson's all about."

Axl responded to the criticism by wearing a red Manson T-shirt, along with a red baseball hat worn backwards in defiance, fascistic black combat boots and thick tube socks, and red shorts, while extending a stiff middle finger at his critics. It's one of the most threatening images of any rock star since Sid Vicious strutted down King's Road with a swastika printed across his chest as a mockery of the "Greatest Generation." Axl's besieged soul was translated through the kind of fashionable terrorism that produced the "Cambridge Rapist" T-shirt that would turn Vivienne Westwood and Malcolm McLaren into cultural assassins from 1975 to 1978.

After endless protest, on December 1, 1993, Axl Rose delivered a statement explaining his motivations:

> A lot of people can say I wear the "Charlie Don't Surf" T-shirt for shock value, but I've worn that shirt for the past year on tour, all over the world. Yes, I was trying to make a statement. I wore the T-shirt because a lot of people enjoy playing me as the bad guy and the crazy. Sorry, I'm not that guy. I'm nothing like him. That's what I'm saying. There's a real difference in morals, values and ethics between Manson and myself and that is "Thou shalt not kill," which I don't. I'm by no means a Manson expert or anything, but the things he's done are something I don't believe in. He's a sick individual. Look at Manson and then look at me. We're not the same. Plus, I like the black humor of the "Charlie Don't Surf" line from the movie *Apocalypse Now* . . . Unfortunately, I Don't Surf Either.

The Manson T-shirt was designed by Richard Lemmons, who is pictured smiling alongside Axl Rose in the *New York Times* editorial titled, "A Song Slipped In Enriched a Killer." In the photo, both Axl and

Lemmons are wearing the Charles Manson T-shirt, with similar-looking bandanas, which made them look like entrepreneurs starting an upstart Charles Manson fashion label. The following caption is used: "Mr. Manson gets royalties of 10 cents a shirt." Each shirt was said to cost $17 dollars, according to Dan Lemmons of Zooport Riot Gear in Newport Beach, who co-produced the shirts, claiming that it was all "a joke"—even though the brothers wrote to Manson at Corcoran State Prison and offered him 10 cents per T-shirt in royalties. The Lemmonses—said to be fundamentalist Christians—were then invited on-set during the filming of "Estranged," which debuted the T-shirt to the masses.

America was still trying to figure out how to talk about Charles Manson in 1993. For musicians, he had become a punkish symbol of rejecting the bourgeois establishment. Underground punk bands were attracted to the true-crime morbidity and hippie-killing appeal of Manson. Sonic Youth and Lydia Lynch wrote about the Manson murders on "Death Valley '69." The Ramones sang about Manson on "Glad to See You Go." Trent Reznor shot NIN's video for "Gave Up" at the Cielo Drive home, where the Tate murders occurred. Marilyn Manson based his postmodern persona partially on the American obsession with Charles Manson. In the years following his death, Manson's countercultural spiderweb began to wrap itself around the minds of naive and ignorant artists who were children in 1970, when *Rolling Stone* described Manson in outlawish terms as "the most dangerous man alive." Seventeen years later, the editors of British rock tabloid *Kerrang!* described Guns N' Roses as the "most dangerous band in the world."

The Manson T-shirt, which became Axl's most publicized protest, had also cemented his legacy as the Tony Montana (aka *Scarface*, 1983) of hard rock, who always told the truth, even when he lied. "You need people like me," Montana explained to a restaurant filled with WASP elites. "You need people like me, so you can point your fuckin' fingers and say, 'That's the bad guy.'"

"Negativity sells," Axl told *RIP* in 1992, "And the media knows that. 'Axl Rose is rock 'n' roll's bad guy.'"

In truth, Axl had spent a lifetime turning himself into the overly candid bad guy, but by 1993, he had completely lost control of his image. Axl Rose had become a monster, and Dr. Frankenstein was his Vietnam: an inescapable 194-date Use Your Illusion Tour. For Slash, his Vietnam, if you will, was his inability to accept a more sober reality. His breaking point was a hallucinatory meltdown in an Arizona bungalow. For Axl Rose, his childhood trauma, which was magnified by his own war with the media, had turned him into the rock-and-roll equivalent of Colonel Kurtz (Marlon Brando), who had removed himself from reality, believed he was doing the right thing, and had begun to lose himself in the jungle. By the mid-90s, Axl had disappeared into the wilderness. While he was less strung out than Slash, he was heavily intoxicated by demons that were, like the shadows chasing Slash, buried deep within his subconscious. The pressure to assert control over them would cause Axl to randomly explode like an untested minefield. The mirror that Willard would shatter with his fist would appear on the walls of Axl Rose's West Hollywood condo in 1989, when he exploded by smashing the glass all over his coffee table and couch, as he sat there with an Uzi semiautomatic machine gun behind him, similar to the one from *The Terminator* (1984), as well as a 9-mm pistol nearby, as he smoked through a pack of Marlboros. "I'm not paranoid," he told friend and journalist Del James in 1989. "This is how I choose to live. This is comfortable," like crawling along the edge of a straight razor, like Brando in *Apocalypse Now*.

2

FACES OF DEATH

The leering male gaze of slasher cinema is splattered across their oeuvre. They are a replay of the '70s that's been edited by the hyper-masculinity of the Reagan-era. To experience the filmic appeal of Guns N' Roses, you first have to retrace their DNA to the cinema of their childhood, or today's pulp TV on Cinemax, for example. If you're walking into a video store in 1987, the year they first appeared on MTV, Guns N' Roses are the slasher film displaying a gory font and a screaming cheerleader. They are the VHS cover that traumatizes children, like *Snuff* (1976), which seemed real. One VHS cover for *Snuff* includes a graphic illustration of a man swinging an axe towards the tied-up wrists of a woman; another includes a woman who is about to be beheaded by a director's clapboard, which has been equipped with a straight razor. This sort of misogynistic camp is intrinsic to Guns N' Roses, who evoke *Evil Dead* (1981), where a horrified woman is chocked by a zombie's decomposing hand. They hearken back to the cover of *Thrashin'* (1986), with the Valley girl gazing at "Hot. Reckless. Totally Insane" skaters. They're the vigilante action film, where black leather, cleavage, and machine guns threaten you like dominatrix Linda Blair on the cover of *Savage Streets* (1984), a feminist take on *Death Wish* (1974):

"They raped her sister . . . an eye for an eye." They are the pulp maga-zine that advertises female corporal punishment in the form of a tied-up temptress in a ripped blouse. Guns N' Roses are what film critic Pauline Kael described populist cinema as in her 1969 essay: "Trash, Art, and the Movies": "a tawdry corrupt art for a tawdry corrupt world." They "fit the way we feel."

The original cover of *Appetite for Destruction* combines vintage pulp art with Cold War–era paranoia. It is a lowbrow painting titled "Appetite for Destruction" by artist Robert Williams, 1978, which depicts a bombshell with her underwear pulled down below her knees, with her right breast exposed, and a crime scene that indicates that she may have been raped by the robot in the trench coat. In many ways, she's symbolic of American innocence being raped by the industrialism and mass-media propaganda. "Appetite for Destruction" recalls the creepy allure of *A Nightmare on Elm Street* (1984), where Freddy Krueger's steel claws violate a teenage girl from beneath a bubbly bathtub. By using the Williams's painting as their first album cover, Axl Rose bluntly reminded the music press that he was a by-product of the same sickness that gave us the damaged duo in *Natural Born Killers* (1994), who were the warped brats of a bloodthirsty and soul-less reality—not Norman Rockwell's beautiful illusion.

The original cover of *Appetite for Destruction* was like a VHS box art of a B-movie about invading aliens and rapist robots. It fit the way they felt. Guns N' Roses were the sadistic drag queen caper, where crime and beauty become inseparable, like John Waters's *Female Trouble* (1974), which is dedicated to the Manson Family. When *NME* declared that Nirvana was the Guns N' Roses you were *allowed* to like, they meant that Guns N' Roses were the VHS cassette you would camouflage in a brown paper bag as you exited through the back. They were the thing you were told not to like, which made you like it even more, like the campy horror of *Friday the 13th* (1980) or Cinemax after midnight. They occupy a porn section that's been curtained off from polite society. Guns N' Roses evoked the sort of uncom-fortable thrill of watching Tarantino turn the act of slicing off a cop's ear into a pleasurable dance routine. This is why a certain type of critic will always hold their nose while listening to (or watching) Guns N' Roses. "Quentin Tarantino is interested in watching somebody's ear getting cut off; David Lynch is interested in the ear." This is how writer David Foster Wallace viewed the difference between the ear as a gag in *Reservoir Dogs* (1992) versus the human ear as something deeper in *Blue Velvet* (1986)— with Lynch being the artist and Tarantino being the purveyor of trash. Note the theme for Waters's *Female Trouble*: "Crime is beauty," which was inspired by Waters's prison visits of Manson Family member Charles "Tex" Watson.

"To me, violence is a totally aesthetic subject," Tarantino told Graham Fuller in 1993. "Saying you don't like violence in movies is like saying you don't like dance sequences in movies."

Guns N' Roses are a homicidal dance sequence, which produces a good–bad thrill that resonates in the same way Pauline Kael received *Bonnie and Clyde* in 1967: "What looks ludicrous in this movie isn't merely ludicrous, and after we have laughed at ignorance and helplessness and emptiness and stupidity and idiotic deviltry, the laughs keep sticking in our throats, because what's funny isn't only funny."

Yes, I'm suggesting there's a certain amount of art to the lowbrow ludicrousness of Guns N' Roses. Even though they feel divorced from "art house," there's something about them that haunts you in a beautifully convincing way, like watching *Faces of Death* (1978) for the first time. In the early '80s, Axl Rose partook in a hobby every adolescent from his generation can relate to: he'd regularly rent VHS tapes of adult horror films like *Carrie* (1976), where a menstruating redhead (we literally watch her bleed) turns her high school prom into a fiery bloodbath. Axl watched *Carrie*, read Stephen King novels, and inhaled the carnage as if it were a cologne strip inside a men's magazine. When he moved to Los Angeles in 1982, Axl would rent snuff and horror films from local video stores. He had a peculiar interest in *Faces of Death*, a mondo horror film of death scenes advertised as being "banned in 46 countries" (a gross exaggeration, but the kind that would become a part of Axl Rose's own marketing strategy in 1987). The cover art of *Faces of Death*, the one Axl was most likely to have rented, includes a skull dripping with blood from font that glimmers like the scythe on the cover of *Savage Weekend* (1979). *Faces of Death*'s tagline reads: "Experience the graphic reality of DEATH, close-up . . ."

Former Guns N' Roses manager Vicky Hamilton discussed the importance of the *Faces of Death* tape in her book, *Appetite for Dysfunction*:

"One of his (Axl Rose) favorites was when a guy was getting electrocuted and his eye-balls pop out. He would watch this over and over, as if he was studying it. Later when Guns N' Roses made the video for 'Welcome to the Jungle,' I think he tried to emulate the structure of the *Faces of Death* video . . ."

The skull is omnipresent throughout their iconography. In their sophomore year of high school, Jeff Isbell (Izzy Stradlin) and William Bailey (Axl Rose) sat together in Jane Boswell's Arts and Crafts Pottery class in 1977. "Gotcha, little bastards!" said Boswell, as she caught Axl and Izzy drawing something they weren't assigned that day, which combined death with natural beauty ("crime is beauty"). "They were combining opposing elements into a beautiful whole," says Boswell. "The whole—it's funny now that I think about it—was a skull-like figure with guns and roses." It was the early draft of a Guns N' Roses logo. Like Van Gogh's painting of a skull with a lit cigarette in its mouth, it wasn't a doom prophecy, it was a macabre rejection of traditional values. It was juvenile. It was anti-authoritarian. It was an expression of their teenage psyche. Whenever Axl Rose tried to reach beyond the damaged teenage psyche he expressed in Jane Boswell's classroom, the results were less punk.

Unlike Freddie Mercury and Keith Richards, Axl never went to art school. At 28 years old, he was not Mick Jagger at the same age, who was the philosopher king of the Rolling Stones; a boho-capitalist who had begun to handle the band's internal affairs and publicity with the tact of a shrewd statesman. Jagger's comic displays of sexism always had the punch of Victorian humor, rather than "white trash" rage (his luscious lips and dangling limbs made him seem like a court jester or sexist game show host). He provoked anxiety in the hearts and minds of parents the way Elvis once had before him, but he never seemed legitimately deranged.

He was never Max Cady in *Cape Fear* (1991), a fiendish rapist who seduces naive young girls and kills their puppies (crimes Axl Rose would be accused of in the tabloids).

The teenage girl who is seduced in 1991's *Cape Fear* is played by Juliette Lewis, who listens to Guns N' Roses' ballad "Patience" in her bedroom. In *National Lampoon's Christmas Vacation* (1989), the Griswold's teenage daughter, also played by Juliette Lewis, has a Guns N' Roses poster on her wall. Teenage girls between 1988 and the emergence of grunge in 1991 viewed Axl Rose as their Mick Jagger. In makeup and lipstick, both Jagger and Axl looked androgynous, but only Jagger looked like a dandy; Axl looked like a homoerotic Dracula or one of Warhol's strung-out groupies in 8mm. In his 20s, Jagger had already graduated from a prestigious grammar school and had attended the London School of Economics. Axl Rose was a high school dropout with a rap sheet that was as long as Jagger's reading list. Mick Jagger's first arrest was in 1967, for the charge of marijuana possession. Jagger's mug shot looks like the passport photo of a British financial executive. Now compare that to any one of Axl Rose's mug shots, where he looks like the various stages of the American dream failling before you.

Guns N' Roses were symbolic of America decaying into the corporate dystopia of *RoboCop* (1987), a satirical example of fascist liberalism. They were a *Midnight Cowboy* (1969) or a doomed Brian De Palma ending (the wrecked car on the opposite side of the highway). Like Tarantino, Guns N' Roses reinterpreted their influences so cavalierly that they were often viewed as art thieves or revisionists. They were postmodern. An early report in *LA Weekly* described them as the "American Led Zeppelin," while others compared them to Aerosmith (*The Fresno Bee* described them as "reheated Aerosmith"). The *L.A. Times* said that Axl Rose was "the most compelling and combustible superstar in American hard rock since Jim Morrison." Guns N' Roses could never escape the shadows of the rock bands that came before them. They were initially viewed as a simulated snuff-film version of their predecessors. They were described in terms of clichés from the '70s: sleazy, dangerous, street level, pissed, unhinged, rabid, cocky, and—in practically every review—the "bad boys."

But there was something about Guns N' Roses that felt like a photo depicting both the wasteland and paradise of post-Vietnam America. While they weren't modern art or part of a new wave, they were, like Jean-Luc Godard, a protest of artistic homogenization. For Godard, it was the Hollywood studio system; for Guns N' Roses, it was MTV's "new wave" aesthetic of sharply dressed supermodels and vogue pop stars. Godard's films were semi-documentaries that seemed driven by the poetic belief that true beauty is found in blazing imperfection. His scripts were often handwritten notes he'd shove down his coat pocket. He shot on location, without permission (frequently without professional actors). It was an unorthodox approach that was disconnected from the engineered star system. It was daredevil filmmaking. Godard poured petrol over American commercialism, flirted with morbidity, criticized mass-media manipulation, and prostituted his subjects the way Guns N' Roses would in choosing a "robot rape" painting by Robert Williams, who, like Godard, drew heavily on cynicism and anti-commercialism.

Before Guns N' Roses became high-concept cinema in the '90s, they kept your heart thumping like the opening chase scene in *Mad Max* (1979). They were unapologetically vulgar and moody, like the sadomasochistic suffering of William Friedkin's *Cruising* (1980), which left bruises on the subject of their video for "It's So Easy." They were shockingly frank. They kept their audience's mouths agape, as if they were watching replays of Evel Knievel nearly killing himself by jumping over a row of double-decker buses. Unlike their contemporaries, Guns N' Roses did not hide their exploitation behind a blur of special effects. Like Tarantino sketching a Japanese bloodbath in *Kill Bill: Volume 1* (2003) using elements of *Lady Snowblood* (1973), the image of Guns N' Roses were a transparently obvious pastiche of the art that mutated their post-boomer brains, which included everything from '70s horror films, American pulp magazines, rock-and-roll tabloids, pornography, skating culture, Stephen King, and *Faces of Death* on VHS. "I was really into early Stephen King," Axl told the *L.A. Times* in 1988. "He was writing science fiction or horror stories, but he made everything seem so realistic that you felt it could really happen.

The stories were up-to-date and sometimes very brutal in their frankness." Unfettered exploitation fueled the early Guns N' Roses' philosophy and their impulse towards self-destruction; it was what longtime friend to the band and writer Del James once described as a "brutal honesty" that came out of the rebellious art movements of the '70s, which ranged from UK punk to New Hollywood.

Even before mastering the guitar, Saul Hudson (aka Slash) would obsessively watch horror films. It's a fact that occasionally makes his nickname confusing, as it has no relation to Michael Myers or his favorite horror films, which include *The Thing* (1982). Slash's horror-tinged image was transformed by Axl's diabolical gleam during their 1988 concert at the Ritz: "Half man, half beast. I'm not sure what it is, but whatever it is, it's weird and it's pissed off and it calls itself Slash." Axl's introduction is a reference to the bearded dog handler in John Carpenter's *The Thing*, who peers into a shadowy dog kennel occupied by a shape-shifting alien and says, "I dunno what the hell's in there, but it's weird and pissed off, whatever it is."

"I was introduced to rock and roll, and horror movies pretty much at the same time," Slash told *Rolling Stone* in 2015. "My mom was a huge horror fan and weaned me on all the horror movies from the '50s and the '60s . . . both my parents took me to see everything through the '70s."

Beyond camp, Guns N' Roses' blending of violence with humor can be compared to Tarantino films that invite its audience to chuckle along with a sharply dressed sociopath in *Reservoir Dogs* (1992) who gyrates his hips to Stealers Wheel, while holding a straight razor in his hand. As his victim stares at the edge of the blade approaching his ear, we momentarily grind our teeth like Axl Rose in an electric chair in the video for "Welcome to the Jungle." Tarantino is doing this intentionally, as he aestheticizes sadism into darkly satirical pulp fiction. Tarantino does this again in the coda of *Once Upon a Time in Hollywood,* when TV cowboy Rick Dalton uses a flame-thrower to turn an already mutilated Manson girl into a hippie barbecue.

Guns N' Roses' aesthetic is a by-product of a teenage boy's most perverse desires. They provide the uncomfortable enjoyment of reading a 1980 *National Lampoon* piece by Ted Mann and John Hughes, titled "Sexual

Harassment and How to Do It!" Guns N' Roses weren't as witty as *National Lampoon*, but they certainly tried with 1988's "Used to Love Her," which is a satirical acoustic sing-along about a nagging girlfriend who "bitched" so often that the only remedy left was killing her and burying her in the backyard. To be able to be tickled by such misogynistic camp, you must digest it with the understanding of Axl Rose reading Stephen King and watching Sam Kinison specials; Slash watching campy horror films; and Izzy occupying the same dazed-and-confused orbit as Jeff Spicoli from *Fast Times at Ridgemont High* (1982). You also have to remember that Andrew Dice Clay was to Axl Rose what the French symbolist poets were to Jim Morrison.

"I'm not into gay or bisexual experiences," Axl told *Rolling Stone* in 1989. "But that's hypocritical of me, because I'd rather see two women together than just about anything else." It almost sounds like the punch line to an Andrew Dice Clay bit.

"Used to Love Her" feels like an homage to both Kinison and Dice Clay. But we still have to draw our own conclusions about what it really means (though it probably means very little). It could have been about a dead dog or an ex-girlfriend, like the Vandals' "My Girlfriend's Dead." It could be about a movie. Privately, Axl had told friends in 2016 that "Used to Love Her" was written with Izzy as a diss track directed at metal band Great White (which Axl seems to have had a grudge with). The cultural impact of "Used to Love Her" is Al Bundy in a donut-stained "NO MA'AM" T-shirt. It produces outrage in feminist circles who simply refuse to accept it as anything other than the aestheticization of violence against women (which is raised each time Tarantino releases a film). In the summer of 2016, when Canadian metal band White Lung covered "Used to Love Her" on indie-rock channel SiriusXMU, the lead singer, Mish Way, was criticized by feminists who viewed "Used to Love Her" like a reaffirmation of the patriarchy in rock and roll. Maybe it is. Because of its lowbrow directness and campy horror imagery, the song fails to persuade their critics the way the Rolling Stones did with "Under My Thumb" and "Yesterday's Papers." Jagger was also able to soften his chauvinism by balancing sophistication with a mischievousness that was captured in a photo from 1973 where Jagger is pictured holding a children's sand bucket and toy shovel. He was often seen leaving posh hotels in top hats and velvet coats with Marianne Faithfull, a chanteuse with choppy bangs and fur coats, and like Jagger, upper middle-class. He didn't produce a music video where he whipped, gagged, and sexually violated his muse—as Axl did in the video for "It's So Easy."

Axl was no Don Juan or even Brando in *Last Tango in Paris* (1972). "Used to Love Her" doesn't possess the meloncholic poetry of the Smiths' "Girlfriend in a Coma." It also feels too closely aligned with Axl Rose's scandalous biography. By the end of 1988, Axl had already developed a reputation for being the sort of brutish wolf who forced nice girls to do bad things. He blended the masculine American cowboy image with that of a Hells Angel biker. He was like Rudolph Valentino wielding an art-deco dildo as a seedy murder weapon. Mick Jagger was a debonair Cary Grant insisting on spanking his costar with a humorous twinkle in his eye. Jagger's sexism, if we can define it as much, seemed traditional, as if it were part of postwar paternalism. Axl Rose, on the other hand, was a domestic violence police report being played through six different octaves. He had more dirt under his unmanicured fingernails. He was the alienated oil rigger in *Five Easy Pieces* (1970), played by Jack Nicholson, who was frustrated, lost, annoyed by the woman in his life, and unable to find his place in an America divided by class.

The blue-collar disillusionment of Axl Rose became an existential crisis that exhibited itself the moment he arrived in L.A. There was pathological self-hatred distorting his views of the opposite sex. It festered in his veins—it was part of his DNA. When he first arrived in LA in the early 80s, Axl had shoulder-length ginger hair, a flannel shirt, blue denim, no makeup (yet), a scowl on his face, and almost no sense of humor about that fact that he looked like an extra who'd just walked off the set of *The Dukes of Hazzard*. Axl Rose was a Midwestern transplant who had come to L.A. chasing the same fantasy that had brought Charles Manson to L.A. in 1967, to be "bigger than the Beatles." Axl wanted to release an album that would make a bigger splash than Boston's 1976 debut.

Axl, like Manson, was an outsider who was ostracized by the inner circle of L.A. music intelligentsia. From 1966 to 1968, it was Dennis Wilson and the hippie aristocrats in Laurel Canyon; in 1982, it was glam metal bands who melded the theatrics of KISS with the virtuosity of Van Halen. Axl was ostracized for not wearing the right heavy-metal uniform, in much the same way Kurt Cobain was mocked by the Seattle punk scene that Duff McKagan once played in. Unlike Kurt, Axl never wrote tortured poetry about feelings of alienation and angst—he adapted like a prisoner, ruthlessly, in fact. He would exact revenge through a screeching instrument and a pugilistic strut. The critics were shocked, just as they were with John Carpenter, who was initially described as a "pornographer of gore" in the aftermath of *The Thing*. But horror fans would fetishize his practical effects, music, storytelling, and genius use of Kurt Russell as an American antihero. Guns N' Roses were similarly polarizing for the critics, which permanently gifted them with a populist appeal.

As to be expected, the band's earliest reviews are a confusing blur of either puritanical protest or lustful mania. Just as Robert Hilburn at the *L.A. Times* spoke of the "thematic intelligence and honesty" of their music, the *Village Voice*'s Robert Christgau pilloried them for their drunkenness and misogyny. At first, the sheriffs of popular culture, from the editors at *Rolling Stone* to the *Village Voice*, had decided that Guns N' Roses were, to coin an old Hollywood term, an "unlikable property." They were what critics like Christgau held their noses at and described as "testosterone poisoning" that was driven by alcoholism and the same unintellectual ethos of other fleeting hair bands. They weren't completely wrong, but in L.A. the scene was thirsty for the next Doors, with the British music press enlisted to help develop the sequel. New York was pressing the mute button on what they viewed as another dim L.A. band that was more hedonistic than artistic. Christgau's *Village Voice* would rank *Appetite for Destruction* 26th out of 40 albums in the 1988 Pazz & Jop Critics Poll, which was the same year in which Guns N' Roses had a *Billboard* number-one hit single and a number-one album. Guns N' Roses talked back to the prejudice of the highbrow music critics in New York on October 23, 1987, when Guns N' Roses first played the Ritz, which was coupled with appearances on

Headbangers Ball and an acoustic set at CBGB on October 30, 1987, which included a rare performance of "One in a Million."

What made Guns N' Roses seem so lowbrow to the critics was what Slash described in the *L.A. Times* in 1986 as "extremities of violence and sex." By the summer of 1987, *Kerrang!* had officially labeled them the "most dangerous band in the world." As one of the first L.A. rock bands to emerge out of the ashes of The Doors and the '60s, this meant they would be colored by the shadow of Manson. In 1989, a reporter asked Manson to describe himself in a sentence, to which he replied: "I'm a tramp, a bum, a hobo . . . I'm a boxcar and a jug of wine and a straight razor—if you get too close to me."

The symbolic significance of the straight razor comes from '50s greasers who wielded it on the schoolyard; frontiersmen; Mr. Blonde in *Reservoir Dogs*; GIs; mafia assassins; skinheads; and Brando's insane Colonel in *Apocalypse Now*. It was what Judy Garland was rumored to have used to cut her throat in the '50s, in an attempted suicide. It is a classic Hollywood prop and masculine instrument that's both precise and deadly in unreliable hands. The straight razor was what Axl Rose would use to graze the throat of a trucker who tried to sexually assault him in a hotel circa 1980, when Axl was 18 or 19. Hitchhiking from Indiana and L.A., Axl was offered to share room by a man who would forever distort his view of homosexuals. "I went to sleep and woke up while this guy was trying to rape me," Axl told *Rolling Stone* in 1989. "I pinned him between the door and the wall. I had a straight razor," Axl added. "I pulled the razor and said, 'Don't ever touch me! Don't ever think about touching me! Don't touch yourself and think about me! Nothing!'"

"I'm proheterosexual," he added.

The big city would reinvent Axl Rose into a masculine nativist; the kid from dime novels who gunned down those who violated him. He was transformed by the grotesqueries he would photograph with his eyes as a bum, hobo, snuff-film fetishist, and white working-class punk who suffered from a manic form of depression that gave him a *straight razor* personality.

Axl was a blue jean–wearing rebel who felt alienated from the jocks. He was "the kid" in Cormac McCarthy's *Blood Meridian* facing the jagged edge of a cowboy's bottleneck. The straight razor was simultaneously his defense mechanism and sidearm. By his 18th birthday, Axl was a survivor of rape, a physical assault at the hands of his strictly Pentecostal stepfather, and the scars of hitchhiking from Middle Indiana to L.A. He was the origin story of a vigilante action film protagonist.

Axl would go on to become the hard-rock prototype of the deranged stuntman in Tarantino's *Death Proof* (2007), who uses a black '69 Dodge Charger as a phallic murder weapon. Guns N' Roses was *Grindhouse* (2007) scored to Axl Rose's supercharged falsetto (like a Harley with too much torque) and Slash's slithering guitar, which seemed unharmed by the poison being injected into his arms. Slash was a daredevil junkie. Even though his nickname was not a reference to the slashing effect of a knife or the edge of a straight razor, it produces vivid recall of slasher film imagery. "Slash" evokes the image of Michael Myers's kitchen knife on the cover of *Halloween* (1978), which is a John Carpenter classic that was fetishized by the second-most famous Guns N' Roses guitarist, Buckethead.

Slash soloed like a wasted zombie, always with a cigarette dangling from his bottom lip that would occasionally collapse onto his glistening skin. Leaning back with his curly hair swinging sweat into the air, the burning cigarette could travel from stomach down into skintight leather pants like a torch being waved at the head of a hissing cobra (as observed once by photographer Robert John). Slash was the reboot of the unkillable junkie persona of Keith Richards, but more Faustian, like Johnny Blaze in *Ghost Rider* (2007), an imperishable daredevil who had negotiated a deal with the Devil.

Slash's flaming skull was his bootleg '59 Gibson Les Paul that glowed like a comet flying through space. It was a handmade guitar constructed by a luthier from Greenfield, Massachusetts, who was the humble architect whose bones were eventually buried under the Celtic cross on the more mainstream cover of *Appetite for Destruction*. The story of Slash's guitar has a mythological weight behind it that will be explored in the proceeding chapters, but for teens who discovered him in a voodooist's top hat that sat over a wilderness of curls, where a lit cigarette seemed to be the only camp-fire for miles, Slash looked like a B-movie parody of a zombie rock star. He had a *Rocky Horror*–style caricature of himself tattooed on his arm. His top hat would become as inseparable from his myth as the brown fedora is to Freddy Krueger, or the black suede hat is to Stevie Ray Vaughan—one of Slash's guitar heroes.

Guns N' Roses might have been an '80s metal band, at least in terms of their earliest definition, but they strutted into the Reagan-era tattooed with the malaise and gore of '70s culture. The individual traits of each member would combine into an explosive reaction that ignited on the Sunset Strip, circa 1985, when the Gun met the Rose. They would turn the Strip into a stylish diorama of *Faces of Death,* with five skulls placed over a Celtic cross that looked like the neon marquee hanging over the strip club in a Reagan-era erotic thriller, e.g., *Fear City* (1984).

3

RUNNIN' WITH THE DEVIL

"THERE'S THAT WORD AGAIN: HEAVY. WHY ARE THINGS SO
HEAVY IN THE FUTURE? IS THERE A PROBLEM WITH THE
EARTH'S GRAVITATIONAL PULL?"

—BACK TO THE FUTURE (1985)

The '80s began with the scandalous image of a 15-year-old Brooke
Shields stretching on a pair of Calvin Klein jeans. "Do you know what
comes between me and my Calvins?" asked Shields, "Nothing." It was
amplified by Morton Downey Jr.'s nicotine-laced lips, which used the
First Amendment as an ashtray. In conservative America, Vietnam's
weltschmerz produced a desire to go back in time to Rockwellian white
picket fences and station wagons—a country defined by Ronald Reagan's
1984 "Morning in America" campaign ad. The '80s were a ray of simulated sunshine and Pepsi Fresh capitalism being injected into a darkened
wasteland. NASA's planned launch of the *Challenger* was designed to
boost morale; instead it produced seven dead astronauts and yet another
reason to distrust the government. The '80s were launched as an idealistic
campaign to purge Vietnam from the American consciousness. "Why
would we ever want to return to where we were, less than four short
years ago?" asked the narrator from Reagan's campaign ad, which was
satirized in *Back to the Future Part II* (1989), where at Café '80s, a digital
Reagan welcomes Marty McFly to a place where it is "always morning in
America, even in the afternoon."

In terms of popular culture, the '80s were suffocated by libidinousness men sculpting their abs as if they were pro wrestlers using David Lee Roth posters for motivation. This isn't merely a comical metaphor, it is eyewitness testimony provided by former Poison manager Vicky Hamilton, who would watch Bret Michaels perform ab crunches in front of a David Lee Roth poster. David Lee Roth was the role model for what would become the most pornographic and mannerless period in rock history. If the '80s were a decade dominated by men overcompensating with gladiatorial levels of toxic masculinity, then David Lee Roth was their sensei: a charismatic cokehead who continuously jumped off his drum riser, some 10 feet in the air, and injured himself like an inebriated trapezist.

David Lee Roth was the illogical blending of Fred Astaire with a circus promoter. "Van Halen is entertainment," he once said, "delivered at maximum impact, but it's entertainment." In the early '80s, Eddie Van Halen's guitar solo was as critical to defining youth culture as Michael Jackson's moonwalk and Calvin Klein. It was Van Halen's stylized Stratocaster that helped deliver Michael Jackson's "Beat It" into millions of white suburban homes in 1983 (which reached number one in April). In fact, MTV had initially wanted to promote "Beat It" ahead of "Billie Jean" because of Van Halen's solo. It wasn't entirely prejudice on the part of MTV (even though most MTV's playlist was still overwhelmingly white). In 1983, Van Halen's guitar was an instrument of liberation, and in just 30 ear-melting seconds (on a track he rearranged with an added chord progression), it managed to scorch a hole through the color barrier separating R&B and heavy-metal on MTV. Legend has it that in the studio, the powerful sound of Van Halen's guitar blew a hole through a monitor speaker. This may have inspired the exploding amp in the opening scene in *Back to the Future* (1985), which is caused by a single guitar chord.

"Eddie was playing and so on," said Bruce Swedien, the sound engineer on *Thriller*, "And the monitor speakers literally caught on fire."

In *Back to the Future*, Marty plugs a tiny humbucking Chiquita into a colossal eight-foot amp, strums a chord, and gets blown across the room into a giant bookshelf. He slowly rises from beneath a pile of books, removing his reflective aviator sunglasses, "Whoa . . . rock n' roll," he says. This was the future of heavy metal.

Van Halen was sent here, according to David Lee Roth in *Circus*, 1978, to "drag the kids across the finish line right into the 1980s." Van Halen's guitar was like the DeLorean flux capacitor. It was the musical equivalent of a secretly engineered spy plane or an alien spacecraft (in *Back to the Future*, Eddie Van Halen's distorted guitar transforms a Walkman into a terrifying transmission from the future. The scene from *Back to the Future* was a reference to the extraterrestrial experience of hearing Van Halen's "Eruption" in 1978, which was one minute and 43 seconds of what it sounded like to nuke the stagnation of the '70s and build a high-speed race course over it.

"Eddie Van Halen is the first guitar hero of the eighties," David Lee Roth told *Circus*.

As a guitar player, Eddie Van Halen had taken the blues and transformed it into a convergence of rocket science and kinesthetic brilliance. He would invent his own sound—a cybernetic extension of his arm; part human, part machine, like RoboCop. He blended the virtuosity of Paganini with the overconfident ambition of John DeLorean (it was never "Built to Last" like Ford). No guitarist in history wanted to patent his own sound as much as Eddie Van Halen did. His fingers were faster than any other guitar player in the '80s. He was, in the Old West sense, the fastest gun in the West. He not only produced a new way of hammering his fret and manipulating the vibrato of his guitar, but he studied the mechanics of his instrument like an engineer building a space shuttle. Eddie would tinker with the voltage controls of his Marshall amps, the pickups, the wood, and fingering techniques that would produce a sound he described in *Guitar Player* as a "Gibson-type of sound, but with a Strat vibrato." It was as if he had taken all his knowledge of his instrument and turned it into a computer program that only he could code. His tone sacrificed melancholy and emotion for the sharp-edged perfectionism of a German sports car. There was no alternative to this, until Slash, who transported the guitar back to the '70s. Van Halen had a sound that *MTV News* host Kurt Loder would describe as "faster, less heavy." It became the most exploited musical innovation of the decade. If Jimi Hendrix had transformed the electric guitar into an instrument of psychedelic experimentation, then Eddie Van Halen had turned it into an instrument of mass production, like Air Jordan basketball sneakers. Between 1978 and roughly 1985, every headbanging guitar solo was infringing on Eddie Van Halen's trademark. When Slash emerged from the asphalt jungle in 1985, it were as if he was trying to sound like the bluesy alternative to Van Halen.

In his book *Fargo Rock City*, writer Chuck Klosterman described the impact Eddie Van Halen's guitar had on music: "Though the term wasn't yet applicable, those first two Van Halen albums created a future where metal would be 'glamorous,' both visually and musically. Marc Bolan knew how glam rock was supposed to look, but Eddie Van Halen invented how it was supposed to sound."

If Van Halen was the new designer drug, then Mötley Crüe was the mouth-frothing overdose. They would offer Guns N' Roses the wardrobe, but not the sound. Mötley Crüe was the band that turned metal's flirtation with the occult into a *Hustler* magazine version of Satanic porn. It's been said that Mötley Crüe singer Vince Neil—permanently trapped in Freud's phallic stage—would blow kisses to posters of supermodels the way WWII GIs would stare bug-eyed at Betty Grable's legs. Crüe managed to hook Midwestern teenagers with 1983's *Shout at the Devil* by combining the branding of KISS with horror-film tropes—which were buried in the DNA of Guns N' Roses. Crüe ruled the Sunset Strip from roughly 1981–86, before Guns N' Roses would emerge as cynical antiheroes who would provide an alternative to Mötley Crüe and David Lee Roth, who lived like a porn star with a nose for cocaine and expensive cars, specifically a black Mercedes-Benz with a skull painted on the hood.

David Lee Roth was like a male stripper with the slick boardroom panache of a Fortune 500 marketing exec. Even in 1986, after he had the nerve to leave Van Halen, the kids were masturbating to Van Halen solos.

Writer Charles Bukowski predicted the temporal junction point of David Lee Roth in an issue of *Creem* from 1975: "This generation loves cocks. The next generation we're going to see huge pussies, guys jumping into them like swimming pools and coming out all red and blue and white and gold and gleaming about 6 miles north of Redondo Beach."

If metal was a diverse and flourishing marketplace in the '80s, then Slash's imitable guitar on *Appetite for Destruction* presented the first serious competition to Eddie Van Halen's monopoly.

In one of their first radio interviews from December 1986, Guns N' Roses appeared on L.A.'s heavy metal or "pure rock" fountainhead, KNAC-FM, which was hosted by Lady Di, one of the station's popular female disc jockeys. It was just eight months after the band had been signed to Geffen by A&R wunderkind Tom Zutaut (who jumped over from Elektra), and the band was promoting their first live EP, *Live ?!*@ Like a Suicide*, which was about as live as a laugh track on a family sitcom (in a cost-cutting measure, the band overdubbed live crowd noise from a '70s rock festival called the Texxas Jam). The EP was limited to ten thousand copies, a move that would advertise them like the *rara avis* of the Sunset Strip—the first glam band that was being sold like a grainy underground smut film, or an art piece, rather than a mass-produced product. They were being promoted as radio unfriendly, with a purposefully misanthropic EP title.

When Lady Di asked the band what direction the local scene was going in 1987, Slash jumped in with, "towards a more '70s-type of sound . . . " that was less about laser-fast guitar solos than a crackling flirtation with Joe Perry's attack on "Walk This Way." Izzy Stradlin continued, "East, east . . . heading east," as he rhetorically pointed to CBGB, as his musical awakening was with the Ramones, who appeared on *Don Kirshner's Rock Concert* on September 19, 1977 and introduced punk to a TV dinner audience. "The Ramones were my favorite," he would tell TuneCore's Jeff Price in 2006. The disobedient minimalism of the Ramones would become part of Izzy's identity. "I like to keep it really simple," Izzy told the Lafayette *Journal & Courier* in 1993.

Axl contextualized their retro ethos:

"A lot of bands seemed to come out of the '80s where everybody was jumping on some kind of bandwagon . . . in the '70s there was a lot of bands that were getting in touch with themselves . . . "

In other words, Guns N' Roses were a postmodern Frankenstein stitching together elements from the '70s, which separated them from the "bandwagon" sound of the '80s. Axl did not have a David Lee Roth poster hanging on his wall. Axl had wrapped himself in snake- and lizard-print fabrics and screamed with the emotional prosody of Janis Joplin on *The Dick Cavett Show*. Axl sounded like a wounded animal's last fight for survival. Something inside him was screaming to be unchained. His pharyngeal resonance created a kind of sandpaper rasp that turned his tight vibrato into the combination of immense control and animalistic unpredictability.

In the glam scene of the mid-1980s, Axl's falsetto would become as genre-defining as Eddie Van Halen's guitar. It would eventually become an *SNL* parody in 1991, when Adam Sandler, as Axl Rose, and Kiefer Sutherland, as Slash, performed classic children's songs as "Kiddie Metal" covers. Though it would become a cliché, Axl Rose's voice began as a bluesy shock-and-awe on the Sunset Strip. Axl could sing two notes at the same time (i.e., overtone singing), which produces a sustained hum in the lower register, like a bagpipe. Climbing towards the top of his register, Axl sounded like a distorted World War II air-raid siren blasting through the London sky. His smoky baritone was so deep that in later interviews, circa 1991, it became resonant and distinctive, almost like actor Yul Brynner's smoky voice. Axl's alto singing voice, from roughly 1980–94, unleashed a torrential downpour of internal revolt, sexual violence, trauma, and a barbarian response to the first line in Rousseau's *Social Contract*: "Man is born free, but everywhere he is in chains."

In the early days, Axl Rose's falsetto was a declaration of independence from the precision of Van Halen, as well as the high camp of Mötley Crüe. In one of the earliest-known recordings of a Guns N' Roses rehearsal, recorded in 1985 (prior to Slash joining that summer), they can be heard working through a ballad Axl had co-written with Izzy, titled "Don't Cry," which is the first song Izzy and Axl wrote together.

There's a tattoo on Axl Rose's right arm of a woman's face. It looks like a painting by Patrick Nagel; something you'd see plastered on the window of a modern hair salon. It has Italian traits. The face belongs to Monique

Lewis. "Don't Cry" is about Axl and Izzy's infatuation with Monique Lewis, an enigmatic model who dated Izzy and brought Axl to tears. "November Rain" is not about her. Axl had been working on "November Rain" from 1983 until it was recorded as a demo in 1986. But "Don't Cry" was written in the spring 1985, when they were still engineering their sound. According to Guns N' Roses fan Kevin Belasco (the owner of the rare recording from 1985), this was the original lineup of Guns N' Roses, which included Tracii Guns on guitar and Rob Gardner on drums. The tape was probably recorded at a rehearsal space operated by Willie Basse in the San Fernando Valley. You can hear Axl flexing his undamaged vocals on the recording. To get as high as Axl does, it indicates his larynx is highly placed, according to one vocal coach I talked to. At 23, he sounded like an aged blues singer, like John Fogerty crooning "Pagan Baby" in a hyper-masculine power posture.

At the age of five, Axl began singing in his Pentecostal church (not in the choir, but as an ensemble with his brother and sister). His stepfather, Stephen Bailey, forbade the young boy from listening to rock and roll or watching TV. If he disobeyed, he would strike him. As a young adult, Axl would occasionally listen to music on a transistor radio (either on the playground or at the park), which introduced him to Elton John's "Bennie and Jets," one of the first songs that would inspire him to chase stardom. "That's when I decided I wanted to play for big . . . in front of big crowds," he told *Interview* magazine in 1992. One of the first tunes he connected with on a deeper level was John's 1975 hit "Someone Saved My Life Tonight," which he listened to on an old electric radio. It was the only single released off *Captain Fantastic and the Brown Dirt Cowboy,* and John refused to cut the song down from six minutes and 45 seconds (Axl fought a similar battle of artistic integrity with both "Sweet Child O' Mine" and "November Rain"). The song tells the story of Elton John's suicide attempt through metaphors of bondage, torture, and domination. Keep this in your notes, as Elton John would shape Axl's desire to compose his torment through the both the keys of a grand piano and his distinctively male gaze.

"I was brainwashed in a Pentecostal church," Axl told *RIP* in 1992. With a tendency to pontificate, particularly during the *Use Your Illusion* era,

Axl's detailed his upbringing in the final portion of a three-part interview with *RIP*:

> My particular church was filled with self-righteous hypo-
> crites who were child abusers and child molesters. These
> were people who'd been damaged in their own childhoods
> and in their lives. These were people who were finding God
> but still living with their damage and inflicting it upon their
> children. I had to go to church anywhere from three to
> eight times a week. I even taught Bible school while I was
> being beaten and my sister was being molested. We'd have
> televisions one week, then my stepdad would throw them
> out because they were satanic. I wasn't allowed to listen to
> music. Women were evil. Everything was evil. I had a really
> distorted view of sexuality and women. I remember the first
> time I got smacked for looking at a woman. I didn't know
> what I was looking at, and I don't remember how old I was,
> but it was a cigarette advertisement with two girls coming
> out of the water in bikinis. I was just staring at the TV—not
> thinking, just watching—and my dad smacked me in the
> mouth, and I went flying across the floor.

With the tape recorder rolling during one of the earliest known Guns N' Roses rehearsals, Axl would growl, *"Ahhhhh*, no, no, no," as if in that small rehearsal space, he was facing down a smoke-filled blues bar. It was nothing more than practice for Izzy Stradlin, a wandering gypsy who preferred to live in the shadows, while Axl Rose was the fire-breathing dragon who wanted to conquer all Seven Kingdoms. It was a struggle for control over the tone of Guns N' Roses—which was quietly being waged between Axl and Izzy—that would give Guns N' Roses such an unstable energy—the convergence of "opposing elements."

The two met in 1976 as freshman at Jefferson High in Lafayette, Indiana, where Izzy was described by one of his teachers as a more introspective and damaged figure who had a "pall hanging over him" and who seemed to withdraw from his classmates by his senior year. Izzy and Axl were Midwestern loners who came to L.A. and immediately felt alienated by its superficiality and cliquishness. Axl Rose would explain these feelings in the interview with KNAC: "A lot of the bands seem to come in . . . I'm gonna be heavy metal, or I'm going to be new wave . . . because that's what it takes to make it. And a lot of people forgot about feeling; forgot about why they were writing the music and what it did for them." The two boys from Lafayette wanted to plant their roots in the cold asphalt of the big city.

In 1997, Ice-T described albums as time capsules "sealed up and sent into space so that when you look back you can say that's the total reflection of the time." This is what *Appetite for Destruction* has become, but upon its release in 1987, it felt like it was a time capsule from the era of Led Zeppelin and Aerosmith. It was also one of the first metal albums that depicted L.A. like a '70s filmmaker, as opposed to self-immolating mockumentary. *Appetite* would hold a cracked, graffitied mirror up to L.A. and force it to see every blemish, zit, scar, and the needle mark of contemporary society. They were reintroducing the polluted '70s into the simulated Reagan-era atmosphere of sunshine and *Saturday Evening Post* propaganda.

"We sang about California and being young," said Dean Torrence of '60s rock duo Jan and Dean, who would contribute to the myth of a girl-crazy and bouncy California beach that was as much a fantasy as the picture on Doc's wall in Thomas Pynchon's *Inherent Vice*, which depicted a "Southern California beach that never was—palms, bikini babes, surfboards, the works." Pynchon describes the picture hanging on the Doc's wall as a "window to look out of when he couldn't deal with looking out of the traditional glass-type one in the other room." Guns N' Roses were forcing the neon '80s to confront the grim realities of contemporary life.

Appetite for Destruction depicted an American city covered in needles, severed body parts, used condoms, half-empty bottles of whiskey, and macabre skulls. It was depicting a Southern California city as it *really* was. Like Albert Camus, it understood that "at the heart of all beauty lies something inhuman." It was the dystopian alternative reality of the Venice

Beach depicted in Oliver Stone's stylized rock bio, *The Doors* (1991), where a golden patina creates a psychedelic experience that removes you from the infernos of Vietnam, as a beautiful woman adjusts her flannel bikini and stares aimlessly at the molten sun, which looks like a gold medallion melting into the Pacific Ocean. *Appetite for Destruction* produces the effect of being accosted on the streets of a sunless dystopia decorated with burn barrels and hypothermic corpses. This was a band that was exposing the phoniness of Reagan's "Morning in America." This is what made them so different from Mötley Crüe, who wrote about L.A. as if it were a modern Babylon, as opposed to a graffitied wasteland. Guns N' Roses were alternative before the word alternative was ever used in popular music. Like so much of popular culture in the '80s, they were shamelessly revisionist, like Tarantino after them, but they were also a jarring reminder that the American dream was overdosing on nostalgia.

By 1984, it had become increasingly voguish to resurrect images from the Eisenhower era. The cover of *Esquire*, March 1986, depicts a completely plastic image of Marilyn Monroe: "America on the Rerun!" The editors of *Esquire* would argue that America was experiencing a kind of cultural time warp, where Madonna was recreating Marilyn Monroe in *Gentlemen Prefer Blondes* (1953), while MTV was recreating looks from the past three decades (e.g., Queen as Fritz Lang characters in the video for "Radio Ga Ga"). It all coincided with the birth of classic rock radio, which was ignited by the popularity of the CD as a way of reexperiencing classic albums through high fidelity. The price of CD players dropped from $900 in 1983 to less than $150 in 1987. Cassette tapes were still the most popular format at the time, which was how most fans would first experience *Appetite for Destruction*—an '80s metal album that felt vintage and modern, a rupture in the space-time continuum. My generation discovered them on CD, which is to say that by the early '90s, *Appetite for Destruction* was already classic. It aged quickly because it was born preaged with a '70s patina.

"We're not doing anything that I would call original—it's all been done before," Axl told *Music Connection* in 1986.

Even before Soundgarden, Guns N' Roses peered into the "black sun of melancholy," as it was written in Gérard de Nerval's 1853 poem "El Desdichado," as their generation had seen the American dream turned into the noxious clouds hanging over Vietnam. The Old West revivalism of the '80s was America's move to reclaim its masculinity. The American outlaw would influence not only Guns N' Roses' look, but also their ethos. They were not alone, of course. In the world of fashion during the mid-to-late 1980s, Claude Montana would draw from the Old West with his cowboy in Bat Masterson black; Valentino would include a string tie and 10-gallon hat on his runway. The Clint Eastwood look was momentarily in vogue. Guns N' Roses were revisiting the culture of both the '70s and the Colt revolver mystique of the Old West. It is simply no coincidence that their first appearance in a film was as a neo-Western gang attending a funeral in Clint Eastwood's *The Dead Pool* (1988), a forgettable installment in the Dirty Harry franchise that was highlighted by a Jim Carrey lip sync of "Welcome to the Jungle."

Axl was communicating to the KNAC metalhead that Guns N' Roses were a muscle car with some rust on its chrome, chipped paint, sun-burned leather, not a Beamer with beige-leather interior, and certainly not a Benz with a skull printed on it.

As bands like Mötley Crüe and Van Halen were being described as "bubblegum metal" in the rock magazines, Guns N' Roses were being advertised in local zines (and in their publicity materials) as contraband that was too *dangerous* for terrestrial radio and MTV. They weren't bubblegum, they were chewing tobacco. Speaking to the UK's *Sounds* magazine on April 4, 1987, Izzy Stradlin described Mötley Crüe as "more teen metal," declaring that Guns N' Roses wanted to go for a more "roots-oriented sound than most other bands." Though it's worth noting that Geffen had assigned Tom Zutaut to find the next Mötley Crüe, which was, in his estimation, Guns N' Roses. Without Mötley Crüe, Guns N' Roses may never have inked a deal with Geffen. But Izzy was protesting the fact that the rock tabloids were continuously comparing Guns N' Roses to Mötley Crüe, which was simply lazy reporting. Guns N' Roses would define their point of difference during every media interview between 1986 and 1988. They were going for what Axl described in *LA Weekly* as a more "depressing" sound, and what Slash described in a 1987 issue of *BAM* as "very realistic," which Axl echoed in his interview with Steve Harris. They were going back into the jungle. Mötley Crüe bassist Nikki Sixx would define his band very differently in a *Rock Beat* interview from 1987: "Our reality is a lot of people's fantasy."

In a July 1986 interview with the *L.A. Times*, Axl would describe the theme of "Welcome to the Jungle" as being based on "a lot of violence in the world. That's the environment we live in, and we like to show what we live in rather than hide it and act like everything is nice and sugary." They were promoting themselves as brutal realists, like John Cassavetes if he was doing a seedy road movie (e.g., Vincent Gallo's *The Brown Bunny*, which, like "Rocket Queen," included an unsimulated sexual act). Like Cassavetes, Guns N' Roses wanted to manipulate their audience into viewing their world as an expression of reality. It was a slaying of the glossy MTV fantasy in order to slice deep into some kind of truth. "I hate entertainment," Cassavetes once said, which is the message Guns N' Roses wanted to communicate in 1986. They blurred the lines between MTV and the streets.

Guns N' Roses began with a juxtaposition that defined The Doors early on, a band that chose to play a brooding and psychedelic version of the muddy blues amidst a crowd of colorful flower children. This would cause rock critics to turn Guns N' Roses into the next Doors. Writer and former Doors' manager Danny Sugerman argued in his book *Appetite for Destruction: The Days of Guns N' Roses* (1991) that Axl was a rerun of Jim Morrison. Sugerman mythologized Axl in such a way that it made him seem more mystical than other glam metal singers. The more I study their relationship, it seems no writer pushed Axl closer to imperceptive narcissism than Danny Sugerman, who would charm the singer by overstating his importance in the pantheon of rock gods. Through Axl, it seems, Sugerman was looking for a vehicle that could help him reexperience the orgiastic feast that was Morrison; what 19th-century French poet Arthur Rimbaud described in "A Season in Hell" as the "key to the ancient feast where I might find my appetite again."

Sugerman wanted to use Guns N' Roses to repair the timeline that was broken when Jim Morrison died in 1971. "I really wanted to believe that Axl could succeed where Morrison had failed—that he could survive the abyss . . . that there is a place to go that Morrison stopped short of," wrote Sugerman in *Spin*. Sugerman would feed Axl quotes from William Blake, Joseph Campbell, and recite for him Greek myth (Icarus and Dionysus), hoping, in some bizarre way, to groom Axl into the new Jim Morrison. "Danny Sugerman would compare him to Jim all the time; he schooled me on Morrison, since I'd never see him, and Axl was that. Had the rest of the band sucked, I would have signed just Axl. It's a mythological thing that nobody in rock has possessed since," Tom Zutaut told me.

Former Poison and Guns N' Roses manager Vicky Hamilton would make similar comparisons, often citing a rumor that Axl once threw girlfriend Erin Everly into a closet and set it on fire, which may or may not have happened. It certainly did happen in Oliver Stone's fantasy of The Doors, where Jim Morrison pushes Pamela Courson into a closet and lights it on fire. The original source of the story is Doors' photographer Bobby Klein, as it was told to him by Courson one evening. Guns N' Roses photographer Robert John would describe a similar story involving Axl and Erin.

Here's Alan Niven (who managed Guns N' Roses from October 31, 1986, to April 1991) discussing Sugerman's influence on Axl's psyche: "Danny Sugerman did immense damage. Axl, and his susceptibility for sycophancy, was not ready for Danny's musings, and I did my best to keep them apart. Danny was full of metaphysics and *Axl you're a trickster* . . . Axl wasn't ready for that." On April 21, 1991, the *L.A. Times* would publish a letter from Alan Niven regarding Danny Sugerman's 1990 *Spin* profile on Axl, in which Niven refers to Sugerman as an "exploitive sycophant" and "an opportunistic parasite." Sugerman would later admit that his profile was rushed by the editors at *Spin*, and thus contained misquotes. "They never showed me a final draft of the piece," he told the *L.A. Times*. The publisher of *Spin* at the time was Bob Guccione Jr., who along with *Kerrang!* writer Mick Wall, would be smeared into history with 1991's "Get in the Ring," a diss track that declared war on the music press.

Sugerman explained his fetish in his *Spin* profile: "The reason I wanted to do a book on you guys was to show that we need Guns N' Roses," he told Axl, "to show that even if everyone on the planet 'just said no' tomorrow, our culture, our society, would still need someone to celebrate and act out the great self-immolation trip." *Spin* would publish the profile with a photo of Axl in a T-shirt advertising a "Drug Free America." Sugerman sounded like he needed Axl Rose to transform into a more extreme version of Jim Morrison. This is from his biography on the band: "Although Guns N' Roses had been transubstantiating the light and energy of life into the immortality of music, the day was soon coming when Dionysus would require a more substantial demonstration of loyalty in exchange for his blessings."

Sugerman romanticized Axl as a doomed prophet who was born to sacrifice himself for his art, like Jim Morrison, and that Guns N' Roses were the sort of band Lester Bangs argued the Stooges were in the 1970s: "most authentic originals," a band that delivered "mass psychic liberation" from the industrialized system of corporate rock. There was a religious need in Sugerman to have Axl fill the vacuum that was left behind when Morrison was found dead in a bathtub in Paris on July 3, 1971, whereas Axl had a far more sustainable life planned for himself. In his own way, Axl Rose was rejecting the trip, as well as the "live fast, die young" philosophy of a previous generation of rock stars.

"I went to Morrison's grave site last year," Axl told Sugerman in *Spin*. "I knew I could go the same way Jim did, that I could go down in flames; crucify myself on the altar of rock 'n' roll . . . I could sacrifice myself like Morrison did, if I wanted to." Sugerman would quote William Blake: "The path of excess leads to the palace of wisdom."

"Not if you die," said Axl, who allegedly visited Morrison's grave at age 27, the same age Jim Morrison was found dead in Paris. "If you die, the path of excess leads to a dirt plot in a foreign land that people pour booze on and put out cigarettes on."

Axl Rose never wanted to be a martyr. He was asserting his independence as an artist, and yet, when you study the myth of Morrison, you see the mold of the kind of rock star Axl Rose would *almost* become. "I've always been attracted to ideas that were about revolt against authority," wrote Morrison in his 1967 Elektra Records bio. "I like ideas about the breaking away or overthrowing of established order. I am interested in anything about revolt, disorder, chaos . . . The world we suggest is of a new wild west."

Guns N' Roses saw themselves as the "new wild west." Maybe Sugerman had a point that he oversold to Axl Rose. After all, when Axl would take off his shirt to reveal his cut physique and translucent pallor; when he'd tightly close his irradiating eyes and melt into his mic stand; when he'd continuously express his annoyance with this audience—was he not, at least in *brief* glimpses, the Jim Morrison of the MTV generation? He began as a physiologically flawless marble statue of a rock star; emotionally fragile, almost childlike, like Morrison as interpreted by Oliver Stone, who would portray his subject not as he was, but how he wanted him to be. Danny Sugerman was a consultant on the Oliver Stone film. The truth is hardly as important as the effect these kinds of myths have on the public perception of a rock star. I believe that you have to understand Jim Morrison in order to grasp the outlaw-shaman mythology of Axl Rose, which is based mostly on a Hollywood fantasy that we still live with today. It was a cinematic portrayal that Axl Rose himself found entertaining.

"Oliver Stone has assassinated Jim Morrison," wrote Ray Manzarek in the *L.A. Times* in 1991, criticizing Stone's focus on the salacious myth, instead of reality. The cinematic portrayal of Morrison as an Apache raindancing madman who saw beauty in self-sacrifice—a noble savage who was escaping the wounds of his past—is now mostly how the public views Jim Morrison. Oliver Stone may have *assassinated* the character of Jim Morrison for his bandmates, but not in terms of the culture. For most Americans, Oliver Stone reinvented Jim Morrison. This is what Danny Sugerman tried to do with Axl Rose, and failed, as Axl never fulfilled the "self-immolation trip." After publishing his book in 1991, and responding to Alan Niven's criticism in the *L.A. Times*, Danny Sugerman never wrote about Guns N' Roses again. He died from lung cancer in 2005, though most people just assume he overdosed. That's his myth.

For Axl Rose, the nihilism wasn't shamanic or spiritual. From 1986 on, he was inflicting severe damage onto himself in order to kill whatever was left of his childhood. The mythological portrait of Jim Morrison in Oliver Stone's film was an exploitation film. Stone's Morrison was a psychedelic cartoon; Axl Rose was pummeling us with stone-cold anxiety and fear. Sugerman wanted the two to converge on a voyage through the doors of perception. In 1987, all we saw was a Middle American redneck who had pulled himself out of poverty with the determination of a gunfighter. "He was much more educated," Axl said of Morrison during a *Rockline* interview in 1991. Axl would go on to say that he was flattered by Sugerman's comparisons. Like The Doors emerging just as the "Summer of Love" was decomposing, Guns N' Roses would break during the final days of Aqua Net hair metal. That's when they appeared on KNAC, as they were launching their careers at the perfect moment. In 1987, KNAC would stop playing new wave and began populating their playlist with more local rock music. They were fishing for a more local following during a period of time when the Sunset Strip was a mile-and-a-half stretch of flyers advertising glam metal bands like Poison, who'd often staple their flyers over those of Guns N' Roses—it was prime real estate, the beachfront condo for emerging metal bands. It's what Vicky Hamilton described as the "flyer wars." Guns N' Roses were both visually and philosophically symbolic of not only where the L.A. scene was headed, but also where KNAC wanted it to go: a rejection of new-wave fashion and East Coast snobbery, and a very clear and present threat to Reagan's "Morning in America." Guns N' Roses were a pastiche of rock's origins at the crossroads where Robert Johnson struck a deal with the Devil, what Axl described as possessing a "blues edge," which wasn't original, but had been previously blown away by rocket-powered Van Halen solos. Van Halen was so disgustingly popular during Slash's teenage years that they likely inspired his six-string rebellion towards a more blues-tinged sound.

In an interview from the Hotel Chelsea in New York, which first aired on *Headbangers Ball*, Axl Rose would describe his desire to find a guitar player who wasn't trying to be Eddie Van Halen:

"I came to L.A., and I saw all these people trying to be Eddie Van Halen," said Axl. "And it took five years to find somebody who played more from the heart, rather than just trying to be the fastest . . . "

If Van Halen had turned rock and roll into a speedboat skidding across the shores of Miami, then Guns N' Roses was dropping it onto the dirt roads of the Mississippi Delta, bringing it back to the jungle rhythms of Africa; a sound that had been exported to England and electrified in America with bands like Aerosmith—who Guns N' Roses were disciples of, the way the Rolling Stones were disciples of Muddy Waters and John Lee Hooker. This is, again, what made Guns N' Roses sound so vintage, and yet modern. By 1991, this was part of a dated sound (and look) that would push Guns N' Roses towards "dad rock" extinction. In terms of their image, Guns N' Roses were advertising themselves as a black-leather motorcycle gang; they were Motörhead without World War II memorabilia. It important to note that they were waving a black flag in a milieu occupied by bands that were embracing a neon-colored aesthetic that Guns N' Roses, rather astutely, had begun to remove from their wardrobe closet.

Their primal and bluesy branding is rooted in a *Music Journal* definition from 1958, describing rock and roll as a "throwback to jungle rhythms" that would incite "youth to orgies and violence." Guns N' Roses were a vehicle of rebellion for young people who had begun to see through Mötley Crüe's thinly veiled gimmickry. In *Fargo Rock City*, Klosterman described Mötley Crüe as "ephemeral, coke-addled deities." Del James, now a road manager on the Guns N' Roses reunion tour, described Mötley Crüe to me on Facebook as, "the most overrated band in the history of rock & roll! All flash and no substance . . . they sing about strippers and fighting and dazzle the kids with a stage show that makes people forget just how bad the music is . . . with the passage of time, Mötley Crüe have been exposed and we've become more objective. Simply put, they were never very good." Mötley Crüe was a stunt show. Their riffs felt like special effects; their lyrics romanticized a pyrotechnic adventurism that would melt down the peace symbol and mold it into the Mercedes-Benz logo on David Lee Roth's car.

Sigmund Freud viewed art as both an "illusion" and a "narcotic." For the egoist '80s rocker, cocaine was the perfect encapsulation of the two. But there was a doomed and darkly poetic quality to the drug that would differentiate Guns N' Roses, which they dubbed "Mr. Brownstone." Even though Morrison himself snorted copious amounts of cocaine and altered his consciousness with LSD (which he described as a "new kind of wine"), heroin was the drug that may have turned him into a martyr for rock and roll. Jim Morrison died at 27 in a bathtub in a Paris apartment of heart failure (but some believe he accidentally overdosed after snorting heroin).

It was a slightly more sophisticated and mystical fix. Heroin was poetically written into the tapestry of Persian mysticism and Charlie Parker's devilish horn. To get hooked on heroin pushed you closer to the spirit of surreal French poets hovering over the poppy groves of Afghanistan; whispering towards plumes of burning *teriak* rising towards the sun. Heroin is a derivative of opium, a drug that seduced poets like Baudelaire and influenced Rimbaud's "A Season in Hell," an artistic predecessor to Guns N' Roses' "Mr. Brownstone," which are both written as confessions of suffering. "One evening I seated beauty on my knees. And I found her bitter. And I cursed her," Rimbaud wrote. Guns N' Roses were turning Reagan's "Just Say No" puritanism into a seedy tale of spiritual poisoning. "Mr. Brownstone," no matter the misconceptions and protests from the religious right, is a song about the struggle to rid yourself of a very bitter kind of skin-poking orgasm. It was written as Axl Rose was shunning heroin in 1986. For Rimbaud it was the smoke rising off opium, a more organic prescription from the devilish poppy plant. For Rimbaud, it was necessary to "derange all senses," like the spiraling guitar and tribalistic drums on the intro of "Mr. Brownstone." Take a moment to study the photo of Guns N' Roses that appears on the back of their 1987 debut, *Appetite for Destruction*: it's as if you're looking into an opium den, as the five members melt into the threads of a sumptuous Persian rug at Take One Studio in Burbank, as a leather newsboy cap on Izzy Stradlin creates a shadow around his eyes that make him look like a terminally ill gunman (the Doc Holliday of his day), while Slash looks zombie-like and detached from the living. Izzy looked more like the guitar-collecting vampire from

Jim Jarmusch's *Only Lovers Left Alive* (2013). "I haven't been out in the sun for ages!" Izzy told *Circus* in 1989.

The blackened mood used by Guns N' Roses produced a thicker, black tar stickiness in the era of fast cars, fast women, fast guitar solos, and "Too Fast for Love." Drug associations often define the mythology of a band: LSD lifted Pink Floyd to a different level; crystal meth fueled Motörhead's firepower; alcohol lubricated the roaring engines of Metallica. In 2013, Aerosmith's Steven Tyler admitted to Australia's *60 Minutes* that he "snorted half of Peru." But for Guns N' Roses, it was the tortuous aroma of heroin—or the perception of its spiritual toxicity on "Mr. Brownstone"—that pushed them closer to the blues, and further East.

Axl Rose, who was prescribed lithium to combat his manic depression, seemed like he was incautiously self-medicating with heroin and other downers (which produce a toxic reaction when combined with lithium). On May 13, 1986, at Raji's, a rock club in Hollywood, Axl was being heckled by a drunk woman in the crowd. He proceeded to bash her over the head with the heavy cast-iron base of the mic stand. Axl Rose was like a rabid animal that needed to be put down.

"I don't care if my mother came up and started punching me," he told *LA Weekly* in 1986. "I'd hit her with the stand."

Heroin may have helped numb his more violent impulses, which may (or may not) have resulted in him throwing out of the band's rehearsal space and into the alley a traumatized 15-year-old girl. Axl's version of events, as reported in the *LA Weekly* in 1986, described a "hippie chick" messing with the band's equipment at their Gardner storage space, which was located behind Guitar Center, which Duff McKagan one described as their "gang headquarters—a place to rehearse, party, and, much of the time, to spend the night." The "hippie chick" apparently triggered Axl, who allegedly ripped her clothes off and sent her "running down Sunset naked, all dingy, doesn't even know her name." The incident occurred in 1985. It's been said that the girl's name was Michelle. In Stephen Davis's biography, he suggests the victim was Michelle Young who was later immortalized in the song "My Michelle," or as Davis described her, "prime Hollywood jailbait at fifteen." Though the girl's name was Michelle, she was not Michelle Young, whose sordid lifestyle was tattooed into the grooves of *Appetite for Destruction*. In 1985, Michelle Young was an adult, not a minor.

"He grabbed Michelle, tore her clothes off, threw her out into the alley, and locked the door. They didn't have sex, at least then," wrote Davis, who titled his subchapter: "The 'Rape' of My Michelle."

Slash would provide his recollection of events in his autobiography:

"My memory of the events is hazy, but from what I remember, she had sex with Axl up in the loft. Towards the end of the night, maybe as the drugs and booze wore off, she lost her mind and freaked out intensely. Axl told her to leave and tried throwing her out. I attempted to help mediate the situation to get her out quietly, but that wasn't happening."

The story varies from accounts of Axl and Slash chasing a nude woman down Sunset Boulevard, to Axl Rose throwing a girl out of their rehearsal space after having sex with her consensually, or not, depending on who you ask. If the girl was 15, Axl, 23, would have been committing statutory rape. When the police finally showed up, the timing of this varies, Axl was behind a block of guitar amps, "going at it" with another girl, gloating like an outlaw evading the town sheriff. Michelle's parents eventually filed a statutory rape charge. Axl was facing a mandatory five-year stint in prison. He decided to go into hiding. Vicky Hamilton would later say that she helped hide Axl in her apartment. "He said it was consensual," she told *The Daily Mail* in 2015. "But he'd thrown her out of the studio and locked her out without her clothes and she was mad. He went to court for it months later but the charges were dropped."

Vicky Hamilton believes it was consensual sex. "No one would go up there with a band member if they were not planning to," says Vicky. "As a woman, I do believe no means no, but I just don't think that was the case. Why would you go there? It's a dark rehearsal spot." In 1987, while be interviewed by *Music Connection*, Vicky would say that she felt like she was "harboring a rape fugitive!" What if she really were? All the available reports suggest the girl in question was 15. Maybe she shouldn't have helped Axl dodge a statutory rape charge, but she wasn't just the manager who helped book their shows or make introductions to record labels—she was also their surrogate mother. For a period of six months, Guns N' Roses lived in Vicky Hamilton's one-bedroom apartment on North Clark Street.

"There were pizza boxes and cigarette butts in the carpet, mounds of Marlboro Reds in the ashtray, empty Jack Daniel's and beer bottles all over the table, black hair dye all over the bathroom wall," she told *Rolling Stone* in 2016.

By the end of 1986, Vicky Hamilton would be shunned by Guns N' Roses. Once the band was signed to a record label, she was unceremoniously replaced with Alan Niven. Soon after, in 1987, she filed a $1-million lawsuit to recoup $25,000 she had been loaned to buy equipment and clothing for the band. She collected $35,000 in a private settlement with both Geffen Records and the band. After paying her lawyer and relinquishing her debt, she was left with $5,000 in her pocket. At one point in 1987, Axl Rose left a voice-mail on her answering machine threating to kill her (she had said something unflattering about him to *Musician* magazine). He also claimed she never managed Guns N' Roses. Vicky Hamilton had sacrificed herself so that Guns N' Roses could live long enough to make it. She booked their shows, fed them, pitched them to record labels, and gave them designer clothes, like a Ray Brown snakeskin belt that Axl would wear over black leather chaps. Once they were signed to Geffen Records, she was shunned and forgotten, a footnote in their history, whose biography has been rewritten by everyone who came after her—like biased Greek historian accounts of the scheming and manipulative women of Ancient Persia. Vicky Hamilton became a victim of the patriarchy in heavy metal. She was what Danny Sugerman would had described as a more "substantial demonstration of loyalty in exchange for his [Dionysus] blessings."

"She busts her ass 24 hours a day," Slash told *Music Connection* in 1986. "She doesn't get to pay her rent 'cause she spends all the money she can possibly get her hands on trying to get us off the ground."

In various interviews where they were questioned about the rape charges, they would often reply with cruel irreverence: "Rape charge? What rape charge?" Axl Rose in a July 6, 1986, interview in the *L.A. Times* would say that the "charges were dropped eventually, but for a while we had to go into hiding. We had undercover cops and the vice squad looking for us. They were talking a mandatory five years. It kind of settled my hormones for a while." The experience would partially inspire track number four on the "Guns" or "G" side of *Appetite for Destruction*, which was titled "Out Ta Get Me."

The sordid publicity was also *exactly* what the band was trying to produce in 1986: headlines as moral felonies. They were bikers ducking rape charges, fleeing the cops, and pummeling hippies at a Stones concert. The publicity derived from such events were exploited to advance the darkly de-glamorized image of Guns N' Roses as an anti-hair metal band. "I think sex is a great sell, but fear is even better," former Guns N' Roses and Geffen publicist Bryn Bridenthal told *Billboard* in 2017.

In a *Rock Scene* interview from October 1988, Axl was asked if being controversial was part of the band's mystique: "Yeah, obviously it is, but I mean, we don't go out of our way to be controversial. If we do something that is controversial, we'll use it to our best advantage. We'll use it in the press and stuff like that, but we don't sit around thinking up ways to be controversial." They certainly had the blueprint. Former Rolling Stones bassist Bill Wyman wrote about the publicity tactics of Stones' manager Andrew Loog Oldham in his 1990 autobiography, *Stone Alone: The Story of a Rock 'n' Roll Band*:

"Our reputation and image as the Bad Boys came later, completely there, accidentally. Andrew [Loog Oldham] never did engineer it. He simply exploited it exhaustively."

Did *Appetite*-era manager Alan Niven help shape Guns N' Roses into an anti-glam band the way Andrew Loog Oldham positioned the Rolling Stones as the "anti-Beatles"? I believe he contributed to the exploitation. "I wanted the band to be a contemporary version of the Rolling Stones," Niven told me. "With an equal catalog of brilliant statements. I believed that was their destiny, but that's just my point of view. I could be wrong." Bryn Bridenthal told *Billboard* in 2017 that, "If [Geffen] got stuck on a point, our go-to phrase was frequently 'would the Stones do it?'" During the KNAC interview, Axl would note that Geffen executives insisted that Guns N' Roses never censor their explicit lyrics. David Geffen wanted to keep Guns N' Roses authentic and crude (he would later regret this decision). Geffen was like Leslie Hill signing the Sex Pistols to EMI in '76 and actually *supporting* Malcolm McLaren's "cash from chaos" strategy.

Alan Niven was pitching them as a more hyper-American version of the Rolling Stones. Guns N' Roses were advertised as a scandalous marriage of violence and romance—which challenged the balance of order in a repressive bourgeois society that viewed sexual liberation as "pornography." Side two of *Appetite for Destruction* was named "R" for "Roses," which included the ballad "Sweet Child O' Mine," while side one, "Guns" was crafted like 2Pac's introduction on *All Eyez on Me* (1996), in which he declares that the police are chasing him, but that they can't touch him. 2Pac throws gangs signs in Kevlar. He spits at the camera. He's a Nietzschean outlaw who threatens to murder the future children of his rivals. He's also an earnest poet with the svelte body of a young ballet dancer, with Bambi eyes, and venerates his mother. Americans are drawn to these kinds of cinematic contradictions. Axl Rose was revitalizing the duality of Jimmy Cagney's hoodlum, who was paradoxically both delicate and tough. Axl personified this on one arm: a tattoo of a woman's face; on the other: the bloodthirsty battle cry of "Victory or Death."

This is how Axl Rose would introduce "Out Ta Get Me" during their MTV broadcast of *Live at the Ritz* in 1988, which was recorded on February 2, 1988: "We want to dedicate this song to the people who try to hold you back," said Axl, with an urban twang, his hair wrapped tightly underneath a blue bandana, while wearing Harley-Davidson suspenders and proudly displaying the "Victory or Death" military tattoo on his glistening arm. "To people that tell you how to *live*, people who tell you how to *dress*, people that tell you how to *talk*." By this point you can hear the band scoring his speech with a heavy humming sound. It's a terrifying speech, when you think about Axl's childhood, as his face nearly turns purple and transforms him from Bill Bailey into W. Axl Rose (aka WAR), the Charlie Manson of glam. "People that tell you what you can say, and what you can't say . . . I personally *don't* need *that*. I don't need that shit in my life," he starts peddling back, as his eyes begin to close, his shoulders tense up. Axl Rose, like Manson and Cagney's hoodlum, was the sort of charismatic criminal you could not take your eyes off. "Those are the kind of people that get me down. They make me feel like somebody, somebody out there is *out ta get me*."

By combining the Rolling Stones with an American biker gang, Niven was promoting Guns N' Roses as a nondenominational chapter of the Hells Angels, which made them seem more road-tested. They seemed like the subjects once glorified in Hunter S. Thompson's 1967 book, *Hell's Angels: The Strange and Terrible Saga of the Outlaw Motorcycle Gangs*: "Even people who think the Angels should all be put to sleep find it easy to identify with them. They command a fascination, however reluctant, that borders on psychic masturbation."

In their Geffen press kit, there's a quote from an executive that gives you a sense of how similar they were to a lawless biker gang: "These guys will be huge, if they live long enough." It was the classic trope of the rock star racing towards death; a limited-time engagement, what Danny Sugerman defined as their "doom philosophy." "The label was betting the band would be huge, and also that some of them wouldn't live long enough to cash their first royalty checks," wrote Stephen Davis in *Watch You Bleed*.

Guns N' Roses were going back in time in order to derange the senses of the present. It was a strategy that created bleeding headlines that made them seem more frightening than their contemporaries. They were promoted like an NC-17 tape found in the uncharted section of a video store. And it worked, for a while. For a brief moment in time, between 1987 and 1991, they were the Rolling Stones of their generation.

4

NOT A GLAM BAND

"WEST, HUH? WELL, WEST IS THAT WAY [POINTS HIS GUN].
AND THE BASTARDS WE GOTTA KILL ARE THAT WAY
[POINTS HIS GUN IN THE OPPOSITE DIRECTION]."

—*YOUNG GUNS* (1988)

How did a "reality-based" band like Guns N' Roses manage to appeal to an audience as colorfully incongruent as teenage prom queens, doltish skaters, Valley girls, metal shop students, strippers, insult comics, and gay executives at MTV?

"We do shoot straight from the hip; we're very realistic. We're not putting up some facade to sell records," Slash told *BAM* in November 1987, just as the band was beginning to aggressively sell themselves to a national audience. For anyone to suggest Guns N' Roses weren't being strategic when it came to their PR, I refer you to Axl Rose's letter to *Music Connection*'s Karen Burch in 1986, where he protests the magazine's refusal to be an "ally," claiming that Burch had agreed to give Guns N' Roses editorial and photo approval (a somewhat ludicrous claim). This would have been unprecedented. Axl described the cover photo taken by photographer Kristen Dahline as a "hideous representation of the artist's abilities as a photographer." Burch responded: "As for the foul taste in Rose's mouth—may I suggest he try a little soap to wash away what appears to be a severe case of sour grapes." This was the beginning of Axl Rose's irrational war with the media.

To understand the roots of Guns N Roses' anti-glam marketing strategy, it's important to examine the cover of the first Rolling Stones album, released on April 16, 1964, where each member is wearing a different outfit. You see a shadow painted over the eyes of each member to form a fatalistic stare. The background is black. They're a band with a very clear expiration date. Compare that to the *Please Please Me* album cover of the Beatles, from 1963, where they stare down at us from a brightly illuminated stairwell in vivid colors, wearing matching coffee-colored suits that make them look like door-to-door salesmen who were, as Paul McCartney once said, "spokesmen for a generation." The Rolling Stones were "psychic masturbation" for teenagers who felt suffocated by postwar conformity. "Rejecting matching clothing was one step," said Stones' manager Andrew Loog Oldham.

The outfits of each member of Guns N' Roses were never synchronized. Their album covers were designed as symbols of insubordination, not cooperation. Compare the cover of *Appetite for Destruction* (both the original Robert Williams painting and the Celtic cross) to Poison's 1986 debut, *Look What the Cat Dragged In,* which is a sardonic drag-queen parody of the Beatles' cover for *Let It Be.* On the Poison debut, each member occupies their own floating mirror, in full makeup, like a sample photo album you'd find at a one-hour photo in a shopping mall. In contrast, the *Appetite for Destruction* covers are both steeped in symbols of death and dystopia. For Guns N' Roses, each cover or band photo is a representation of their anti-glam image. It is never a centerfold for a teen gossip magazine. They never appear in photo shoots with the coordinated maximum-impact advertising of Poison (who were the "boy band" of metal).

Comparing the Guns N' Roses aesthetic to Poison is like comparing a sunny Gene Kelly musical to the men's room brawl from *The Warriors* (1979), which feels like a surrealist-pop accompaniment to "Welcome to the Jungle." These are important comparisons to make for a variety of reasons, the most immediate being the writer's need to determine how the iconic Guns N' Roses logo—depicting two conjoined Colt pistols wrapped in bleeding roses and vines, attached to a giant bullet—became as culturally pervasive as John Pasche's tongue logo for the Rolling Stones, AC/DC's thunderbolt, and Madonna's blonde hair in 1985, the year Bette Midler introduced her at Live Aid as a "woman who pulls herself up by her bra straps . . . and who has been known to let them down occasionally." A year later, gigoloing for pizza money on the streets of Hollywood, Guns N' Roses inspired the Kelly Bundy's of America to drop their bra straps with the speed of the Dow Jones Industrial Average on Black Monday, October 19, 1987, when it fell 508 points, five days before Guns N' Roses would make their debut on MTV as a rejection of the "new wave" that had made MTV so fashionable.

"What were the Eighties like, Daddy?" *Esquire*'s Tom Shales wrote in March 1986. "Well, here, take a look at this videotape of MTV." Guns N' Roses would be videotaped into the history of MTV in 1987, which would crescendo in 1988 with the video for their first and only number-one hit, "Sweet Child O' Mine." Their MTV origin story has become stuff of legend, which began with their controlled demolition of the *Headbangers Ball* set on October 24, 1987. To infiltrate MTV's number-one metal platform, they would spend two years grooming themselves to be the alternative to Poison, who did not appeal to the hard-core segment of metalheads tuning in to the *Headbangers Ball*. They began by posing for band photos in abandoned construction sites, suburban landfills, boiler rooms of recording studios, liquor store fronts, Slash lounging amidst the rubble of a demolished building (which is by photographer Gene Kirkland), or playing live in Hollywood, as Slash's childhood friend Marc Canter would photograph them.

He captured Guns N' Roses between 1985 and 1987. Canter's photos were compiled into a glossy coffee-table book titled *Reckless Road: Guns N' Roses and the Making of Appetite for Destruction* (2008), which featured a band that looked both masculine and androgynous from the moment the Gun met the Rose on the stage of the Troubadour on June 6, 1985.

Some of the most vivid photos from Canter's book include a blonde woman named Pamela Jackson (aka Pamela Manning), who looked like a more voluptuous Debbie Harry photographed by Trix Rosen. Dancing on stage in black lingerie and white ankle boots, with Heather Locklear sex appeal and dark eyeshadow, Pamela would fall to her knees and softly graze her nails over Axl's leather pants, practically molesting him on stage—occasionally topless—as he attempted to undersell the foreplay. Beautiful women like Barbie Von Grief (the inspiration behind "Rocket Queen") and Pamela Manning were the one-handed magazine image for Guns N' Roses fans. Pamala managed to add to the perception that Guns N' Roses were one of the more sexually provocative bands on the Strip. She helped enhance his erotic image. "Sex sells," Marc Canter said in a BBC documentary about the band. "And everyone likes to see a stripper."

Perhaps the most iconic early photo of the band was taken by Jack Lue, who captured them in 1985 sitting together inside a booth at Canter's Deli, where they looked dazed, confused, and downright menacing. There's nothing particularly glamorous about them. The booth is now a tourist destination. But it was the photography of Robert John that would define their popular aesthetic. He shot them at a gas station on the corner of La Brea and Romaine. He shot Axl Rose in a thick brown leather belt over black leather pants, with a black leather cowboy hat (the same one he'd wear on the *Headbangers Ball*), when he's leaning against hardwood like a seasoned gunfighter. He shot Izzy in a leopard-print coat leaning against a decaying wall and doing his best James Dean with a pocketknife. ("He would smoke cigarettes in this very interesting way. Like it was the '40s or something. He was James Dean to me," said Chris Weber, the former guitarist of Hollywood Rose, a band Izzy Stradlin belonged to before Guns N' Roses.) Robert John shot the band as early as 1985, with Axl sticking his head out of the broken windshield of a demolished automobile, and Slash hanging off the edge, with a black cowboy hat, the visual personification of Hollywood gypsy. The Robert John photos, now owned by Axl and filed away in his vault, depict a band that's trapped inside a dystopian landscape reminiscent of the hardcore punk backdrop of 1984's *Repo Man*, where Otto Maddox is Axl Rose with a buzz cut (Axl had shorter hair in 1982). Guns N' Roses is depicted as graffiti being sprayed over the architecture of glam.

Like the Stones before them, Guns N' Roses didn't smile in their establishing photos, which were grim portraits of a city decaying into crack houses, typhoid scares, skid row, gangland arrests, AIDS, and the fear of nuclear annihilation. In 1987, there were twenty-five thousand nuclear warheads aimed squarely at strategic targets in both the United States and the Soviet Union. MTV was offering a fantasy that bypassed the paranoia of the period. Guns N' Roses were a symptom of the paranoia, not just in their photos, but also in their music, attitude, and press materials. They weren't MTV-friendly. Like the Rolling Stones before them, they were the band that forced the American media to ask the same question the British tabloids had asked in 1964:

"Would you let your daughter go to a Guns N' Roses concert?"

But if Guns N' Roses were being marketed as the American Rolling Stones, who were the Beatles? Or more accurately, who were the Monkees? Poison were like tanned Barbie dolls dancing around a wasteland that was being graffitied by Guns N' Roses. They were Pennsylvania transplants led by a former hairdresser named Bret Michaels, the precise breed of band that Guns N' Roses was trying to slaughter in order to assert their authority. There's an anecdote from Marc Canter's collection dated August 30, 1985, from the Stardust Ballroom. Poison's Bret Michaels was scattered among a crowd of Guns N' Roses fans, as Poison had played earlier in the evening. As part of their set, they covered Grand Funk Railroad's "We're an American Band." Bret Michaels sang it the way it was written, with an emphasis on partying down. When Guns N' Roses took the stage, they covered "American Band" and replaced "party down" with "fuck around." That's the difference between Guns N' Roses and Poison.

Poison was fashioned entirely in pastel-colored glamour photos, where Michaels puckered his cherry-red lips behind a hazy filter that makes their photos look like foggy dream sequences or colorized Old Hollywood publicity photos. Though this will become clearer as you read on, for a period of about a year-and-a-half, Guns N' Roses were aesthetically similar to Poison (Axl was described by *Sounds* in 1987 as having "Farrah Fawcett hair"). But Guns N' Roses were clumsy and blue-collar; they weren't as focused on defining themselves through their drag personas. Poison viewed their extravagant outfits and choreographed dance moves the way actress Gloria Swanson viewed her publicity strategy: wish-fulfillment for the working class. "The public didn't want the truth, and I shouldn't have bothered giving it to them," Swanson once said. "In those days they wanted us to live like kings. So, we did—and why not? We were in love with life."

Axl Rose wasn't stable enough to entertain his audience in that way. Watching him pound his boots across the stage like a cowboy on crystal meth must have been an absolutely jaw-detaching experience for the Reagan-era. Every single one of Axl's body movements seemed as unpredictable as the collateral damage from a ballistic missile strike. Though none of it was particularly original. We'd seen the snake dance executed by Davy Jones of the Monkees. Axl would swing a mic stand like James Brown; he'd throw himself into each song like Janis Joplin. His falsetto was the product of Led Zeppelin's Robert Plant and his most apparent vocal influence, Dan McCafferty of Nazareth. Axl's vocals and stage presence were tattooed by his influences and self-created myth, which made him a postmodern performer in the league of Madonna. But there's one name that won't appear in an Axl Rose autobiography.

"Axl would go to Gazzari's and study Richard's performances," Vicky Hamilton wrote in her autobiography, "and pretty soon, he had developed what we all now call the 'Axl Shuffle.'"

Richard Black, lead singer of '80s metal band Shark Island, has been credited as a source for some of Axl's trademark dance moves. Everyone from former manager Vicky Hamilton to drummer Steven Adler have made the claim that Axl would study Shark Island shows. In 2006, Richard Black accused Axl Rose of artistic plagiarism in MelodicRock.com: "He's really a piece of work for the dregs. As far as I'm concerned, he's never done anything original in his life. Him and his cronies would come every week and watch the show. One day before GnR's debut, I went to his place . . . as I walked in, I saw a video of me playing on his TV and on top was a stack of VHS tapes all labeled Shark Island with dates and times. I remember being mortified. It was obvious he was studying my shtick, and I knew there was nothing I could do."

Axl has mentioned Dan McCafferty, Elton John, Johnny Rotten, Angry Anderson, Michael Monroe of Hanoi Rocks, Phil Lynott of Thin Lizzy, Freddie Mercury, Steven Tyler, and Robert Plant as influences, but never Richard Black.

On a mainstream level, for the average American male who had never heard of Shark Island, the introduction of Axl Rose would have the effect of Elvis on Eisenhower-era teens. Axl would liberate teenagers from feeling like they had to conform to the standards and practices of the bourgeoisie. If the *big bang* of teen pop was Elvis's swinging legs on Ed Sullivan, then 30 years later, Axl Rose was the post-apocalyptic mutation. Most of the popular hair-metal bands seemed choreographed like pre-Elvis vocal groups who snapped their fingers and swung their guitars with the unison of synchronized swimmers. Guns N' Roses were semi-civilized Gauls who struck fear in the hearts of the Romans of 1st century BC. They were the jungle yelling back at the machinery seeking to civilize it, which included bands like Poison and Ratt, who had taken the wicked flamboyance of Little Richard and turned into a corporate form of drag queen exploitation. Guns N' Roses may have been too dark to find on heavy rotation on MTV, but they could, in small doses, work as one of the alternative bands presented on *Headbangers Ball*— (which diversified its playlist with different genres of metal).

"They say you guys are insulant," said VJ Adam Smash, as Guns N' Roses sat frozen on the couch of MTV's *Headbangers Ball*. "They say, honestly speaking, that you guys are a bunch of wackos . . . That's the image you guys have got as far as the critics are concerned." They presented themselves not as showmen or dandies (though Izzy's look was partly influenced by English dandyism), but as the Sex Pistols of the Reagan era, who had, in the most commercial sense, orchestrated a more pro-wrestling version of what the Sex Pistols had done on the BBC in 1976, when the fledgling punk band appeared on Bill Grundy's *Today* show and called the host "a fucking rotter," which was the most vulgar thing ever said on BBC up to that point.

On *Headbangers Ball*, Guns N' Roses looked like a juvenile street gang.

"We just don't take any garbage off anybody, that's all, it's simple, and a lot of people think that's problems," was Axl's ineloquent response to Smash. Axl wore a leather jacket covered in pins, along with a leather cowboy hat. Smash proceeded to introduce their music video for "Welcome to the Jungle," a screaming depiction of urban decay that had yet to be put into heavy rotation by the executives at MTV, including John Canelli, who would advocate for Guns N' Roses inside MTV's glass conference rooms. In *I Want My MTV: The Uncensored Story of the Music Video Revolution*, Canelli described the first time he heard "Welcome to the Jungle": "I was taking a ride through Central Park on my ten-speed, and I put the Guns N' Roses cassette on my Walkman. When I heard 'Welcome to the Jungle,' I almost fell off my bike." Guns N' Roses had found their first fan at MTV, whom Doug Goldstein described as a gay man—which only becomes important in apropos to "One in a Million." Canelli's introduction to Guns N' Roses was all too common for his class. On the cover of *Newsweek* on December 31, 1984, was depicted a comic of two yuppies in their natural habitat: the city, where a woman in New Balance sneakers takes a stroll with her Walkman, while a man rides his 10-speed like John Canelli quietly discovering "Welcome to the Jungle." Guns N' Roses were like a dirty smut film for the thirtysomething yuppie looking for the next wave, who was hooked to a word processor, which would make the experience of viewing a video like "Welcome to the Jungle" like discovering an illicit drug.

"What kind of 'jungle' we talkin' about here, fellas?" asked Smash just before playing the video. Axl responded, "the streets, the city, basically, what being exposed to news and everything else in the city and what that can do to you." Axl was like Paul Verhoeven planning a dark satire on American culture. He was like William Friedkin directing *The Exorcist* (1973) with the intention of producing a film that felt so real that it might actually cause seizures. In fact, it did. *The Exorcist* made demonic possession seem terrifyingly possible. The first time you watch the video for "Welcome to the Jungle," you are completely convinced that Axl Rose is out of his mind.

"Welcome to the Jungle" is a raffish street poet's merciless view of a rotting Babylon, which began to alienate its own inhabitants as poverty and crime rates began to skyrocket. In "Welcome to the Jungle," Axl seems like William Blake surveying the darkness of London during France's Reign of Terror. While MTV was trying to sell Manhattan as a photogenic new Rome, Guns N' Roses were documenting city life as they saw it: a morally ugly clash of police brutality and L.A. noir. Being from the rural Midwest had poisoned Axl's view of the city, making him view it as a distrustful dystopia. On the other hand, MTV was broadcasting a much more mellow and cosmopolitan mood, one that was fueled by bohemian art snobs occupying the skyscrapers of the big city. At the 1987 MTV Video Music Awards (VMAs), which aired on September 11, 1987, Peter Gabriel won 10 awards. His video for "Sledgehammer" depicted Gabriel being animated into surrealistic visuals, dressed sharply, and melting into wallpaper that produced a narcotic effect for the viewer—as if you were walking through a modern art exhibit wearing 3D glasses. For MTV's fashion-conscious demographic, who had been conditioned by depictions of wealth and supermodels in Christian Lacroix, "Welcome to the Jungle" must have been like taking the wrong train from uptown into Soho in 1978, or being suffocated by the city, like Jon Voight in *Midnight Cowboy* (1969), which is very much the story of Axl Rose hitchhiking through the Bronx, which looked like what Patti Smith once described as a "piss factory." New York was the same slum where Madonna was raped when she was 19, when she was led to the top of a building with a knife being held at her back. Madonna told *Harper's Bazaar* in 2013 she was initially terrified by the sprawling metropolis and the "smell of piss and vomit everywhere." Axl Rose's entire *Appetite*-era psychology was the aggregate of the estrangement he felt in the big city.

Manager Alan Niven would cinematically capture Axl's alienation by using a collage of cinematic images that reflected the vulnerability he felt arriving in Los Angeles for the first time. "I used stills from 'Midnight Cowboy' [innocence] 'The Man Who Fell To Earth' [discovery] and 'A Clockwork Orange' [the horror]," says Niven, who is credited by the video's director, Nigel Dick, for coming up with the creative vision for "Welcome to the Jungle," which may have also borrowed from the electric chair scene in *Faces of Death*—one of the more famous scenes from the film.

Niven had purposefully selected films from New Hollywood, from the '70s, which communicated Guns N' Roses' intention to assault MTV's sterilized view of culture. The music video for "Welcome to the Jungle" would show a side of L.A. that was foreign to the rest of the country, as MTV had never introduced it, who still viewed L.A. as a sun-soaked beach community that lacked the grit and character of New York. But L.A. has always been foreign to outsiders. Poet Luis Rodriguez said that "to truly love L.A. you have to see it with a different eye, askew perhaps, beyond the fantasy-induced Hollywood spectacle." On the Sunset Strip, Guns N' Roses weren't exactly counterculture, but on a national level, for the MTV audience, they were presenting a grimmer portrait of L.A. The video for "Welcome to the Jungle," as a series of scenes, produced the effect Francis Ford Coppola would describe in the press kit for *Apocalypse Now*, which was a project that "put an audience through an experience—frightening but violent only in proportion with the idea being put across—that will hopefully change them in some small way."

"Welcome to the Jungle" was a nearly perfect debut film, which possessed only a few hair and wardrobe flaws, namely the fact that Axl had teased, Farrah Fawcett hair, a powdered face, and eyeliner, which made him look like a hypocrite when he'd deride glam in subsequent interviews. Still, it was the visual personification of Guns N' Roses as an *idea*, or a brand. It also felt boldly original, while most of what they were performing on Strip—including covers of Aerosmith and Elvis—felt like reruns of the past. There are those who claim that "Welcome to the Jungle" was lifted from a lyric in a Hanoi Rocks song titled "Underwater World," but what we can file away as fact is that the song was Axl Rose having his first honest, albeit confusing, conversation with his audience about his views on culture, media, race, women, and violence. In many ways, Guns N' Roses were analogous to what Black Flag presented in the L.A. punk scene in the mid-1980s. John Doe, co-founder of L.A. punk band X, would describe Black Flag as being on the "realistic side of things. If realism is dark, then they're on the dark side of things."

"The dark side of things" is what Guns N' Roses were going for, which was an apolitical protest of MTV's mood-enhancement effect, and yet, just like Elvis in 1957, Guns N' Roses produced a *very* political reaction. The "Jungle" video was a demonstration against the pseudo-pleasure culture that MTV was profiting from. In the context of MTV, the "Jungle" video was a preposterously off-brand statement. For Guns N' Roses, it was how they would immediately distance themselves from the shiny and plastic image of glam. They were creating their own black-leather rebellion. Even professionally manicured magazine shots of Guns N' Roses evoked the "dark side of things."

"Glam sucks," Axl painted onto the front of his black leather pants in a photo that appears in *Hit Parader* in July 1987. "I don't consider us a glam band. We weren't trying to do anything with that," he told the *LA Weekly* in 1986. "Guns N' Roses used to wear more makeup than Poison ever wore, and like a year later, they have on their pants, 'glam sucks,'" Bret Michaels told Steven Blush in *American Hair Metal*. "We don't want to associate ourselves with glam, and the main reason is because that's what Poison associates themselves with," Axl told *Kerrang!* in June 1987.

Guns N' Roses were a band that *Music Connection* reporter Karen Burch described as being allergic to image; in fact, she claimed they *refused* to discuss it. Yet in their earliest interviews, that's about all they were concerned with. As drummer Steven Adler put it, they were anti-image, which *was* their image. Their progenitors the Rolling Stones were described in *Melody Maker* as being ". . . against the boss, the clock, and the clean-shirt-a-day routine" and looked like "five indolent morons who give one the feeling that they really enjoy wallowing in a swill tub of their own repulsiveness." The same description would fit how the rock tabloids explained Guns N' Roses, who, like the Stones before them, would eventually abandon their crime-ridden personas and become the sort of slick corporate revolutionaries who'd "be sitting in a country house with four Rolls-Royces and spitting at everyone." This is how Keith Richards cheekily described it in a *Time* interview in 1964, and roughly 30 years later, that would become Axl Rose in his secluded Latigo Canyon compound at the top of the winding hills of Malibu.

"I hate it when other bands say they don't care about image. What a pile of poop that is!" said Bret Michaels in 1988. In his 2007 autobiography, Slash would indirectly swing back at Michaels's "calculated rebellion": "There was no concern for the proper poses or goofy choruses that might spell pop-chart success, which ultimately guaranteed endless hot chicks. That type of calculated rebellion wasn't an option for us; we were too rabid a pack of musically like-minded gutter rats." Duff McKagan's autobiography argues that Guns N' Roses had a kinship to '70s punk, while Slash's autobiography was married to the Alan Niven view of Guns N' Roses as a street-fighting rock band in the tradition of the *Beggars Banquet*-era Rolling Stones.

Guns N' Roses were, by all observable accounts and decades of history to guide us, both extremely calculated and thoroughly raw, like the Sex Pistols (though they never had a Svengali-like Malcolm McLaren designing their image). Their anti-image marketing would be repeatedly communicated in the '87 interview with *BAM*, where the headline read: "Glam Band – No Thank You, Ma'am." The interviewer would claim that he was advised to never ask the band if they were a glam band, which seems to indicate that Geffen's flacks had been busy working over journalists who dared mischaracterize Guns N' Roses as anything other than "hard rock," which was a throwback to Led Zeppelin and Aerosmith; a retro-sounding group that fed off the dust-covered LPs of smoky blues musicians from the past. But prior to 1987, Guns N' Roses looked like the definition of a glam band. In a *Recycler* ad created by Axl and Izzy in 1985, they were looking for a "Heavy Punk Metal Glam Guitarist." According to Axl in a *Kerrang!* interview from June 1987, they wanted "someone who wore make-up and put their hair up. That was the first glam ad I think I ever saw. And then we quickly got rid of that, but it stuck."

Early in 1985, prior to cementing his position as the lead guitarist of Guns N' Roses, Slash auditioned for Poison (by this point, he had seen Poison perform live at least three times). Some reports indicated that Slash refused to join the band because of their theatrical stage introductions and more flamboyant outfits. Slash wore lipstick in the street drag mode of the New York Dolls. But he never wore neon spandex and certainly never embraced the stripper outfits of so many glam bands. He never danced like one of Judy Garland's male backup dancers in *Summer Stock* (1950). Slash may have embraced elements of the glam aesthetic, but he didn't allow it to become his gimmick. What actually happened when Slash auditioned for Poison is mostly lost to history. We know that in preparation for his audition, Slash had learned five Poison songs, and during his audition, he wore jeans, a plain T-shirt, and moccasins. When Bret Michaels asked Slash what sort of costume he'd wear on stage, Slash knew he wasn't going to be "Poison enough" for Poison. The unanswerable question is just *why* Slash would audition for Poison and then, a year later, proceed to make fun of them in the press, as if they were the antithesis of everything he stood for. Michaels would later claim that Slash was too much of a virtuoso to play in Poison, the way, for example, Les Claypool was probably too experimental to join Metallica following the death of bassist Cliff Burton.

The guitarist who would get the part in Poison's glam production was a Brooklynite by the name of C.C. DeVille, which is a portmanteau of Old Hollywood director Cecil B. DeMille, with a Cadillac Coupe DeVille. History would be unkind to C.C. DeVille, while Slash would transcend the vapidity of Sunset Strip's star-making machine. For Slash, the gender-bending look was more of a Machiavellian strategy to infiltrate the scene, than any desire to spend a career applying makeup and performing for the same demo as New Kids on the Block. This seems to have been the case for Axl Rose, as well.

"It seems because you have the makeup you're thought of as less than a musician," DeVille once complained. Bret Michaels would later say that Guns N' Roses' transformation into a leathery biker gang was merely a well-planned rebrand from their hair-metal days, which was a derivative of the glitter-and-cum stained bell jar of L.A. in the '80s. Bret Michaels had a point, as androgyny was a part of the sexual persona of Guns N' Roses. It was undeniable, as seen in their early concert and candid photos of Axl Rose. Axl became notorious in the L.A. music scene for wearing leathery homosexual fetish wear on stage. He wore assless leather chaps over a black G-string that revealed his pale butt (which comes up in their

KNAC radio interview). Biker fetish wear was not part of the hair-metal uniform. Axl's shredded abs and vainglorious obsession with showing the world his butt was clearly an appropriation of the gay club culture that defined Freddie Mercury's homoerotic motif. Axl looked like what one writer described to me as a "gay twink."

"The band I became obsessed with was Guns N' Roses," wrote trans punk singer Laura Jane Grace in her 2016 autobiography, *Tranny: Confessions of Punk Rock's Most Infamous Anarchist Sellout*. "Their music appealed to me because it felt dangerous. I was afraid of my parents seeing the liner note artwork. The look of the band, particularly that of wiry lead singer Axl Rose, excited me most because it was androgynous. Hair was big, clothes were tight, lines were blurred. I often couldn't tell if the band members were boys or girls, and I liked that."

Axl Rose may have been too heteronormative to embrace his androgyny in the press, but in images it was potent, glamorous, and oscillating between the vulnerability and toughness of a young Brando, which made Axl seem more like a damaged sex symbol, than a party animal. Axl Rose would become Bette Davis fighting for respect in a scene full of vacuous blonde bombshells. "Hollywood always wanted me to be pretty, but I fought for realism," Bette Davis once said. Axl was a white working-class version of Oscar Wilde's Dorian Gray, an Adonis "made out of ivory and rose-leaves." To pretend, even for one second, that Guns N' Roses didn't exploit Axl's eroticism would be completely dishonest.

The roots of their more masculine transformation remain one the most debated topics among the first generation of Guns N' Roses fans: a group of purists who believe that it was Izzy Stradlin who first defined their aesthetic, which is only partially true. Izzy arrived in Los Angeles in 1980 in a Chevy Impala—two years before Axl finally made the move. Izzy studied photos of guitarist Andy McCoy, as well as Johnny Thunders, as he proceeded to dye his hair as black as a wild stallion, costuming himself in faux leopard-skin fabrics, pink sports coats, '50s creepers, leather cowboy belts, and his famous mug shot facial expression. It was understated and less flamboyant, as Izzy, even when he was playing in drag punk band

Naughty Women, never fell into the trap of becoming a parody of the New York Dolls. According to ex-Hollywood Rose bassist Steve Darrow, Izzy was the band's unofficial stylist: "He had us meet up at his place, then fix up everybody's hair and makeup before anyone left the room. Axl, too." And as guitarist Chris Weber told me, "Izzy was the mastermind. In the beginning, it was all him. Axl assumed that role later on." The history of Hollywood Rose (originally known as Rose) is complicated, but for the uninitiated, it's only important to know that they were an early version of Guns N' Roses. As Vicky Hamilton told Marc Canter, "They were trying out bands like they were trying on clothes."

It's been said that in those early days Izzy would share pictures of Finnish glam metal band Hanoi Rocks with Axl, who would initially design his frizzy hair to look like Hanoi Rocks' lead singer, Michael Monroe. Axl would talk about his hair in a June 1987 *Kerrang!* profile: "The only reason I put my hair up is because Izzy had these pictures of Hanoi Rocks and they were cool, and because we hung out with this guy who studied *Vogue* magazine hairstyles and was really into doing hair."

"They [Hanoi Rocks] were an influence on Guns N' Roses and are still an undervalued rock and roll institution as far as I'm concerned," Slash wrote in his autobiography. Though historically ignored as one of the chief architects of the band's aesthetic, Slash's upbringing seems to suggest that he had a sophisticated nose for style. His father, who was white, was a visual artist who drew the cover for Joni Mitchell's *Court and Spark* (1974). He was also what writer Katherine Turman described in *Music Connection* as a close business associate of David Geffen. His mother, a Black woman, was the costume designer for David Bowie (Ola Hudson was also one of Bowie's former lovers). His mother is where Slash got his sense of style. His father is where he got the talent to draw, as would be apparent when Slash illustrated the earliest version of the Guns N' Roses logo, which depicted two intertwined Colt pistols wrapped in bleeding roses—what teacher Jane Boswell may have described as, "combining opposing elements into a beautiful whole." It's as if Slash were there, in 1977, sitting with Izzy and Axl in Jane Boswell's Arts and Crafts Pottery.

"If you put us side with an actual 'glam' band," Slash told *Concert Shots* in May 1986, "you'll see there's a big difference. I mean, we wear leathers and jeans. Their hair's always spiked up and they have a full time makeup job. And they wear a lot of frilly stuff. It's just a different look."

Slash was the offspring of Jimi Hendrix and Joe Perry. He was also the most subversive visual statement Guns N' Roses could have made as an anti-glam band. Try, if you can, to transport yourself to 1986: emerging from the shadows is a Black guitar player fitted with an English gentleman's top hat (which was cheeky, like Dudley Moore, and mystical, like Stevie Ray Vaughan). "While I never thought it was original," Slash wrote in his 2007 autobiography, "it was mine—a trademark that became an indelible part of my image." He wore tight leather pants, cowboy boots or moccasins, along with gypsy jewelry he'd borrow from stylish strippers. He spoke with a Californian drawl, like Darby Crash, or Nicolas Cage in *Valley Girl* (1983). He was too laid back to exude the corporate determination of Eddie Van Halen. Slash transcended the fame game. He released an almost mystical incense from the neck of his 1959 replica Les Paul, while Van Halen's stylized Stratocaster ("Frankenstrat") embodied precision and horsepower.

Slash was perhaps the only guitarist in the L.A. scene who deserved the adoration of Wayne and Garth getting down on their knees and chanting, "We're not worthy!" In 2014, Mike Myers told comedian Marc Maron that the studio and director of 1992's *Wayne's World* (directed by Penelope Spheeris, who was a Guns N' Roses fan) were advocating to have Guns N' Roses score the iconic headbanging scene. But Meyers fought for the more operatic "Bohemian Rhapsody," which would change the course of rock history. Myers did not reveal which Guns N' Roses song was being considered, though it was probably "Welcome to the Jungle." And while Guns N' Roses didn't own a piece of cinematic history the way Queen did, Slash remains the most cinematic guitar player of the past three decades.

Slash burnished his myth by wrapping a dark veil over his celebrity. He seemed like he possessed a carnal secret; perhaps a Faustian bargain with a smoky-eyed devil with black sunglasses and a Southern drawl. Every generation has a guitar player who fulfills the role of Paganini: Robert Johnson, Jimi Hendrix, Jimmy Page, Stevie Ray Vaughan, Van Halen, and Slash, the final contract. He was a sinister image with a guitar that sounded almost foreign to the commercial ears of Van Halen youth. There was also something aristocratic about Slash, which made him a paradox among his peers. He emanated from an unknown shire in England (Stoke-on-Trent), but he was born in Hampstead, London. He grew up in L.A. in an isolated bohemian paradise surrounded by rock stars and socialites. He possessed an ambivalence towards the L.A. punk and glitter-rock scene of the late '70s. Slash was a secular guitarist with no interest in any particular movement or destination. He lived and looked like an outsider.

Perhaps the most neglected aspect of the Guns N' Roses aesthetic is Slash himself, or more specifically, the fact that his Blackness was muted behind the forest of his curly mane and a dangling cigarette that hung from his maw. He was, in the milieu of glam metal, dominated entirely by white men cloning the precise and mathematical guitar solos of Van Halen, a call to African-inspired spirituals that traveled from the South into Chicago's juke joints. Slash's guitar technique was influenced by Joe Perry's playing on *Rocks* and *Toys in the Attic*, but his soul was firmly grounded in the moving trains of Black bluesmen like Muddy Waters, who played an electrified guitar that expressed the melancholy and torment of slaves born in Southern cotton fields, who would teach themselves how to play the guitar by stringing broom wire to cabin walls.

Producer Bobby Robinson once described the blues guitar as the "raw-nerved, spine-tingling picking of the guitar and the agonized screams and soul-stirring of Elmore James. Close your eyes, you'll see the slave ships, the auction blocks, the cotton fields, the bare backs straining, totin' that barge and liftin' that bale. You will smell the sweat, feel the lash, taste the tears and see the blood, and relive 300 years of the blues."

That's what Slash brought to '80s metal. He played the guitar in a way that grounded the jet-engine vocals of Axl Rose, who screamed with such volume and anguish that he sounded like he was experiencing an exorcism. Slash's guitar would interpret Axl's bipolarity the way a poet would their abusive lover or fascistic father. His guitar reflected the confusion of a partially completed city like L.A., which still felt uncharted. Saul Hudson's nickname, "Slash," was a throwback to blues players like Chester "Howlin' Wolf" Burnett, who were given nicknames to reflect how they would augment the rhythm and blues. Slash was cutting right through the facade of hair metal by achieving a more "roots-oriented sound." He was striking a bargain at the crossroads, instead of the boardroom. Slash was the avatar of a less glamorous, more primordial guitar hero, who not only sounded more authentic, but looked more deeply rooted in the origins of rock and roll. His contemporaries must have viewed him the way Axl Rose would later view Kurt Cobain: the symbol of his extinction.

The color of Slash's skin was part of his allure, as well as his struggle. One evening at the Rainbow Bar and Grill, Slash was confronted by the guitarist of a band that was, at the time, bigger than Guns N' Roses. "Niggers shouldn't wear tattoos," the guitarist said to Slash. Duff McKagan, who was with Slash, claims he punched the racist guitarist in the face, which led to him collapsing and breaking three of his ribs. "He reminded me of the bullies back in Seattle," Duff wrote in his autobiography. "The meatheads who beat up punks in packs, who called everyone faggots." This kind of experience is tragically reminiscent of Jimi Hendrix being denied service in the South because of his skin color, while in England, Hendrix was treated like a "Black Elvis." In L.A., though it was never said aloud, Slash was the Black Van Halen.

But Slash never marketed his racial identity. He never used it to secure the adoration of bourgeoise liberal critics at the *Village Voice*. When the band entered the UK in the summer of 1987, Slash's background was still very much a mystery. Guns N' Roses came to England to farm a following from a country that had helped boost the Go-Go's and Metallica in the '80s and the Ramones in 1976—before the US market was ready for punk. Track two off *Appetite for Destruction*, titled "It's So Easy," was released as the band's first single in the UK in June of 1987. It was quickly banned by the BBC for its lascivious lyrics. In their 1987 press kit, Slash would describe "It's So Easy" as being the by-product of being oversexed and fatigued by the mundanity of "chasing normal chicks." Like a drug one builds a tolerance for, normal sex, for the members of Guns N' Roses, no longer produced the desired effect. "It's So Easy" was about exploring the fetishes that emerge out of boredom.

The band fully embraced the censorship, as it allowed them to cook their raw image into the British tabloids. It was part of an overall strategy to turn *Appetite for Destruction* into some more black-market than it really was.

"My strategy with GNR was to break them in England, like Tom Petty, Jimi Hendrix, and JJ Cale before," said Alan Niven, who would never outright deny rumors of Axl being abusive to puppies, which ensured the band would be described as the "most dangerous band in the world" by the time they flew back to the States. Niven, who was from New Zealand but had studied the music business in the UK, had brought to Guns N' Roses the "cash from chaos" creed of Malcolm McLaren. Niven and Zutaut fed dirt to the British tabloids and clipped the headlines into promotional materials that reflected the brash American sleaziness that Guns N' Roses were pushing into the UK rock tabloids. They had gone from being the postmodern Rolling Stones to the new Sex Pistols as they invaded the Marquee Club for their first UK show on June 19, 1987 (they'd play two more nights that month). The first night would create headlines for being both sloppy and on the verge of riotous, as can of beer flew at Axl Rose, who angrily turned to a member in the audience and said, "Fuck you, pussy."

"It was easier to penetrate a small island market then a huge American continent," Niven says. "And the English press, I knew, would connect faster than Americans." On October 5, 1987, five days before Whitesnake's power ballad "Here I Go Again" would reach number one, Axl told a small crowd huddled inside Rock City in Nottingham, England: "In the States, they're too much of pussies to play the fucking thing ["Welcome to the Jungle"]. I think that's why we came over here instead." Axl Rose must have looked like an escaped convict in the eyes of the slightly well-mannered Brits. That was the point. BBC's ban of "It's So Easy" was turned into an informal press release. Alan Niven and Tom Zutaut wanted to make a statement in the country that had turned punk into a fashion statement, and Slash (who had no interest in punk) was their secret weapon. With his hair covering his face and his biography mostly kept out of the papers, Slash would seduce the British rock critics with his bewildering mystique, as if he had attained some kind of secret knowledge, like the snake in Native American folklore. *Kerrang!* critic Mick Wall would stare with mouth agape at such "booze-sodden monsters that feasted on babies for breakfast and spat out their bones," as he wrote in his 1992 book, *Guns N' Roses: The Most Dangerous Band in the World.* The UK tabloids supplemented the fear factor associated with Guns N' Roses with headlines that bled right off the page, packaged into a new drug for Manhattan.

"Guns N' Roses had entered Britain with the image of dog-killing, drug-dealing," wrote Wall, " . . . but they left, though it wasn't yet reflected in record sales, with a growing reputation as one of the foremost rock 'n' roll noise-making machines on God's earth.

It was now obvious that Guns N' Roses had a very defined philosophy, perhaps engineered more by Slash than he gets credit for, but nonetheless, this was a band that wanted everyone to know they were "weird and pissed off." And it seems the British press were willing to hype their underground appeal the way they had Metallica. Early on, Metallica was practically nonexistent on MTV, who achieved a gold record with *Master of Puppets* by touring relentlessly and ingratiating themselves to alterative media outlets like *Spin*, which was one of the first media publications to describe Guns N' Roses as the future of rock and roll, as opposed to a "throwback," as the *Village Voice* had suggested they were. *Appetite for Destruction* had sold two hundred thousand copies with almost no support from terrestrial radio or MTV.

Magazines like *Spin*, *Circus*, *Hit Parader*, *Kerrang!*, and *RIP* had given Guns N' Roses the endorsement they needed to attract an underground following. In the summer of 1987, especially in Germany and Britain, heavy-metal teens were turning up the volume on Metallica's third and most critically acclaimed album, *Master of Puppets*. Guns N' Roses were arguably the only hair-metal band that managed to preserve their artistic credibility in the aftermath of March 3, 1986, when Metallica released *Master of Puppets*, which aggressively converted the youth towards a more anti-glam version of metal, which they did without the support of MTV. Metallica accomplished this with the ground game of a well-oiled war machine. In the process, they created their own genre: thrash metal. Guns N' Roses were trying to establish themselves as a hard-rock band, which was a faded genre in 1986.

"If I had to label this band," Slash told *Music Connection* in 1986, "I'd say that it's a hard-rock band with an R&B base. It's not a glam band . . . "

Without the dedicated support of the mainstream media or culture pubs, Guns N' Roses were focusing on courting controversy, while Metallica operated like a disciplined war machine that was marching across the world map. When Axl was asked by *Metal Edge* in 1988 who he'd like to tour with, and he promptly answered: "Metallica." He'd proceed to tell the interviewer that Guns N' Roses were considering taking "the Metallica route" of focusing on touring heavily, as opposed to producing videos for MTV and writing radio-friendly ballads.

Guns N' Roses were paying attention to Metallica's populist revolution. "Lately, we listen to Metallica all the time. It's cool, 'cause those guys listen to us all the time," Axl told *Music Connection* in November of 1987. "That's where Metallica is amazing—the sincerity. A lot their stuff is more dark, getting out their anger, and we do that in our way, too."

Metallica's success would force tastemakers to pay attention to unsavory bands like Guns N' Roses. In 1986, the same year Def Leppard and Bon Jovi turned metal into Top 40 pop music, Metallica was building an audience that resisted Top 40; they were the band for the acned teenager who wanted to mass murder the intelligentsia. Metallica was a Panzer tank heading towards the mainstream. Guns N' Roses saw them coming. They would negotiate a detente with Metallica, which is what they could not accomplish when grunge threatened their arena-rock supremacy. Here's Slash in his autobiography, discussing a 1987 tour stop in Germany: "I remember that before we went on and the second we got off, the club played nothing but Metallica, nonstop. It was obvious that any American band, or any band at all, that didn't sound like Metallica wasn't going to go over."

In terms of America's youth, it was Metallica, before Guns N' Roses, who had turned the genre of hair metal into a farce. Guns N' Roses were astute enough to recalibrate and create an alliance with Metallica. If heavy metal is truly forged in the factories of the patriarchy, then Metallica had industrialized the genre into an anti-glam killing machine. Guns N' Roses aligned themselves with the future of metal in order to avoid being its past. In their first *Rolling Stone* cover story from November 1988, the introduction by Rob Tannenbaum seems to indicate that their political strategy was working: "You might compare Guns N' Roses to Poison, Ratt, Faster Pussycat, Mötley Crüe and any other of the dozen of neatly identical heavy-metal bands currently being pushed by the music industry. The Gunners engage in the same antics revolving around booze, drugs and women. But Guns N' Roses don't play heavy metal. They play a vicious brand of hard rock that, especially in concert, is closer to Metallica or to punk than to heavy metal."

Guns N' Roses sounded nothing like Metallica, but they wanted to draw comparisons to a band whose authenticity was as undeniable as American's military hegemony. It was the perfect arranged marriage for the rock tabloids. Both Metallica and Guns N' Roses were too menacing for MTV, and yet had managed to create a massive following in the clubs. They were simplistic, pissed off, and remorseless machines with looks that presented an alternative to hair metal. In 1987, before they became mainstream, Guns N' Roses were "alternative." In 1987, Metallica and Guns N' Roses were helping to define a counterculture in heavy metal that was staging a black-gloved assault that had more in common with Motörhead and Judas Priest than it did with Def Leppard and Quiet Riot. "We had intricate songs, we had complex songs, and I think only bands like Metallica were doing anything similar to what we were doing," Slash wrote in his autobiography.

In several interviews between 1986 and 1988, Metallica became one of the only contemporary metal bands that Guns N' Roses would name-check.

Axl said in a *Concert Shots* interview from May 1986: "Metallica were getting banned when they played here [Los Angeles]. And they kept fighting it out, like we were doing. Now it's up to us to make an album that people will like."

Appetite for Destruction was chasing the underground success of *Master of Puppets*. While Slash's ferocity on the album was partially influenced by Metallica's Kirk Hammett, the technical factors that made Slash's sound so inimitable are far more complicated. His guitar tone—the intercourse of muddy blues and thunderous metal—made *Appetite for Destruction* sound bruised with wildly dangerous contradictions.

Appetite for Destruction was one of the last mainstream rock albums that was handmade, without a reliance on Pro Tools, where tracks are cut using razor blades. The album was mixed on a Neve 8068 console. Producer Mike Clink used vintage instruments and microphones. There was no sampling or electronic drumming on the record, which was constructed over the clumsy brilliance of drummer Steven Adler—who created a delightful counterbalance to Axl Rose's perfectionism. "What people don't understand is that there was a perfectionist attitude to 'Appetite for Destruction,'" Axl told Mick Wall in 1990. "There was a definite plan to that. We could have made it all smooth and polished with [original producer] Spencer Proffer, but it was too fuckin' radio. That's why we went with Mike Clink. It just didn't gel having it too tight and concise."

"This was the last great hard-rock record made entirely by hand," Tom Zutaut told me. "No computer assistance or automated faders. It's a piece of imperfect art that will stand the test of time because it was made manually on a console. It captured lightning in a bottle." Slash's '59 Les Paul replica (or "bootleg" in the eyes of Alan Niven) was one of the key ingredients in the unexplainably intoxicating sound of the record. Slash used the custom guitar for most of the overdubbing of *Appetite for Destruction*, including the solos. It was a handmade axe that was cut from maple trees lining the roads of Hillsborough, New Hampshire. The story reported by Matt Wake at *LA Weekly* describes an Allman Brothers fan occupying an old trailer in Redondo Beach. His name was Kris Derrig, a luthier who rummaged through piles of curly maple gathered inside barns in Hillsborough to find the wood to build his guitars. It was a guitar that Wake would describe as a "flame-top beauty," which Derrig's brother Dale would say was constructed from "extremely dense, old wood . . . Mellow, but with a bite to it."

With his graying hair hanging below his neck and rock band T-shirts, Derrig would curve and manipulate the wood into the framework of original '59 Gibson Les Paul guitars, one of which Alan Niven purchased for Slash as a way of helping him find that rare tonal balance between the lush countryside of Led Zeppelin and the steel factories of Metallica.

Niven would pay around $2,500 for the guitar. The Derrig guitar was hand-painted to a faded sunburst finish that looked like rusted gold, rather than graffiti or neon colors that were all the rage in the mid-1980s. Derrig's guitars had an unmatchable quality to them. Niven was drawn to the guitar as if it were the supernatural axe in Slash's quest to reach the final stage of his journey, what Joseph Campbell would have described as an amulet to battle "against the dragon forces he is about to pass." It would become Slash's main guitar captured in the first three Guns N' Roses videos, which evoked Joe Perry, as opposed to the neon-colored, whammy bar–equipped "Frankenstrat" models that felt like science fiction.

"That instrument, and Slash's eloquence, took some kids away from the awful speed guitars," said Niven.

It's been said that Slash was frustrated with the tone of his Gibson SG. There's a Robert John photo of Slash kneeling against a white van with an SG impaled through the windshield. Slash would record with a Firebird, two Jackson guitars, a replica Les Paul purchased from Howie Hubberman (which was later stolen or pawned for heroin), and a B.C. Rich Warlock—none of them had the feeling Slash was going for. In the maelstrom to finish the album, Niven would direct the Derrig guitar to help Slash find what jazzman Mezz Mezzrow described as Bix Beiderbecke's "imitable pickled-in-alcohol" tone.

"Kris had the brilliant idea that he could make a better '59 than Gibson," Niven said. "His conceit was that a single skilled luthier could construct a better instrument than a line of Gibson employees on a conveyor belt.

He was right. He found parts of the period and built 13 of them before he died." Jim Foote, the owner of the Music Works shop where Derrig worked, suggested Derrig switch the original Les Paul pickups with the "zebra-style" Seymour Duncan pickups that produced a tone that was, according to Foote, both "simultaneously classic and contemporary."

Kris Derrig would die tragically from cancer on May 14, 1987; he's now a gravestone sitting under the Celtic cross of *Appetite for Destruction*. He died just two months before the release of *Appetite for Destruction*. For Guns N' Roses fans, the Derrig guitar was their Stradivarius. It was the Guns N' Roses equivalent of Hendrix's forgotten Danelectro Shorthorn, nicknamed "Betty Jean," Joe Perry's Gibson Les Paul on the first solo of 1975's "Walk this Way," and Johnny Marr's sparkling Rickenbacker on "This Charming Man." If the guitar had not vanished from history, it would now sit inside a vitrine at the Rock and Roll Hall of Fame.

Appetite for Destruction was like a rusted six-gun poking holes into the polished steel of Top 40 metal like Bon Jovi's *Slippery When Wet*, which was the best-selling album of 1987 behind what *Rolling Stone* described as an image "tailor-made for today's teens." Slash's guitar was blowback from MTV's deification of Van Halen and Bon Jovi. In many ways, the connection Guns N' Roses had to Metallica was rooted in their mutual disdain for the heavy-metal orthodoxy.

Duff McKagan, who had begun his career as a drummer in Seattle punk bands like the Fartz and Fastbacks, took what was a more traditionally punk look (bleached hair with a padlock chain around his neck) and blended it with a long red-and-black trench coat he'd wear in countless photos, along with a vintage military hat. Duff's punk roots were used to push Guns N' Roses in the UK, as it were Duff who had gone through the crucible in Seattle. In Duff's autobiography he continually draws comparisons between himself and the working-class Seattle punk scene, as he reminds us that he shared a gene pool with Nirvana, while criticizing L.A.'s more glamorous scenester culture. He talks about the jocks that assaulted him for being a "punk rock faggot." He described Guns N' Roses as playing "sped-up punk versions" of Stones and Elvis songs. For Duff, Axl Rose was punk. One can only imagine what mohawked anarchists from Seattle felt when they saw Bret Michaels sitting on the hood of a red Corvette wearing a ridiculous choker, tie-dyed jeans, and cowboy boots that look like they were purchased from the Sherman Oaks Galleria. Duff's punk-rock identity was yet another way to separate them from the mall-friendly aesthetic of Poison.

"We're not going to cop-out and do drugs and just lean against a wall and looked strung out like Johnny Thunders," said Michaels in an interview, knowing, perhaps, that punk guitarist Johnny Thunders was the biggest influence on the look and style of Izzy Stradlin—who was widely known for selling dope to local rock bands. Izzy was described by *Music Connection* as the "cynic" of the band. "There's a lot of bands picking up on the negative side of glam," Michaels complained. "It's like that total glittered-up person that dressed up and rolled around in dirt, saying we're poor souls and complete drug-problem people, mixing the death with the glam, and that's not what Poison is all about." Between 1986 and 1988, Guns N' Roses did everything they could to represent themselves as the "negative side of glam."

"I don't consider us a glam band," Axl told *LA Weekly* in 1986. "[Guns N' Roses] is non-denominational. We could play symphonic music, and if I had all my heart and emotion and feeling into that, I'd call it rock & roll. I think Mozart was rock and roll."

Michaels seemed like a polished PR executive selling an aspirational brand. Guns N' Roses were asking teens to get ugly tattoos and ditch class; a throwback, in many ways, to the rebel without a cause, as opposed to the '80s teen who lusted for gold cards and sports cars, who was drawn to graphic demonstrations of wealth that writer Tom Wolfe described as "Plutography," where the American dream was being reshaped by sushi diets, Beamers, gold watches, and absurd amounts of cocaine. Guns N' Roses were trying to obliterate the Robin Leach "champagne wishes and caviar dreams" lifestyle that Bret Michaels seemed to be embodying, which Axl Rose would eventually embrace by fulfilling his version of Keith Richards' fantasy of "Rolls-Royces and spitting at everyone."

Poison was engineered to help audiences escape into a haze of cocaine and pyrotechnics. Their videos were invitations to party as they would look directly into the camera in their videos and ask their audience to sing-along and jump to exploding pyro and slow-motion karate kicks and become hypnotized by the ebullient propaganda. They made instructional workout videos with guitars, as opposed to network news footage of riot squads, war, the business end of police batons, and anarchy—which Guns N' Roses would edit into their video for "Welcome to the Jungle." Two years after the release of *Platoon* (1986), director Oliver Stone described his film as being "an antidote to *Top Gun* and *Rambo*." Guns N' Roses were the antidote to MTV's fantasy-based music videos. "Welcome to the Jungle" was essentially what Stone described *Platoon* to be: "a white Infantry boy's view of the war." Poison were the cabaret performers who entertained the soldiers. The best way to understand Bon Jovi is as a hybrid between Poison and Guns N' Roses; an entry-level Guns N' Roses.

In the video for Bon Jovi's smash hit from 1986, "You Give Love a Bad Name," the second biggest video on MTV that year, we see Bon Jovi looking like a caffeinated pre-teen in a jungle gym. It's a xerox copy of Van Halen's video for "Jump," which was then repackaged in Poison's "Nothin' But a Good Time," where rock and roll is portrayed like a house party scene from an '80s teen sex comedy. Speaking to *Masquerade* in 1986, Michaels described Poison as the "soundtrack to a Friday or Saturday night movie." Slash would diplomatically trash Poison in a *BAM* interview in 1987: "I won't slag them, though I'd like to," he said. "The epitome of Los Angeles is Poison, and what's wrong with Los Angeles. Okay? Enough said."

Guns N' Roses were part of a movement to deglamorize L.A. But they weren't alone in their decision to stop wearing makeup and expand their denim-and-workwear wardrobe. After their working-class anthem "Livin' on Prayer" reached number one in February 1987, Bon Jovi began to rebrand with populism. The colossal success of Bon Jovi's *Slippery When Wet*, which began in 1986, was completely rebranded by "Livin' on Prayer," which gave Bon Jovi the Springsteenian appeal that they had always longed-for.

Guns N' Roses didn't follow in Bon Jovi's footsteps, but they certainly rode their blue-collar wave. Looking back at Guns N' Roses' *Headbangers Ball* interview, host Smash began with a question about the band's image, which was well-cultivated by that point, as by October 1987, Guns N' Roses were the John Carpenter alternative to Spielbergian popcorn flicks. In *Time*'s review of *Escape from New York* (1981), Richard Corliss wrote that, "John Carpenter is offering this summer's moviegoers a rare opportunity: to escape from the air-conditioned torpor of ordinary entertainment into the hothouse humidity of their own paranoia. It's a trip worth taking."

Escape from L.A., Carpenter's 1996 sequel, could have been a fitting title for the debut of Guns N' Roses. As previously noted, *Appetite for Destruction* was named after the 1978 Robert Williams painting, which was the original cover and which feminist groups would later describe as a "glorification of rape." The painting was influenced by carnival art and Williams's self-described "comic arrogance"; it's also the painting Axl Rose discovered either a postcard or a page inside a book at a shop on Melrose Avenue in Hollywood. Once submitted to the record label, it was decided that only thirty thousand copies of the vinyl version would use the "robot rape" art as a cover, while every other pressing (both CD and cassette) would include a Celtic cross with each member's stylized skull attached to it—where Slash has unnaturally straight hair—which was originally a tattoo designed for Axl Rose by art student Billy White Jr.

Several record stores refused to carry the "robot rape" pressings of *Appetite for Destruction*, which may have slowed down sales in the beginning, but the controversy certainly spilled enough blood in the tabloids to further enhance the band's obscene image. Axl would say in a 1987 interview that the painting "captures the band." It was a form of semiotic blowback after decades of conservative and family-friendly *Saturday Evening Post* illustrations. The scandal would transform Guns N' Roses into lewd graffiti sprayed across MTV's star-making machine.

"Axl showed it to me and said he was joking," Niven told *Billboard* on July 21, 2017. "I, however, thought his instinct was brilliant and the pair of us drove way out into the Valley to go to Williams' home to persuade him to let us use it. Tom [Zutaut] and I knew it would create a hoo-ha. That's why we only printed 30,000 units of the original cover and had 30,001, the replacement cover [the Billy White Jr. art], printed even before the record was released—we did not lose a beat in transition and we got the attention we wanted—you can count on people to grab the wrong end of the stick every now and then."

In a *Rock City News* interview from January 1988, Slash and Duff corroborated the claim that album number 30,001 would be the first without the "robot rape" artwork. Slash would describe Williams's artwork as a picture of a "chick flashin' her panties at you."

"There were lots of meetings, debating about what was the right thing to do," Bryn Bridenthal told *Billboard* in 2017. "Frankly I was all for [the Robert Williams cover]."

In an interview with Eddie Trunk in 2011, Axl admitted the "robot rape" cover was orchestrated by both Guns N' Roses and the label as a publicity stunt: "All that was kind of planned to sell records . . . first cover gets banned, we go with the second." Axl's original idea for the cover of *Appetite* was the *TIME* cover photo of the exploding space shuttle *Challenger*. He was like Madonna edging the Vatican with "Like a Prayer" and then packaging her nudist art book like it was a condom. Axl was trying to use artwork as an abstract statement about the role of the media, military industrial complex, church, and government. But because of the "robot rape" imagery, any metaphor or symbolism was lost in Axl Rose's edgelord tendencies.

Similarly dystopian symbolism was hammered into the theme of Metallica's cover for *Master of Puppets*, which depicted a cornfield aligned with burial crosses attached to puppet strings. If you study the semiotics of both the cover of *Appetite for Destruction* and *Master of Puppets*, you'll see they share a common theme: *We are not in control.* The two bands would offer teens a special pair of sunglasses, like those in John Carpenter's *They Live* (1988), which allowed them to see the hidden oppressors lurking around their suburban neighborhoods and rural towns.

In the way that Madonna had generated boatloads of publicity with a wedding-cake striptease on the stage of the 1984 MTV VMAs, Guns N' Roses had used the aestheticization of violence against women to provoke the ire of parents, teachers, and second-wave feminists, who would turn *Appetite for Destruction* into the cult movie that every adolescent boy wanted to see.

This is what Tom Zutaut said about the cover:

> Axl showed me a card with the Williams painting and said, "You realize . . . this is the future." Then he pointed to the woman: "This is the victim; this is the media, and above them is the monster that the media creates." He predicted, in 1986, that we were going to live in a world of "fake news," where we'd feed on tragedy. It depicted human nature and the ugly need we have for an appetite for destruction. Axl told me that CNN was going to change the world by feeding that appetite. He saw the future in that painting, and because GNR had one hundred percent creative control in their contract, the label had to use the artwork.

In the unreleased "Red Hand" booklet of *Chinese Democracy*, Axl would include an image titled "Girl Raped by Alien" by Beijing artist He An. The booklet seems to borrow from some of the sci-fi dystopian inspiration behind NIN's art for 2007's *Year Zero*. On the lyrics page for "This I Love," Axl would include a vagina covered in colorful Nerd candy dots that form a heart shape. There's also an image of two skeletons having doggy-style sex. Unfortunately, by 2008, the mainstream appeal of Axl Rose's provocations had worn thin. Both the "Red Hand" and "Grenade" booklets would be shared on internet forums, but never released widely. "Robot rape" remains their most transgressive visual statement—which was simultaneously anti-feminist and anti-glam.

Duff, who first saw the Clash as a teenager in a crowd of 200 people in Seattle, was completely mortified of being associated with L.A. He told *LA Weekly* in 1986 that, "L.A. people think they have to be put into one category, like 'Now we're death rockers,' or we're this or that—which is not bad, but in other cities you're just a band. You're not grouped with anything." Guns N' Roses were renouncing any association with the star system that had developed Poison.

"I've always been a big believer in the Star System," Paul Stanley said in 1988. Stanley was part of the cast of characters in Penelope Spheeris's hair-metal documentary, *The Decline of Western Civilization Part II: The Metal Years*, which documented the Sunset Strip from 1986–88 and unintention-ally became a mockumentary of a scene that Spheeris seemed to want to glorify. When Guns N' Roses chose not to appear in the farcical documen-tary, Poison became its star.

By deciding not to appear in Spheeris's film, it seems Guns N' Roses were dodging the *This is Spinal Tap* treatment. Michaels embraced it fully. "When you look at a city like Los Angeles, or the whole United States in general, you're gonna look and say, man, there's a million bands out there, they look great, they sound great, they're doing their own thing," Michaels told Spheeris. "What's Poison gonna do to stick out to the crowd? We had an outrageous look, and outrageous sound, everything that we did was outrageous, and all of a sudden, people said, 'what a great gimmick, but can they play?' Like you said, you don't sell three million records if you can't play music." Which is a patently untrue statement when you look at the history of popular music from Pat Boone to Britney Spears.

Had they appeared in Spheeris's documentary, Slash and Duff probably would have come off like the air guitar troglodytes who were satirized in *Bill & Ted's Excellent Adventure* (1989). Guns N' Roses have done a marvelous job of protecting their brand from being conflated with hair-metal clichés (though on some level they were the most talented hair-metal band). Sitting on their couch, Beavis and Butt-Head reminded their audi-ence that Axl Rose was "cool," as they proceeded to make fun of Bon Jovi's cheesy video for "In These Arms." In a different episode, the two sang the chorus of "Paradise City" and swung a chainsaw. Between 1993 and 1997, Beavis and Butt-Head's couch was culturally more influential than some of America's top music critics.

In 1993, Geffen Records planned to release a CD compilation of bands that Beavis and Butt-Head had decided were "cool." MTV executive and Guns N' Roses fan John Canelli was behind the comp.

Guns N' Roses, like The Who before them, would use volume as a demonstration of both power and "cool." After Tom Zutaut signed them to a recording contract on March 26, 1986, he said that Guns N' Roses were the loudest band he'd heard since AC/DC. Loudness was a measurement unit for a band's hegemony and authenticity, where decibels were viewed like a kind of "arms race" to determine supremacy. "Guns played louder than bombs," wrote Stephen Davis in his biography on the band. Nobody ever described Bon Jovi as being an especially *loud* band. Slash would advertise his band's volume supremacy in *Music Connection* 1986: "The last band he'd [Tom Zutaut] seen that was *this* loud was AC/DC. And he's been doing this for years."

Loudness was a way of measuring the size of a band's penis. It was also the teenager's way of muffling or even antagonizing their volume-sensitive parents. The louder a band, the more subversive. On the liner notes of *Appetite for Destruction*, the band included notes that read like threatening yearbook messages. The album art, along with the band photos and song lyrics, were all part of their attempt to create a manifesto for teenage nihilism. Axl Rose was Brando in *The Wild One* (1953) being asked by a wide-eyed teen what exactly he was rebelling against, to which Brando responded, while playing the bongos on a jukebox, "Whaddya got?"

Guns N' Roses understood the appeal of the brooding Hollywood rebel—which you can see in a photo of Izzy Stradlin wielding a vintage butterfly knife. The 1987 *Headbangers Ball* interview was their jukebox into the hearts and minds of millions of captivated teens who were watching three to four hours of TV per day. In 1987, MTV was the only platform that could lift a rock band from the underground towards the skyscrapers of Manhattan. They had initially denied Guns N' Roses by refusing to put "Welcome to the Jungle" into heavy rotation, which was the exposure the band required to gain mainstream buzz. The reason for their apprehension was a symptom of cable TV's conservatism. "Half their cable outlets were run by a right-wing Conservative, John Malone, who told MTV's founder Bob Pittman that if he played junky bands, he'd knock MTV off his cable networks," says Zutaut. John Malone, the former CEO of Tele-Communications Inc. (TCI), was described by the *New York Times* in 1990 as a "cable baron" who directly or indirectly provided cable TV to more than fifty million households—a man who would proceed to yank cable networks from TCI's systems if they refused to comply. In order to even consider running "Welcome to the Jungle" on MTV, Geffen was asked to implement edits to the video that would cut down the use of graphic network news footage from ABC, CBS, and NBC. There was also a scene with drummer Steven Adler engaging in sexual foreplay with a woman, which was cut.

Here's Tom Hunter, the senior vice president of MTV, in *I Want My MTV*: "When they submitted 'Welcome to the Jungle,' we accepted it for *Headbangers Ball*, which was typically what we'd do with a video that extreme. Axl was twitching in an electric chair!" Tom Freston, the president and CEO of MTV, and the man who would eventually push "Welcome to the Jungle" into heavy rotation, said that "the programming group decided to put 'Welcome to the Jungle' on *Headbangers Ball* for starters. Not in regular rotation. It was getting played a couple times a week. David Geffen called me and said, 'Every time you guys play this thing at 3 a.m., our sales light up. Please leave it on.' Normally, I wouldn't tell the programming guys what to put into heavy rotation. But this was David Geffen."

Two gay men—David Geffen and John Canelli—were the corporate endorsements "Welcome to the Jungle" needed to machete through the charts. A year later, Axl Rose would refer to gay people as "faggots" and accuse them of spreading "disease" throughout Los Angeles.

"When John [Canelli] spoke up, you listened," said Sam Kaiser, who was a programming executive at MTV in 1987. "He brought us a video by Guns N' Roses, 'Welcome to the Jungle,' and I fell out of my chair." According to former manager Doug Goldstein, at the time, John Canelli and Axl Rose were friends.

The prevailing myth is that MTV had "banned" the video for "Welcome to the Jungle." This simply isn't true. In fact, the video played as early as October 1987—it just wasn't placed into the coveted position of *heavy rotation* (which equals four plays per day). The fiction that MTV had banned "Welcome to the Jungle" served its purpose in their anti-glam marketing campaign. The video for "Jungle" was their anti-glam genre film. In it Axl is seen in various stages of transition from naiveté to madness: first as the flannel-wearing white boy with eyeliner, being hustled by Izzy. Later he's depicted as a cranked-out maniac in skintight leather pants, and finally as Alex DeLarge from *A Clockwork Orange* (1971). In the most shocking scene, Axl is seen shaking violently in a straitjacket, as he's strapped to what looks like an electric chair and forced to endure footage that was not part of the fantasy MTV was selling in those days. This was Axl Rose watching *Faces of Death*. Axl Rose shaking in an electric chair must have traumatized the children who stayed up late to watch MTV. Axl looked like the deformed image of Richard III that grew out of the imagination of Shakespeare.

For MTV, which was launched in 1981 to hook teens who were watching sitcoms, videos were fashion runaways and lifestyle advertising. MTV founder Bob Pittman described MTV videos as "mood enhancers" for "TV babies"; a form of advertising through captivating images that glued you to the TV, what Jello Biafra of the Dead Kennedys described as the moment when "rock and roll and advertising became one and the same."

"Welcome to the Jungle" was an injection of adrenaline right into the heart of the MTV viewer. It's hard to say precisely when MTV put "Welcome to the Jungle" into heavy rotation, but it was probably put into heavy rotation sometime between October 1987 and February 1988, when MTV filmed Guns N' Roses at the Ritz, which would air in April 1988 and become the most watched episode of *Live at the Ritz*. The footage would be introduced by VJ Adam Curry, who would use a series of clichés to introduce the concert, including the now infamous talking point from the Geffen press kit: "Their own record label said that they'll make it, if they live long enough. Well, they have."

David Geffen would discuss the MTV breakthrough in a 2012 PBS *American Masters* documentary: "Zutaut said to me that the only way we're gonna break this record is if we get it on MTV, and MTV did not want to play it, and I called my friend Tom Freston, and said to him 'Just play it in the middle of the night, don't report, just play it . . . and let's see if there's a reaction to it.'" This is what Jimmy Iovine once referred to as Geffen's "magic trick." It wasn't just Geffen; Niven pressured executives at MTV, including John Canelli.

"We have a pretty big role in spreading something from underground to the heartland," Canelli told the *New York Times* in 1992. "We're always looking for whatever the next thing is."

The band would publicly deride MTV and vocalize how exhausted they were with music channel's resistance to playing their video. Behind the scenes they aggressively lobbied to appear on a network they were trashing publicly, until, of course, they had their video in heavy rotation (by 1988, MTV executives were appearing in their videos). In a January 1988 *Rock City News* interview published when *Appetite for Destruction* had sold close to four hundred thousand copies, Slash was asked by the interviewer if they were on MTV. Slash replied, "No. We should be. We gave them the new video." Duff interjected: "We went to the studio in New York to do a taping and we got 30 seconds to thrash the set."

To be clear, by this point, the "Jungle" video was on MTV; it just wasn't on at least four times per day. "I watch MTV and it's hard not to throw shit at the TV set because it's so fucking boring," Axl told *Kerrang!* in June 1987.

In a December 1987 interview published in *Music Connection*, Slash refers to MTV as "just dicks," after suggesting that "Welcome to the Jungle" was being played all throughout the country, except on MTV. It's important to note that the interview took place before they appeared on the *Headbangers Ball*. According to Zutaut, MTV first played the video for "Welcome to the Jungle" at 4 a.m. EST on a Sunday night and then a few more times in the afternoon—this was the first time the video would get multiple plays on the network. While there's almost no way of separating myth from reality, the breakthrough occurred when MTV's switchboards began lighting up like Clark Griswold's house in *National Lampoon's Christmas Vacation* (1989) as Handel's "Hallelujah" chorus played, and Guns N' Roses became the most requested band on MTV.

Zutaut explains the moment Guns N' Roses became an MTV band:

> The album was seen as a failure by the label. They had sold 200,000 units within a few months of release, which any band could have done in those days. Geffen CEO Ed Rosenblatt called me into his office and said the record was dead. That it was time move on to the next one. I went over his head to David Geffen, who called MTV CEO Tom Freston and pulled a favor to get the video on MTV, at 4 a.m. in New York. The next day, I had multiple phone calls from my office. I called my assistant and she said that Rosenblatt and Geffen were looking for me. I got in around four in the afternoon, and the head of promotion told me the video had lit up MTV's switchboards. He was yelling hysterically and said MTV finally added the video into rotation after just one play of "Welcome to the Jungle."

The precise date is nearly impossible to determine. But Guns N' Roses began to break on MTV at a uniquely opportune moment in the history of the network (just like they had in the local L.A. scene, during the rebrand of KNAC). In 1987, in a renegotiating of their playlist, MTV had made room for more metal and hard rock. Created in April 1987 to run from 12 a.m. to 2 a.m., *Headbangers Ball* drew an average of 1.3 million viewers a week. It was the revival of a genre the network had practically abandoned in 1985, but in 1987, it had begun to farm from the loyal audience of heavy-metal magazines like *Circus*, *RIP*, and *Hit Parader*. Prior to this, MTV had briefly tried to be more metal-friendly in 1985, when they test launched *Heavy Metal Mania* as a weekly hour-long interview program hosted by Twisted Sister singer Dee Snider. *Mania* ran at 1 or 2 a.m. and was what MTV CEO Tom Hunter described as a "dumping ground" for metal videos, as curation was not the priority. This was a two-hour platform where Dee Snider would randomly promote metal bands without very much curation. "When I listen to heavy metal," said Snider during an interview with the Scorpions, which was conducted next to a dumbbell rack, "I like to lift heavy metal."

Perhaps one of most forgotten factors in the rise of Guns N' Roses on MTV was the fact that they first appeared on *Headbangers Ball* (which ran at midnight) and not on Snider's juvenile prototype. Think about the awkward moment during the *Headbangers Ball* interview, when Smash asked the band to introduce their video after a count of three, when all five members were asked to say, "Let's rock!" Guns N' Roses didn't want to play. They just sat there, which seemed to surprise Smash—who may not have known that Guns N' Roses would never allow MTV to turn them into a comedy act. Guns N' Roses were asked to destroy the set of the *Headbangers Ball*, and proceeded to throw hubcaps toward the cameras and threaten any sense of normalcy at MTV. It was as staged as pro wrestling, but teenagers watching the *Headbangers Ball* in 1987 didn't know that. Wrestling was still "real" in 1987. There was a period of time when many of us legitimately believed Guns N' Roses had wrecked the *Headbangers Ball* set. That they did it without permission. The *Headbangers Ball* appearance wasn't the Sex Pistols' use of profanity on Bill Grundy's *Today* show. It wasn't Elvis proving that George Bernard Shaw was correct when he said that dancing is a "perpendicular expression of horizontal desire." It wasn't Little Richard colliding with his piano keys and screaming gibberish, or even the Rolling Stones on the *Ed Sullivan Show* on October 25, 1964, prompting hundreds of complaints from parents, along with millions of teenagers screaming for more. But the perception that Guns N' Roses had destroyed the set of an MTV show, along with their anti-MTV comments in the press, worked, like a highly successful pro-wrestling angle. We wanted it to be real. Years later, their *Headbangers Ball* moment was picked as one of the 40 greatest moments in MTV history by *Rolling Stone*.

It was the night that Guns N' Roses informed MTV's audience that they were not the next Bon Jovi, a band who had taken all the Americanism of Springsteen and turned into a Levi's commercial scored by fist-pumping anthems. The way Ronald Reagan had co-opted "Born in the U.S.A." into a campaign song in 1984, Bon Jovi had appropriated Springsteen for as much cultural clout as possible in 1986. "My attitude from the start has been that if this isn't my 'Born to Run,' it isn't coming out," Jon Bon Jovi told *Hit Parader* in November 1986, just as Bon Jovi had begun to switch their spandex for the simplicity and modesty of blue jeans.

By 1987, Bon Jovi had sold twelve million copies of an album that would take metal from being a subculture on MTV into a top billing position. Some of Bon Jovi's success as a pop act on *Slippery When Wet* belongs to pop songwriter Desmond Child (who was brought in to help the band create hooks), including "Livin' on a Prayer," the power ballad that would define an album that had fused together bubblegum metal with Springsteen populism.

To appeal to as many consumers as possible, regardless of socio-economic status, Bon Jovi would abandon the *Tiger Beat* aesthetic and begin branding themselves as the E Street Band of MTV. They would embrace a more egalitarian image, as opposed to metal's traditionally more salacious and male-driven presentation. But this would have been impossible had Bon Jovi's label allowed them to use the original cover of *Slippery When Wet*, which featured a full-breasted, tanned bombshell who was dripping wet, presumably from washing cars, who wore a torn yellow T-shirt that looked like it was going to explode off her chest. Bon Jovi bene-fited heavily from Mercury Records' aversion to the cover. The original cover for *Slippery When Wet* would have made Bon Jovi writing an homage to the Old West feel as outlawish as the Eagles playing cowboys on the cover of *Desperado,* or as Ratt's drag-queen Western, "Wanted Man."

In 1987, Bon Jovi had refashioned themselves from teen idols into cowboys for their hit single "Wanted Dead or Alive," which was the third single off *Slippery When Wet*. In 1990, Emilio Estevez asked Bon Jovi to allow him to include "Wanted Dead or Alive" in the soundtrack of the sequel to *Young Guns* (1988). Jon Bon Jovi instead decided to pen "Blaze of Glory" for the film. Old West pastiche by a hair-metal band was as prepos-terous as Jon's Native American choker. He was from New Jersey, not New

Mexico. Still, the six-gun revivalism continued the move to make Bon Jovi seem less libidinous and neon.

Like Guns N' Roses, Bon Jovi was beginning to use the press to rebrand themselves as something less glamorous. "We never tried to do any of the pin-up stuff," Jon Bon Jovi told *Hit Parader*. "We wanted people to just react to our music. We're very proud of where we come from. New Jersey's a lot different from places like L.A., where things are phonier, and there's tons of hairspray everywhere. I'm from the gutter, and that's where I like it." The cover art for *Slippery When Wet* that was used in North America was decidedly more New Jersey than L.A.: it featured a wet trash bag with the title hand-drawn over the moisture rising off the black bag, which was an album cover for the common man, from the gutters. It felt darkly erotic, like the prose of Raymond Chandler, which is reimagined in the bookstore scene from *The Big Sleep* (1946), where a rain-covered window is used to symbolize the lust Bogart feels for Dorothy Malone.

"Many credit the mass-appeal Bon Jovi's 'You Give Love a Bad Name' last summer with opening programmers' ears to the merits of metal," *Billboard* wrote in 1987. "Others give a nod to Mötley Crüe's 'Smokin' in the Boys Room' for dispelling the notion that Top 40 and hard rock don't mix. Metal and hard rock have fallen between the programming cracks because of their predominantly teen appeal." What would have happened had Bon Jovi used the more exploitive cover for *Slippery When Wet*? Would the album have attracted an audience beyond horny male teenagers? Bon Jovi's *Slippery When Wet* spent eight weeks at number one and became the best-selling album of 1987, turning heavy metal into a mainstream product that even Madonna fans were buying. To understand how Guns N' Roses became an MTV band, we have to go back to 1986, on the high heels of Bon Jovi's box-office success, when MTV increased the amount of heavy metal it programmed, which they had reduced in 1984. Between 1982 and 1984, MTV had mainstreamed metal by playing videos by Mötley Crüe, Def Leppard, and Quiet Riot, and normalizing the horror-film tropes that had, within a year, become so cult that they only appealed to a niche audience. Heavy metal wasn't as culturally appealing to MTV in 1984, which, with the exception of Van Halen, saw a brighter future in the dance clubs of England and the more family-friendly stadium pop of Phil Collins. MTV was a disco with a New Romantics playlist of synthesizer-heavy sounds and pure pop music.

You could argue that the biggest rock star in America before Axl Rose was Michael Jackson. *TIME* in 1984 said that "Jackson is the biggest thing since the Beatles. He is the hottest single phenomenon since Elvis Presley." But unlike Axl Rose, Michael Jackson was more family friendly. He visited Reagan's White House, received public service awards, and seemed as custom-built for the Reagan era as Bon Jovi was for turning heavy metal into dance music. MTV wanted more rock stars like Michael Jackson, who was less polarizing than Axl Rose. In February 1984, MTV founder Bob Pittman spoke to *Rolling Stone* about the state of heavy metal on MTV: "People either love it or hate it. And people who hate it, hate it with a passion . . . We want to play music that's on the cutting edge [such as Talking Heads] . . . I don't think anyone would say that heavy metal is the most creative element in music today. It's a quick, crass, easy buck for record companies. These guys don't deserve to dominate the channel. They're not as popular as the Police or Mick Jagger."

But Bon Jovi changed the perception of heavy metal at MTV. In 1986, "You Give Love a Bad Name" was the second-most played video on MTV, sandwiched between Robert Palmer and Peter Gabriel. When MTV began to struggle in 1985–86, along with the record industry as a whole, there was a recommitment to playing the genre. In February 1987, *Circus* reported that only four of the 30 videos in heavy rotation at MTV could have been considered "metal." Frustrated metal singers like Ronnie James Dio spoke out: "MTV suddenly seemed to desert us all. The sad thing is, when you spend $250,000 on a video and you only see it once." By 1989, when Guns N' Roses were the most talked-about band on the planet, heavy metal accounted for 40 percent of all music sales in the United States. This was timed with the tragic reality that US steel mills were closing down. Just as heavy metal was on the rise—between roughly 1974 and 1986—the steel industry was experiencing a decline. Jennifer Beals laboring in a steel mill in 1983's *Flashdance* was Hollywood's way of turning a working-class tragedy into escapist box-office gold (it was the progenitor of the populism used on "Livin' on a Prayer").

Flipping through pages of rock magazines in 1989, it's very clear that a more blue-collar version of metal had become mass-media culture by the late '80s, and Bon Jovi had cleared the flight path for an anti-glam band like Guns N' Roses. The front page of *Billboard* on October 11, 1986, read: "MTV: Changes at the Channel; More Rock and New Acts, Execs Say." In 1987, a band like Guns N' Roses must have lifted the faces off MTV hipsters like the wind tunnel effect in Maxell's "Blown Away Guy" commercial. Guns N' Roses gave the Wall Street generation a dangerous rush, like they were being chased by a vigilante mob in the mean streets of Soho, like the lonely yuppie in Scorsese's *After Hours* (1985) who went from his computer desk in uptown into the vortex of nightmarish version of Soho. "I just wanted to leave my apartment," he said during the film's nervous breakdown, "maybe meet a nice girl . . . and now . . . I gotta die for it?" This was "Welcome to the Jungle" as a yuppie revenge flick.

For the self-conscious intellectual reading Henry Miller behind the napkin dispenser inside a dimly lit café, Guns N' Roses were a pulp novel that combined sex with violence. In 1983, when Huey Lewis told the new corporate class that he wanted a new drug, he probably had no idea that new drug would be Guns N' Roses, who were going from an NC-17 fetish into the sort of Top 40 that played inside the teenage girl's bedroom in *Cape Fear* (1991).

But for most of 1987, Guns N' Roses would fight for mainstream acceptance. Every interview, photo shoot, and live performance was a potential proving ground. The Ritz '87 concert is mostly unseen, as it never aired on MTV, but it's worth watching, as it's Guns N' Roses at their most uncivilized. The footage exists somewhere, where Axl can be seen stomping around the stage with the energy of a demonic rabbit, pogoing, and pouring with sweat like a male stripper in skintight leather pants and a "wife beater." Axl's soft red hair swings around his face as if he's in the middle of a live sex act. Slash is shirtless, dark, glistening; his face draped with thick black hair. The spotlight is on the two of them for a full hour of complete brutality, as if they're invading Rome and using the blood of their victims to paint messages on the walls. Towards the end of the set, Axl rants with righteous indignation: "In these last few minutes, I'll make a point for what's it worth. Got a lot of people, a lot of magazines going: *It's a glam band, it's a metal band, it's a glam metal band, it's a hard rock band, it's a thrash band* . . . fuck it. It doesn't make a good goddamn difference whether my hair is up, my hair's down, or I'm fucken' bald. It's all fucken' rock and roll to me."

If you study the mainstream media landscape between 1986 and through the summer of 1987, Guns N' Roses, on a national level, didn't really exist. Certainly, they weren't à la mode in New York, where in 1987, the top three most-watched music videos on MTV were by U2, Genesis, and, of course, Bon Jovi. MTV music videos mostly depicted supermodels as fleshly real estate. It was a culture that would turn Donald Trump into a lifestyle brand, which oversold the decadence of getting reservations somewhere exclusive or having your photo taken in an Armani suit, like Alex P. Keaton chomping sushi on the cover of *Esquire*. It's no wonder that in *American Psycho*, Bret Easton Ellis's 1991 satire of the era, MTV and daytime talk were part of the same oeuvre of mindless channel surfing for America's most soulless architects of culture: editors at *Vogue*, producers at MTV, *Village Voice* music critics, investment bankers, and tanned sociopaths like Patrick Bateman (*American Psycho*), who watched Axl Rose on *The Patty Winters Show*: "When I get stressed," said Axl, "I get violent and take it out on myself. I've pulled razor blades on myself, but then realized having a scar is more detrimental than not having a stereo . . . when I get mad or upset or emotional, sometimes I'll walk over and play my piano." Bret Easton Ellis was using part of a 1989 *Rolling Stone* interview where Axl was responding to the following question: "How do you explain your volatile nature?"

While the thought of Axl Rose being relatable to a sociopath like Patrick Bateman is nothing more than fiction, it says something that Bret Easton Ellis would use Axl Rose to symbolize the degradation of

Bateman's sanity. It were as if Axl's psychopathy represented the hidden desires of Manhattan's repressed upper-class. Between 1986 and 1988, as Guns N' Roses became pop, the sushi-obsessed elitist, in his beige trousers and crisply ironed dress shirt, who'd flip through glossy magazine to sniff the latest fashionable fragrance sample from Christian Dior, had finally discovered the gunpowder aroma of Guns N' Roses. They had pulled down their suspenders, whipped out their gold cards, and snorted two lines of Axl's heart attack–inducing falsetto, which exploded through the back of the gelled cranium of *Wall Street*'s Bud Fox.

Around the middle of 1988, the video for "Welcome to the Jungle" would become number one on Dial MTV, which would play the top five most requested videos each day. This was the dial-in predecessor of *Total Request Live*.

In Guns N' Roses' first major print interview, *Music Connection*'s Karen Burch described them as five different personalities linked together by a common thread: cockiness, which was a characteristic embodied in American folklore by the cowboy, the gangster, the biker, the post-Brando teen rebel, and the Wall Street banker of the '80s. The psychological function of Axl Rose was to allow his audience to vicariously rebel through his madcap persona, one that offered what Western historian David Brion Davis would have described as an "instrument for their aggressive impulses." We see this liberating image when Axl preaches the gospel, if you will, as he stomps and hurls himself across the stage with the torque of a muscle car in the video for "Paradise City." Axl is dressed like a televangelist at a biker rally, wearing all white and swinging his red mane around his face like he's tackling his shadowy demons inside a football stadium. "Paradise City" is the first Guns N' Roses song to use synthesizer (which was Axl's suggestion), which gave it a tinge of "Livin' on a Prayer."

In contrast, on "Welcome to the Jungle" Axl Rose is dragging his audience into the infernos to witness a physically menacing street fighter, which Brion Davis would have concluded to be part of his appeal: "Physical prowess is the most important thing for the ten- or twelve-year-old mind. They are constantly plagued by fear, doubt, and insecurity, in short, by evil, and they lack the power to crush it. The cowboy provides the instrument for their aggressive impulses." The Axl Rose in the "Welcome to the Jungle" video looked like what former Rolling Stones' manager Andrew Loog Oldham once described Mick Jagger as: "An adolescent Tarzan."

After two years of aggressively cultivating their image—and benefiting greatly from Bon Jovi's timely breakthrough—Guns N' Roses had forced America to accept them as the rebirth of American hard rock—not the evolution of glam. No band in history had worked as hard to define themselves as the alternative to the genre that had given birth to them.

5

SWEET CHILD O' DIE

**"I LOVE YOU, I TELL YOU. NOW WALK ON ME.
SPIT ON ME. STOMP ON MY FACE."**

—*BELLE DE JOUR* (1967)

If the first encounter most fans had with Guns N' Roses was the video for "Welcome to the Jungle," then the lowbrow lust of "It's So Easy," which never ran on MTV, would become their obscure sex tape. Even when a version of the footage was released on Apple Music in 2018, it had to be edited into a more digestible product. Geffen/UME would describe it as "original" and "newly discovered," but in reality, the video was never completed (it was shot in October 1989).

"The clip never progressed from Nigel's off line and thus was never presented to MTV," says Niven, who hired Nigel Dick to direct the video (and who directed "Welcome to the Jungle").

Some of the uncensored original footage only exists on bootlegged cassette tapes and grainy YouTube clips that appear and disappear with the frequency of tweets by Izzy Stradlin. There's also some dispute over whether the footage was banned by MTV or suppressed by Axl Rose himself. As far as a viewing of the grainy footage, as well as the less smutty released version, "It's So Easy" doesn't seem particularly vulgar, especially when you compare it to the Nazi chic exploitation of Madonna's "Justify My Love," or the 8mm seediness of "Erotica." It certainly isn't any hornier than Duran Duran's "Girls on Film," what feminist Andrea Dworkin would have referred to as "high-class pornography." It's not alarmingly more extreme than the crotch-grabbing rabidity showcased at the end of Michael Jackson's original cut for "Black or White."

I don't believe MTV outright banned the video without asking for an edited version. I do believe that Axl Rose wanted to use the video's "ban" to counterbalance the MTV-friendly video for "Sweet Child O' Mine." This is what artists did in those days: they produced racy videos. They followed by saying it was never meant for a mass audience. They would leak word to the press that MTV had banned the video (even if they hadn't outright *banned* it). The ink would bleed; the record label would watch it bleed. After that, a sterilized version of the video would become the most requested video on MTV. This is essentially what happened with "Girls on Film."

"If we made a nice video for MTV, we could put it out and sell more records and shit," Axl Rose told the extras gathered during the concert shoot for "It's So Easy." "But instead, we're gonna spend a hundred-fifty grand just to make something we want to see." It was not the first time Axl Rose wanted to create something that only "we [Guns N' Roses] want to see." During the recoding of *Appetite for Destruction*, Axl and Adriana Smith, a raspy stripper who was dating Steven Adler at the time, recorded themselves having sex inside a recording booth. Over an hour of tape was mixed into the one-minute bridge and guitar solo on *Appetite for Destruction*'s grand finale, "Rocket Queen." If you listen carefully to the audio, you can actually hear the moment where Adriana Smith's erotic, high-pitched moan melds into Slash's wailing guitar note.

The "It's So Easy" footage bursts with the lustful exhibitionism of a trashier Helmut Newton photo shoot. In its opening a scene, a young woman in a pearl-white dress jiggles her rump along to Duff's plucking bass. It may or may not be Axl Rose's girlfriend, Erin Everly, who is the inspiration behind "Sweet Child O' Mine." The video begins to flicker with slave–master flashbacks that recall *The Night Porter* (1974) or Friedkin's exploitive S&M thriller *Cruising* (1980), along with caffeinated crowd shots, and a glimpse of a woman with "AXL" tattooed across her exposed butt cheek. It's an orgiastic burst of sensory overload. Axl proceeds to use bondage gear purchased from WeHo's Pleasure Chest, which included a handcuff, leather whip, S&M blindfold, ankle cuffs, gothic outfits, and a red ball gag to dominate his girlfriend, Erin Everly, who also appears as an adoring groupie in plain clothes. She is the young woman with the exposed butt cheek. Like Catherine Deneuve in *Belle de Jour* (1967), Erin Everly embodied a high-class maiden being corrupted by her masochistic fantasies. She is the "good girl gone bad" of Hollywood teen cinema; the "dirty tramp" from *Rebel Without a Cause* (1955), who is played by Natalie Wood.

"It's So Easy" is disturbing because of its starlet, Axl's submissive girlfriend, who is the muse who inspired both the tenderness of "Sweet Child O' Mine" and the lashings in the video for "It's So Easy." On an appearance on Eddie Trunk's radio show in May 2006, singer Sebastian Bach claimed to have acquired a tape of the unreleased footage. Axl Rose would make a surprise appearance on the show. "That's fine . . . that's where I'm spanking Erin," replied Axl. "I'm spanking sweet child." With the success of "Sweet Child O' Mine" in the summer of 1988, would it not have been logical to assume that both MTV and Geffen would have been hesitant to release footage of the "sweet child," Axl's beauty queen—a blossoming American sweetheart—being gagged, tied, and forced to endure pain? It would be like reading a love poem, only to find out it was written by a rapist.

The footage was recorded in the fall of 1989 using staged concert footage spliced with Axl Rose's scandalous male gaze. It's fleshly exhibitionism, like an 8mm Warhol, except it's Warhol as a horny redneck in fetish gear. For three decades, "It's So Easy" would only appear in glimpses on YouTube, as GIFs on Tumblr, rarely on underground tapes, but never as an uncensored and complete music video. It's important to understand that the video the band released in 2018 is original, but that's because there never was a final edit—just a collage of footage, most of which remains in Axl Rose's vault. Because it was confiscated from the public eye, for reasons I hope to illuminate, "It's So Easy" became a case study in the Streisand Effect, where the commentary about the unseen footage would slowly metastasize into obsession and theorizing about the true cause of its burial—which may have been an example of the criminal hiding circumstantial evidence of a far more serious crime.

"According to rock folklore," wrote *NME* in 2018, "the video was originally rejected by MTV and has remained in a vault unseen for almost 30 years." What really happened requires revisiting the tragic story of Erin Everly, the debutante who transforms into the scandalized vamp. Axl Rose is her hell-raising Valentino. The video for "It's So Easy" includes flashes of a pancake-faced Axl Rose, who is costumed like a homoeroticized biker from Kenneth Anger's *Scorpio Rising* (wearing a sleeveless leather jacket with a skull on it), as he degrades his girlfriend, who can be seen crawling on red velvet like a purring kitten—as seen through the eyes of a wolf. This is Axl's intensely "pro-hetero" gaze, where he wraps chains around the wrists of a young woman who is the daughter of '50s pop star, Don Everly, and former Hollywood starlet Venetia Stevenson. There's a photo of Venetia with Elvis, still in his youthful rockabilly phase, as his greasy hair dangles over a 19-year-old Venetia, who looks like Erin Everly in the crowd shots of "It's So Easy"—transfixed on the intoxicating blend of innocence and ferociousness that stood before her.

Like Hitchcock, Axl was manipulating his obsession, like moldable clay he could form into the shape of his darkest desires. "Sex was an ego addiction similar to the one felt onstage," wrote Del James in his short story "Without You," which was partially inspired by the turbulent romance of Axl Rose and Erin Everly, written before *Appetite for Destruction* was released. Erin is Axl's doe-eyed "ego addiction," a symbol of the upper-crust society that he wanted to penetrate in order to turn the hayseed in his mouth into a luxurious cigarette holder. She was the heiress that he so desperately wanted to, "rape, pillage, *search*, destroy." We see her submitting to the slave-master relationship that would give Axl, a child who once had the control taken away from him, authoritarian-levels of control. The more you know about their abusive romance, the more you begin to understand the reason why "It's So Easy" was locked inside a vault for 30 years.

With her Windex-colored eyes, and sheltered upbringing, Erin Everly seemed like an uncontaminated sweetheart who could only have been written by Hollywood screenwriters. She was the prom queen who coyly accepted her tiara at a prom attended by pole dancers and prostitutes. She seemed, at least to the public, demure, like the classic "good girl" who becomes contaminated by the "bad boy" e.g., Sandy in *Grease* (1978). She was not introduced to us like Tawny Kitaen doing the splits in a sheer dress. She's what would have happened had Bender and Claire's flirtation in *The Breakfast Club* (1985) led them to Las Vegas to tie the knot, and then, within 24-hours, untie it.

Imagine a sun-kissed prom queen arriving home in a bathing suit, as a high-strung rock star demands her to undress, before hog-tying her, slapping a strip of masking tape over her lips, and blindfolding her with a bandana. He then throws her into a closet, where she remains for hours. She is too afraid to move. It reads like a scenario from a pulp novel, and yet it is taken directly from a deposition given in May 1994 by Erin Everly, who two months earlier had filed a lawsuit charging Axl Rose with "assault and battery, sexual battery, false imprisonment, and intentional infliction of emotional distress." She would claim that Axl repeatedly hit her with "foreign objects." At some point in 1994, Axl Rose and Erin Everly settled out of court for an undisclosed sum.

But before her silence was secured, Erin would describe how Axl Rose "forced himself on [her] anally really hard. Really hard." This is where the footage of "It's So Easy" becomes an exhibit for the judge in a domestic violence case. But before it could be extinguished from the public record, parts of Erin's deposition were published in a *Rolling Stone* profile on Axl Rose titled, *Axl Rose the Lost Years: The Inside Story of Rock's Most Famous Recluse*, a notorious profile which permanently damaged the relationship between Axl Rose and *Rolling Stone*.

"Were you screaming?"

"Yes," Erin Everly said during her 1994 deposition.

"How long did that last?"

"I don't remember."

"What happened when it was over?"

"He took it out and stuck it in my mouth."

Erin claimed that Axl pulled her out of the closet, threw her down onto the bed, and then began to anally penetrate her. The graphic testimony colors "It's So Easy" with bruises and ignored pleas for help (like the overexposed photos of a beaten Nicole Brown Simpson), rather than mere exhibitionism and kink. Erin's deposition turns Axl into the pale corpse-like biker he's playing in the first shot of the edited version of "It's So Easy."

The suppressed video, for those who've seen parts of it, becomes even more provocative. You want to turn your head, but instead, you look on as if you're watching a scrambled sex scene or crime scene footage. You are invited behind the curtained-off section of the Guns N' Roses video store. The cover of this VHS tape isn't a skull that's "banned in 46 countries." What you're now looking at is a blurry glimpse into one of the many layers of Axl Rose's complicated psyche.

Axl Rose has said that he was sexually abused by his biological father (whom he didn't know existed until he was 17 years old). This happened when he was a two-year-old toddler. We know that Axl never completely forgave his mother, Sharon, for allowing the abuse to take place. Axl witnessed his mother allow his biological father and stepfather to abuse him physically (though we only have reason to believe he was *sexually* abused by his biological father). This is when the demons began to breed inside him. There are sources I spoke to who claim Axl's mother never accepted his claim that he was raped by his biological father, William Rose, who died in the '80s. I believe this trauma is one of the causes of his need to dominate the opposite sex.

Axl told *Rolling Stone* in 1992 that he had, "a lot of violent, abusive thoughts toward women." He would watch his mother being abused by his father. "I was two years old, very impressionable, and saw this. I figured that's how you treat a woman. And I basically put thoughts together about how sex is power and sex leaves you powerless, and picked up a lot of distorted views that I've had to live my life with." These were the "distorted views" that inspired the video for "It's So Easy," which bled into his real life. In a separate section of the *Rolling Stone* interview, Axl said, "Basically,

I've been rejected by my mother since I was a baby. She's picked my step-father over me ever since he was around and watched me get beaten by him. She stood back most of the time. Unless it got too bad, and then she'd come and hold you afterward. She wasn't there for me."

He would often experience intense nightmares as a child. One of the nightmares included him as a wild horse, perhaps a mustang, which was unwillingly domesticated and used in Hollywood productions—enslaved by the studio system. Axl was clearly struggling with feelings of powerlessness. He seemed like a beaten dog, which is how producer Moby would describe him during a meeting in 1997. For Axl, women were complicit in his "beaten dog" syndrome, his festering trauma, and manic cycles of depression, which were a gift, in some ways, as they exploded into expressionist modern dance that seemed as wild as the mustangs in *The Misfits* (1960), which struggled to free themselves from Clark Gable's lasso. Axl Rose's turbulent performances were choreographed by his nightmares. After seeing Elvis perform for the first time in 1956, an executive producer of *Stage Show* described Elvis as a "guitar-playing Marlon Brando," whose erotic dance moves had turned Eisenhower's dying small towns into the sexually frustrated ennui of Bogdanovich's *The Last Picture Show* (1971). When America heard Axl Rose's falsetto melt a hole through their stereos, it must have had the effect of white teens in the South seeing Elvis for the first time; or urban teens witnessing Michael Jackson grab his crotch, simulate masturbation, and release a high-pitched scream that felt both orgiastic and a reason to alert the authorities.

As previously noted, when Axl was not dancing like a coked-up Apache, or charring his vocal cords, he could be found channeling his suffering through the keys of a piano. Axl spent seven years working on his melancholic piano ballad "November Rain," which was musically influenced by the dynamic changes of "Bohemian Rhapsody," and emotionally rooted in a memory: one in which Axl walks down Main Street Lafayette, heartbroken, watching the cold November rain trickle off tree limbs and shingled rooftops. Although it wasn't initially written with her in mind, the novelistic conclusion of "November Rain" is written with Erin Everly as its Catherine Barkley (from Hemingway's *Farewell to Arms*, 1929), who associates rainfall with tragedy. "I'm afraid of the rain because sometimes I see me dead in it," says Catherine to her lover, Frederic Henry. In the final scene of Hemingway's semi-autobiographic novel, when Catherine lay dead in the hospital, Henry must walk to his hotel in the rain, recalling the image of her gray, statue-like corpse. "November Rain" was being meticulously arranged just as Axl and Erin's romance withered. Like Hemingway, who rewrote the ending of *Farewell to Arms* 47 times, Axl Rose reworked "November Rain" countless times before it was complete.

He told *Rolling Stone* in 1988 that, "If it's not recorded right, I'll quit the business." Its title may have been a reference to a line from Ray Bradbury's *Fahrenheit 451*: "They read the long afternoon through, while the cold November rain fell from the sky upon the quiet house."

"November Rain" is a noirish expression of what literary critic Mario Praz may have described as "romantic agony." Like Led Zeppelin's "Stairway to Heaven," it begins with a melancholic reflection, and ends in a torrential downpour. It is nine minutes of storm clouds piling up and detonating into a biblical flood of epic proportions. It is decadent, morbid, and tangled in a spider web of symbolism, with the faint glimmer of an explanation appearing in its blackness: "'November Rain' is a song about not wanting to be in a state of having to deal with unrequited love," Axl said in a documentary about the making of their mini-movie for "Estranged."

If "November Rain" is a deluge of intense suffering—thunder, lightning, the levee breaking—then "Sweet Child O' Mine" is the rainbow appearing over a field of sparkling, dew-covered flowers. In terms of its position on *Appetite for Destruction*, it sits at the center of side two, the "Roses" side, like a glowing heart-shaped box in the middle of a metropolitan wasteland. The contrast of cold steel on the "Guns" side, anchored by "Welcome to the Jungle," and the saturated warmth of the "Roses" side, is how *Appetite for Destruction* connected with such a diverse audience.

"Sweet Child O' Mine" was written inside Axl's meticulously cleaned bedroom, which sat above a disordered rehearsal space covered in molded pizza boxes and cigarette butts. His need for orderliness can be studied in the auctioned-off handwritten letters to Erin Everly, in which Axl's precise and measured handwriting contradicts his frenetic dance moves. Axl's handwriting shows us a person who is desperate to control not only his thoughts, but also the physical manifestation of those feelings. Below him, Slash languorously practiced in an unfurnished living room. It was the summer of 1986, and Geffen Records had moved the band into a luxurious two-story house in Laughlin Park, which is gated community littered with Spanish-style homes. Hollywood director Cecil B. DeMille had an estate there in the 1920s.

"Axl had a room with a padlock on it that was *pristine*," Tom Zutaut told me. "He stayed away from the chaos and was sober as a church mouse and overthought everything. But that dichotomy worked because Axl would hear the work ["Sweet Child O' Mine"], sing through it, and make the changes."

Slash's most famous musical moment—the audacious solo he plays in the introduction of "Sweet Child"—was an accident, lightning, if you will, inside a Jack Daniel's bottle. It was a pattern Slash was toying with in E-flat, as he'd rotate his fingers to loosen the tendons while skipping strings (it was a forgettable arpeggio exercise, according to Slash). The "stupid little riff" or "goofy personal exercise," as Slash would later describe it, was both math and art, like Bach's piano, which provided the structure Axl could use to stabilize the child-like energy of his poetry. "Sweet Child" was a diverse bouquet of flowers that combined a poem Axl Rose had penned for Erin Everly with Slash's dazzling legato, Izzy Stradlin's chord progression, and Duff McKagan's hummable melody—which sounded as sweet as a lullaby. Axl had thrown a lasso around Slash's riff and domesticated it for teenage girls who were experiencing their first crushes by watching MTV.

To compose "Sweet Child," Axl would relisten to Lynyrd Skynyrd cassettes. He would blend muddy Southern rock with Izzy's glistening progression (a similar progression is used by Dire Straits in 1985's "So Far Away," Roy Orbison's "You Got It," and Australian Crawl's "Unpublished Critics"). The merger of their "opposing elements" once again created something that would transcend their milieu. "Sweet Child" is now a lullaby sung to children by their mothers. There's a Shakespearian quality to it, too, as Axl is comparing his muse to a summer's day. It's important to remember that Axl's bandmates initially rejected anything that would make them sound like the next Bon Jovi. They would casually mock Axl for wanting to record such an adoring ballad. This is what began the process of Axl feeling alienated from his bandmates, which left dents on his persecution complex. "It was like a joke," bassist Duff McKagan told Q magazine. "We thought, 'What is this song? It's gonna be nothing.'" It was a "joke" to everyone, except Axl Rose. Though Duff's punkness may have caused him to culturally reject the song, on a deeper and more artistic level, he was augmenting it with a danceable bass line that hummed like Van Morrison's groove on "Brown Eyed Girl." It would capture the very quality that made Erin Everly such a "sweet child."

With the music video climbing the charts at MTV, on September 10, 1988, "Sweet Child" became number one. It spread through the Billboard Hot 100 like a Malibu wildfire being nourished by the Santa Ana winds. On August 6, 1988, *Appetite for Destruction* became the number-one album in the country. It macheted through the charts to achieve that position for 50 weeks.

"You should have seen the fucking difference [in crowd reaction] before, and after, that single came out," Duff stated in Stephen Davis's biography. "Before, only the people in front even knew who we were. They came to see us because they were our fans, all two dozen of them. Afterward, when [we played "Sweet Child O' Mine"], everybody was on their feet with their cigarette lighters switched on. It was amazing, night and day. It happened that quickly." For two weeks in the summer of 1988, Guns N' Roses were bigger than Madonna. They did it the way Bon Jovi did in 1986. "Roses" were how they seduced teenage girls, not "Guns." "It makes me sick. I mean, I like it, but I hate what it represents," Slash said in 1990.

Kurt Loder would solidify the band's pop status in an *MTV News* report heading into 1989: "The most important band of 1988 was Guns N' Roses. Their sounds actually had something to say, poetically in some cases." The poetry was cultivated from the unvarnished beauty of Erin

Everly, who would become the warmest color in the frigid palette of '80s metal. "There is a garden in her face. Where roses and white lilies grow," wrote the English poet Thomas Campion. "A heavenly paradise is that place." Erin was Axl's Pre-Raphaelite fantasy of a mystical nymph with an idle gaze. In a polluted urban terrain, Erin was a childhood fantasy that evoked the quaintness of the Welsh countryside that inspired so much of *Led Zeppelin III*. She was the dream that Axl would fall in love with—his "Tangerine."

The "mood-enhancement" video for "Sweet Child" would turn *Appetite for Destruction* into a vogue statement. The band would strategically cast the video with both MTV executives (John Canelli) and models. "Sweet Child" was a glossy magazine version of the band MTV had always wanted them to be: a photogenic and Christian Dior–scented expression of rebellion, which was hatched at party one night in 1986. She was the innocent 21-year-old daughter of a vintage pop star, and he was the lustful 24-year-old rocker who was being courted by every major record label in town. She had eyes that glowed blue like a glacial lake, with curly brown hair with highlighted streaks, and pale white skin. In the black-and-white video for "Sweet Child O' Mine," we are deprived of Erin's eyes in color. The effect is a purposefully toned-down presentation of "sex, drugs, and rock and roll" as a fresh fragrance ad, as opposed to an invitation to party. In a flash, we see Erin in a sports coat, as an industrial fan blows her big hair into a moment of release from zoom-ins of Axl's spectacular ass. The director uses Erin as an evanescent whisper of something we had begun to obsess over: who is the sweet child? She was used like an aroma that sparks a childhood memory. Who's the face tattooed on Axl's arm? The tattoo of Monique Lewis became the sleazy Mona Lisa of hair metal. Millions of teenagers assumed the tattoo depicted a sweet child. The video leaves you obsessing over the biographical details of the subject it romanticizes.

In a stroke of marketing genius, Erin's body is never prostituted like other cheap music video vixens from the era. It immediately made female viewers feel less objectified. One might assume that the suppression of "It's So Easy" was designed to protect the sweet child from being maimed by its misogynistic whip. If it were a strategy, it may have been the savviest PR move Guns N' Roses had ever made. This wasn't a video that had been melded with the minds of horny teenagers. It wasn't a *Penthouse* shoot. Erin was introduced to the MTV viewer as a conservative figure. Like early black-and-white publicity photos of Elizabeth Taylor that deny us the steaminess of *Butterfield 8* (1960), Erin debuted as a more modest portrait of an ingenue, rather than as a kind of "eternal one-night stand," which is how Richard Burton would describe Elizabeth Taylor. It preserved her celluloid mystique, as we waited for her to undress her appeal for us.

Geffen used the video for "Sweet Child" to spray Guns N' Roses into the bedrooms of Valley girls, cheerleaders, *Tiger Beat* readers, Madonna fans, and just about anyone who felt like "Welcome to the Jungle" was perhaps too *uncivilized*. "Sweet Child" turned Axl Rose into a teenage dream. Erin Everly would blend Axl Rose's brutish masculinity with something sweeter and more divine. The heartfelt feeling Axl was looking for when he began composing the song was found in the delicacy of Erin Everly, not Lynyrd Skynyrd.

The sweet child marketing strategy had made Axl more alluring to an audience that was probably too afraid of him in 1987. It's literally the reason why teen gossip magazines began publishing Axl Rose bios attached to feminine-looking photos of the singer with pinkish lips and rosy cheeks. Beauty editors were suddenly turned on to Axl Rose. He was in magazine columns with soap stars, Disney sweepstakes, River Phoenix centerfolds, and *Hot! Hot! Hot!* photos of baby-faced sitcom stars. Axl, who rarely unveiled his discolored teeth, would soon have them whitened and replaced with porcelain veneers or crowns that made him look more like a dreamboat.

"Axl became vain," Colleen Combs, his former assistant, told *Spin*. "Worrying about dyeing his eyebrows and eyelashes and going on prescription drugs for his hair and skin. He had his teeth fixed. He went on all-sushi diets."

Behind the scenes, Axl was kicking his sweet child with his cowboy boots, gagging her, and beating her with "a fuckin' baseball bat," says one source, who also insists, as many Axl apologists have over the years, that, "she got off on it, in a way. She also came from a pretty fucked-up childhood, so it went both ways."

A short time before "Sweet Child" was released as a single, Erin Everly filed a domestic abuse report with the Los Angeles Police Department, dated March 27, 1988, in which she described being beaten with "fists and kicks." There was another episode of domestic violence in 1986, when Axl Rose was writing "Sweet Child."

Axl and Erin's volatility parallels another stormy romance from the period. In the summer of 1987, there were tabloid rumors that Sean Penn had struck Madonna across the head with a baseball bat. The temporal proximity of both Sean Penn and Axl Rose's baseball bat suggests that the two stories might be linked to the same tabloid dirt. There's more: when Axl and Erin were dating, Axl had begun collecting firearms. So did Sean Penn, who was rumored to have a shooting range in the basement of his Malibu home. Axl had acquired an Uzi, a handgun, and a riot-grade shotgun he would frequently take to the shooting range. Like Sean, he had a quick temper and often brandished weapons during moments of duress. Like Sean, Axl had a self-destructive personality fueled by internalized rage. According to Erin Everly in a *People* interview from 1994, Axl threatened to shoot himself in the head if she did not drive to Las Vegas and marry him.

Axl Rose and Sean Penn were two of Generation X's most notorious "bad boys." They were similar figures occupying two very different realities that occasionally blended together. They were both, for example, the reruns of postwar Hollywood teen rebels. They were sensitive yet pugilistic misanthropes who would sit at the Hamburger Hamlet, get sloshed, and lose their cool with the frequency of a hoodlum in a pre-code gangster film. On the cover of *Vanity Fair* in 1986, Sean is pictured kneeling down with a lit cigarette, as he penetrates the camera lens with a diabolical gleam. In his black leather jacket, like Axl Rose in his oft-worn leather trench, Sean Penn looks like perfect blend of Casanova and Jack Dempsey, and naturally, he's being photographed by Herb Ritts. The *Vanity Fair* headline reads, "Bad or Just Misunderstood?" This was the alluring dichotomy that had sold Axl Rose to the masses. Inside the magazine, there's a pull quote under a photo of Penn pressing a bottle of beer against his cheek: "There's a drunken rebel Irish poet in his soul that he intends to keep fueled and fighting." I believe that occasionally two figures in popular culture, especially in the interpretative gallery of the mass media, begin to blend together, smudge, and decompose into the darkest attics of our memory. Our recollections of these similarly aligned icons swap traits, headlines, images, accusations, and scandals. Our weakness for nostalgia will blur the two images together in order to supply us with something we can cling to. Understanding how popular culture in the late-80s interpreted Sean Penn is important to understanding how Axl Rose was injected into the mainstream consciousness. It's not simply that both figures have been accused of abuse; it's about deconstructing our memory of popular culture, the chemtrails of its traumatic episodes, replaying it, and then using it as a flashlight to uncover things we've lost. Understanding Sean and Madonna helps decipher the complexities of Axl and Erin's cinematic romance.

They were no longer living together, when at around 4 p.m. on December 28, 1988, Madonna Louise Ciccone contacted the Los Angeles County Sheriff when Sean Penn, her estranged husband, had broken into their home in a drunken and jealous rage. It's important to note the original story was reported by the British tabloids, specifically *The Daily Mail*. But something did happen on Malibu's Carbon Mesa Road. What that was exactly is unclear. "Madonna Found Bound and Gagged," read a headline in a January 8, 1989, issue of *The People* (a British tabloid). It was followed by a deliciously dished pun by gossip columnist Liz Smith: "Brits Tell a Tale of Madonna Bondage." The tabloids were practically inviting us into Madonna's bedroom, which seemed like a scene from "It's So Easy" or a horrific detail from Erin Everly's deposition. Madonna biographers and reporters would paint similar portraits of the event, in which Sean Penn broke into the Malibu estate he still co-owned with Madonna, who was alone after giving the household staff the evening off. Sean was allegedly frustrated by Madonna's flirtatious relationships with stars like Warren Beatty and Sandra Bernhard (Axl Rose would experience similar bouts of jealousy when he began dating Victoria's Secret model Stephanie Seymour). Madonna is said to have refused to be domesticated by Sean. According to the gossip writers of the day, Sean did a number on her by tying her up with leather straps (or twine, maybe even a lamp cord) to a chair, slapping her, berating her, and leaving her in a state of bondage for nine hours. Madonna would come away with a bruised lip and makeup smeared all over her face. Sean returned a few hours later with a bottle of tequila. Madonna convinced him to untie her. She then ran into her 1957 Thunderbird that Sean had bought her on her birthday, locked the doors (as he pounded on the windows), and dialed for help on the car phone. This account is taken from Christopher Andersen's biography, *Madonna: Unauthorized*. It might as well have been written by a Hollywood screenwriter. Anderson writes that Madonna drove to the sheriff's station to file an assault report, which she would withdraw days later. Lieutenant Bill McSweeney would say that he "hardly recognized her as Madonna, the singer. She was weeping, her lip was bleeding and she was all marked up. She had obviously been struck. This was a woman in big trouble, no doubt about it." Madonna would spend the night at Herb Ritts's place.

"Sean has never struck me, 'tied me up,' or physically assaulted me," Madonna said in 2015. "And any report to the contrary is completely outrageous, malicious, reckless and false." She also said that any claim that Sean Penn had struck her with a baseball bat was "completely outrageous, malicious, reckless and false." On January 5, 1989, Madonna filed for divorce (she had also served him with divorce papers in 1987). Their combustible marriage can be best understood with a *People* cover from December 1987, where a tightly ponytailed Madonna has her arm around her glassy-eyed husband. "The Diary of a Mad Marriage: Jealousy, booze, and brawling sink Hollywood's most outrageous couple." Filming the *Truth or Dare* documentary in 1990, Madonna was asked who she considered to be the love of her life. "Sean . . . *Sean*."

Remember this, because Erin Everly, regardless of the abuse she sustained, *never* stopped loving Axl Rose. But Erin couldn't write a song about it the way Madonna did on 1989's "Till Death Do Us Part," which she described in *Rolling Stone* as a song about a "sadomasochistic relation-ship that can't end." She couldn't fire off a press release; summon an army of fans to her defense; or book an interview with Oprah. While she was the subject of one of 1988's most popular love songs, she never became a mega-celebrity in her own right. Erin Everly has only conducted one inter-view. Her silence was broken in a July 1994 issue of *People*, which ran with the following headline: "Battered Beauties: With domestic abuse in the headlines, the ex-wife and a former lover of Axl Rose reveal their shocking stories of his violent and physical rages." The story seems to have only been approved for publication because of its timely connection to the O.J. Simpson trial. *People*'s Steve Dougherty was hooked by the same editorial bait: "Everly describes a pattern of abuse frighteningly similar to Simpsons's relationship preceding Nicole Simpson's murder."

Several sources have told me that Erin considers Axl to be her soulmate. Perhaps he feels the same way, though we may never know. He is said to have forgiven her decision to auction off their collected history to Julien's in 2013. Erin would sell love letters, items of clothing, private photos, legal documents, a recording of their wedding, and other ephemera. A three-ring binder filled with 23 pages of private notes sold for $16,640. It's unclear how much she earned, but based on the hammer price of each item, her collection was valued at somewhere around $160,000. Julien's collected a 20-percent commission.

"Erin [Everly] spoke very highly of Axl and was not worried about a lawsuit," said Darren Julien, founder of Julien's Auctions. "She knew that she could sell these items and likewise we would not have sold them if there were any issues."

She's forgiven him for allegedly, according to her own words, beating and sexually assaulting her. In a private conversation with friends at the Roosevelt Hotel in 2016, Axl Rose said that he talks to Erin on the phone. Because she is either muzzled by an NDA or her own privacy concerns, Erin Everly remains an enigma that may never be solved. Her melancholic image fades into the bittersweet music of "Sweet Child," it stalks us with "It's So Easy," and bemuses us with "November Rain."

She's only talked twice. All we have is an issue of *People*, where she's photographed by Deborah Feingold to look purposefully grunge, and a few lines from a deposition that was sealed and later purged from the courts. All we have are fragments of her domestic nightmare. On April 27, 1990, according to Erin's own words in *People*, Axl showed up to her West Hollywood condo at about 4 a.m. Axl had a gun and threatened to use it on himself if she refused his wedding proposal. Axl forced Erin to take a five-hour drive from West Hollywood to Las Vegas, to the Cupid Wedding Chapel, to gamble on his illusion of domestic bliss. He promised, several times, to never hit her again. Three months later, Axl beat her so violently that she was hospitalized. This would have been towards the end of the summer of 1990.

"I used to go into the bathroom to cry. I'd turn the water on so he couldn't hear me, because that would set him off too," she told *People*. This is what I imagine now when I listen to "Don't Cry," which isn't about Erin Everly, but like "November Rain," it might as well be.

Axl would regularly explode into fits of hellish rage. New York City modeling agent Faith Kates claimed that in 1987, Erin had to cancel a lingerie shoot after Axl dragged her outside their apartment and left her body covered in scrapes. "It was sad," said Kates. "She'd had this sparkle in her eye, and it was gone." Axl would strike Erin, like a "rabid dog," one observer said, dragging her by the hair in front of others, throwing a TV set at her, and even kicking her with his cowboy boots, according to other witnesses.

The police were called when neighbors heard Axl trashing their house in the hills, which was followed by the previously stated LAPD investigation of domestic abuse, dated March 27, 1988. The actual report, along with a purchase bill for her wedding ring, a Van Cleef & Arpels Beverly Hills card signed "I love you Erin – Axl," and two receipts for damage caused by Axl (one for repairs to a TV that Axl smashed) were auctioned off by Erin Everly.

A lot people believe Erin would provoke Axl, which is how they viewed Madonna, who was a material girl, after all, who seemed like she was incapable of being committed to the banality of domestic bliss. Erin was seen as a child, and like a child, she was often blamed by other adults for doing thing she never did. Erin's father, Don Everly, is often described as a mentally unstable and abusive husband who would become violent with his wife, Erin's mother, actress Venetia Stevenson. "Their relationship was a powder keg," Tom Zutaut told once me. "You had two kids [Axl and Erin] who were drawn to each other because of their fucked-up childhoods."

According to *Entertainment Weekly*, neighbors would report various events that would mimic tabloid reports of Sean and Madonna. One morning, Erin was chased out of their Laurel Canyon home by Axl yelling, "Psycho bitch!" as she ran into her Jeep. The next morning, there was graffiti on her garage door: "'Sweet Child O' Die' . . . You R 1 of many, nothing special." The vandalism included a drawing of a gravestone with "R.I.P. 'X'" followed by "Erin Rose." It was like a sordid *Desperate Housewives* episode, and to this day, there's no way of verifying who was responsible. A photographer named Laura London, who lived in the area, took a few photos of a garage door. Twenty-two years later, she would display the photograph in an art show titled, "Once Upon a Time . . . Axl Rose Was My Neighbor." The photos were described as, "documentary photographs of a circa 1990 graffiti vandalization of the residence of Erin Everly by her then-husband Axl Rose."

"Erin would call me and say, 'Axl's crazy—he's throwing things around.' She pushed his buttons, but I know he loved her," mutual friend Michelle Young told *Spin* in 1999.

In 1992, Great White would release an album titled *Psycho City*. At the end of the opening track, you can hear the faint sound of a woman screaming on an answering machine. She's crying. It's unclear what she's saying or doing, but some people have suggested she's fighting off her abuser. The voice is said to belong to Erin Everly. *Psycho City* was produced by former Guns N' Roses' manager Alan Niven.

In *People*, Erin describes Axl removing the doors inside their house in order deprive her of any privacy. He'd occasionally lock her out of the house, only to let her back in when she complied with his various demands. In September 1990, Erin Every found out she was pregnant. "I thought it could have been a cure for Axl," she said. According to *People*, she miscarried between November and December 1990 (other reports suggest she miscarried in October). Erin had to sell her Jeep to cover some of her medical costs. Soon after that, she would leave Axl, this time for good. In January 1991, the marriage was annulled, but for the next few months, Axl would write letters, send flowers, deliver caged birds to her doorstep, and call her in the middle of the night. "Hello, it's Axl," he said on a phone call in 1991. "I moved the next day," Erin told *People*.

When Sean and Madonna were separated, he called her, constantly. When he couldn't catch her, if you believe the story to be true, he broke into their estate and tied her up. Like Sean Penn, Axl Rose was trying to domesticate his lover with dangerous displays of affection. They were both products of a generation that viewed male-female relationships as power struggles, rather than partnerships, where men would seek to cage their lover and never allow them to sing for anyone else. "The joy of a caged bird was in her voice," wrote Oscar Wilde in *The Picture of Dorian Gray*. "Her eyes caught the melody and echoed it in radiance, then closed for a moment, as though to hide their secret. When they opened, the mist of a dream had passed across them."

The sparkle in her eye, as Faith Kates observed, was gone. "It was the first relationship I had had," she told *People*. "I felt like we were two people who didn't have much but who had found each other."

"Sweet Child" still glitters with her feminine energy, which wraps itself around Axl's adolescent poetry. It creates a romance between the listener and Erin, who would become the cinematic *main squeeze* for Guns N' Roses fans. We pictured Axl like John Garfield gently reminding Beatrice Pearson that, "you're a sweet child" in *Force of Evil* (1948).

The final track of *Appetite for Destruction* is similarly paradoxical. "Rocket Queen" is a beguiling song about a sharp-tongued madam who has control over her racket, and for the first three minutes, it's a diary entry about her sordid lifestyle, which crescendos with a stripper's orgasm. It "substitutes sexual fulfillment for a change of heart," which is how film critic Pauline Kael described *Bonnie and Clyde*'s lack of maudlin sentimentality. The final three minutes of "Rocket Queen" bridge the gap between crime and beauty, like "Sweet Child," as it explodes into a love letter that is arguably the most anthemic coda Guns N' Roses ever wrote. It is this marriage of "opposing elements" that makes Guns N' Roses such a magnet for our contradictions. It is the duality between hot steel with bleeding rose petal that makes Guns N' Roses so intoxicating.

"I've been hell on the women in my life, and the women in my life have been hell on me," Axl Rose told *Rolling Stone* in 1992. "And it really breaks me down to tears a lot of times when I think about how terribly we've treated each other. Erin and I treated each other like shit. Sometimes we treated each other great, because the children in us were best friends. But then there were other times when we just fucked each other's lives completely."

When they first met, Erin looked like a teen idol. Axl looked like a criminal. It was the beginning of a John Hughes script. She was a Wilhelmina model, and she dressed like one, with a designer feel to her outfits that made her look almost like an Ivy League sorority girl in a scene full of aspiring leopard-printed *Penthouse* Pets. Erin appeared in modeling campaigns for Guess, Bebe, Jordache, and Gasoline jeans. In the same way "Sweet Child" was disconnected from the pyrotechnics and gaudiness of '80s power ballads, Erin would never become the objectified candy depicted in videos like 1990's "Cherry Pie." Her portrayal in "It's So Easy" made you want to call her parents, not unzip your trousers. She possessed an innocence that Axl Rose wanted to protect, at first, which was evocative of Oscar Wilde's Sibyl Vane, or the third stanza of Oscar Wilde's poem, "Requiescat," which poetically describes a sweet child:

> Lily-like, white as snow,
> She hardly knew
> She was a woman, so
> Sweetly she grew.

In their Las Vegas wedding photo, Axl looks like someone who's just entered the Witness Protection Program. He's holding a cigarette with dark sunglasses hiding his gimlet eyes. She's smiling with a pink corsage gripped tightly between her hands. It looks like a prom photo taken before a crime occurs. The saccharine of "Sweet Child" becomes bitter once you investigate its ingredients. Erin Everly wasn't just Axl's muse, she was also his victim. In 2015, Erin Everly posted her wedding photo on Instagram with the following caption:

"25 years ago today. And to this day is the only picture I have of a wedding day. My one and only wedding picture. Thank you for that Mr. Rose."

"The last time I talked to her," says one source, "She told me that she had come to accept her responsibility in the failure of their marriage. She still loves him very much."

But what if Erin Everly was a much more complicated figure than merely a "sweet child" who was tormented by a "bad boy"? What if she were more like Shannen Doherty, the Hollywood "bad girl" who allegedly threatened to shoot her boyfriend with a pistol, before trying run him over with a BMW? She may have been a "young woman on the verge of spinning out of control," as Doherty was described in *People* on June 14, 1993. What if Erin was not Sandy as a milkshake schoolgirl in the beginning of *Grease* (1978), but Sandy as a snarling dominatrix in the last scene of *Grease*?

There's a story in Andy McCoy's 2009 autobiography, *Sheriff McCoy: Outlaw Legend of Hanoi Rocks*, where Erin is depicted as swerving her Jeep through the Hollywood Hills in an effort to crash it. "She'd tried to crash her car off Mulholland Drive at a spot where there's a 150-yard drop down the cliff," he writes. "It's a perfect spot if you want to commit vehicular suicide." McCoy would describe Erin as an attention-needy socialite who had begun to abuse prescription painkillers like Valium, and seemed capable, according to McCoy, of fabricating abuse stories. Erin, according to McCoy, would often come to his home and visit his girlfriend at the time, Angela Nicoletti, and according to McCoy, Erin would regularly threaten self-harm. "Angela told me she thought Erin was disturbed enough to rip off the ring herself, just so she could blame Axl and get attention," writes McCoy. The "ring" McCoy is referring to is a nipple ring.

What if Erin were the quintessential jezebel? What if Erin fabricated the cause of one of her 1990 hospitalizations? According to *People*, she was hospitalized twice that year: once when Axl struck her and a second time, when she miscarried. This would have placed her in a hospital bed in the summer of 1990 and once more at the end of the year (according to her version of events). But what if there were a third visit that spring?

According to McCoy, and other sources, at some point between the spring and summer 1990, Erin overdosed on either Valium or heroin at the Laurel Terrace home of Guns N' Roses drummer Steven Adler, who was McCoy's next-door neighbor. Axl has suggested in past interviews that it was a speedball (a combination of cocaine and heroin) that caused her to overdose that day. According to McCoy's version of events, Erin would arrive at his home high on prescription Valium, threatening to kill herself. Erin would then sneak out of the house and walk next door to Steven Adler's house, who looked like a scabbed junkie with sunken-in cheeks and pinpoint pupils. At some point, Adler allegedly helped Erin shoot up heroin, or heroin with cocaine. This would have been the first time Erin had tried heroin or, for the matter, a speedball. After injecting her, according to McCoy, Adler was casually walking around the house in a druggy haze, as Erin overdosed in his bathroom. Adler neglected to call an ambulance and decided instead to hide in the shower, while McCoy attempted to inject a shot of buprenorphine into Erin's arm. It had very little effect in countering the heroin in her system.

McCoy's version of the story includes him banging on her chest and rubbing ice all over her waif-like body. Her pulse was faint, but McCoy managed to keep her alive until the paramedics arrived and used a defibrillator to regain her pulse. "She was like a small child," he writes, "a very naive person, who always needed somebody around. I think Axl had written their huge hit 'Sweet Child O' Mine' about her for that reason . . . When I saw her there with her pants down and almost dying, I couldn't help wondering if Steven had done something to her while she was out cold."

Did Erin Everly almost die in Andy McCoy's arms? Was she raped by Steven Adler? For the record, everyone I interviewed in the process of writing this book denies that Steven Adler assaulted Erin Everly. That's also just one perspective of what happened that day. In his own autobiography,

My Appetite for Destruction, Adler claims that Erin arrived at his house with Angela, who he refers to as "Laura" in order to protect her identity. According to Adler, Laura asked Adler to give Erin something to calm her down. She had taken Valium after a fight with Axl, and began OD'ing at Adler's doorstep, who claims he dragged Erin into his bedroom and tried to keep her alive. "I called an ambulance and tried not to freak the fuck out," writes Adler. "She was Axl's bride-to-be for Chrissakes." The paramedics arrived and induced vomiting. "Later I discovered that Erin already had heroin in her system. When questioned, they said that I was the one who had given it to her. Axl Rose called and threatened me . . . Axl told the press that I shot Erin up, and no one had any reason to believe otherwise."

"I kept myself from doing anything to him [Steven Adler]," Axl told Del James in 1992. "I kept the man from being killed by members of her [Erin Everly's] family. I saved him from having to go to court, because her mother wanted him held responsible for his actions." Axl's account of the story, according to biographer Stephen Davis, was that after one of their usual fights, Erin escaped to Steven Adler's place, where he injected her with a speedball. "Erin turned blue," writes Davis, "and Adler dialed 911." The timeline in Davis's book is the "California spring of 1990." According to Davis, Erin spent the next few days in a coma. A clear date of Erin Everly's overdose remains foggy. But on July 11, 1990, Steven Adler was fired from Guns N' Roses.

"Had he [Steven Adler] been smacked up but consistent on the kit," says Niven, "he would still have been in the band. It was poor performance in pre-production [*Use Your Illusion*] that brought everyone to exasperation."

Erin's overdose likely happened in the spring or earliest part of the summer. But we don't know Erin's version of events, which leaves us permanently lost in a vortex of gossip, lies, fractured timelines, and the narratives of men who've had their memories discombobulated with junk. One lingering question is whether her hospitalization for battery, as per the *People* interview, may have been for an overdose. In her 1994 lawsuit, Erin claimed that Axl had hit her so hard that she passed out. The next day she woke up in the hospital with a doctor telling her she had been injected with heroin and cocaine. We're also left with the "robot rape" image of a nearly comatose Erin Everly, with her pants below her knees, being raped by a junkie. Whether it is true or not, as Adler himself as stated, it flashes past our eyes when we think about the tragic coda of Erin and Axl. All of this happened when Steven Adler was under probation by his own band.

In an interview on Kurt Loder's *Famous Last Words*, Axl insisted that the decision to fire Steven Adler included "other things besides the band . . . very dangerous and scary. I want nothing to do with him."

In August 2010, Erin Everly was arrested on charges of aggravated assault with a knife, when she attacked her boyfriend Matthew Klyn. Erin's mug shot—with its glassy eyes, vacant stare, and hard edges—became the *proof* Axl apologists required to convict her of being a "psycho bitch." In 2011, a couple cellphone photos began to circulate around the internet that looked like Erin Everly at a Guns N' Roses concert in Atlanta, Georgia. It has since been confirmed to be her.

In one of his letters to Erin, Axl writes, "Sorry for being so hard on you . . . you didn't do anything wrong I just became frustrated with my predicament and didn't know how to verbalize my feelings." On a piece of paper found on pile of auctioned-off letters, he wrote her a poem:

> *No love was there*
> *More true*
> *Erin I love you*
> *Goodbye sweet child –*
> *Love Always, – Axl –*

6

DAYS OF THUNDER

"CONTROL IS AN ILLUSION, YOU INFANTILE EGOMANIAC,
NOBODY KNOWS WHAT'S GONNA HAPPEN NEXT."

—DAYS OF THUNDER (1990)

"There's imperfections in any mechanics," Slash told *Total Guitar* in 1996, when he was asked whether Guns N' Roses could ever function as a well-oiled machine. They were romantic, raffish, loud, hyper-sexual, and like Nicolas Cage's snakeskin jacket in *Wild at Heart* (1990), they were a gaudy representation of individuality gone haywire. They were a rock band derived from the demolished remnants of B movies and men's magazines. By the '90s, when Axl Rose began to lose himself in an avalanche of headlines, they would begin to transition from lowbrow cult film to high-concept blockbuster that seemed to be gambling with its credibility—what Slash would describe in 1995 as a "Las Vegas" direction.

During the *Use Your Illusion* era, Guns N' Roses were the cock-rock equivalent of *Days of Thunder* (1990), a Tom Cruise vehicle about an over-confident stock car driver with a death wish. Guns N' Roses would include their cover of Bob Dylan's "Knockin' on Heaven's Door" on the film's soundtrack, which was released in the US by Geffen Records. According to former manager Alan Niven, Guns N' Roses recorded "Heaven's Door" purely as a favor to David Geffen:

"I received a call from Geffen while I happened to be in New York at the Capitol offices. He wanted a song from *Appetite* for a Cruise movie . . . I suggested we maybe think about recording something non-*Appetite*, for David [Geffen]. He [Axl Rose] agreed and suggested 'Knockin' on Heaven's Door.'"

In order to savor the high-concept evolution of Guns N' Roses, you have to take a bite out of their filmic equivilant, *Days of Thunder*. It's in this gap between reality and illusion that I believe Guns N' Roses began to lose control of their own illusion. They had gone from the alternative to the mainstream and then strapped themselves with booster rockets and launched into outer space—never to return. I suppose to really grasp the symbolic importance of the *Use Your Illusion* era, one must think of it as a grand production that begins with something blowing up, climaxes with something else blowing up, and ends in memoriam of a rock band fading into a molten-orange sunset.

In *Days of Thunder*, Cole Trickle drives with Nietzschean indifference for the norms of NASCAR. Like Axl Rose, he lacks the hardwired circuitry that introduces the brain to fear. He's a brash rookie who knows nothing of the mechanics of a stock car that he continuously redlines and pushes beyond the limits of the tires, engine, and chassis. He has it, but it hasn't been honed. "I'm an idiot. I don't have the vocabulary," he tells his crew chief in a rare moment of vulnerability where we discover that Cole Trickle knows as much about race car engines as Axl Rose did about preserving his vocal cords.

Throughout his career, Axl would push the throttle of his vocal cords to the point of burning the tread right off them. He was born with a gift that he tore through like the rubber on the rims of a stock car. Like the arrogant stock car driver who doesn't know a lick about engines, Axl's unrestrained wailing caused damage to both himself and his band. In the '90s, he would regularly cancel shows, or abandon them midway, as his worn-out instrument had begun to be covered with jagged growths and scars. His pit stop—consisting of masseuses, throat elixirs, and oxygen tanks—was the first stop. Even though the crowd would roar at the sound of his distorted and nicotine-laced rasp, Axl was screaming beyond his mechanical limits. This would cause immense damage to Guns N' Roses. At times, Axl's scream sounded like coarse squawking; a guttural scream in the league of the head-spinning wail of Linda Blair in *The Exorcist* (1973).

Axl's instrument was an engine nearing its final race—his "last note of freedom," which is the David Coverdale theme for *Days of Thunder*. "Find your scream!" Courtney Love told *Pitchfork* in 2014. "Even if you don't release it, find a scream. It's so liberating. You can do anything then. It's like you can fly. It gives you superpowers." Axl's "superpowers" were beginning to diminish.

Like Axl leaning back and melting his vocal cords with guttural torque, Cole Trickle abuses his race car in order to exorcise his demons. In the first scene of *Days of Thunder* — shot during a cloudy sunset — Trickle arrives at the racetrack on his fuel-injected steed, a Harley-Davidson Softail, wearing a flowing black trench coat, black-leather gloves, and dark sunglasses, like Axl or Izzy in photographs by Robert John. Axl even had a dog named after the turning power of an automobile, Torque, while Slash would eventually become an amateur race car driver who would punch the pedal on his own shiny black 1966 Corvette Stingray, which he bought in 1988 and auctioned off in 2011 for $115,200. Going fast and never really arriving at their destination was Guns N' Roses' destiny. "No future," Johnny Rotten would snarl through his deformed teeth, who is the postmodern embodiment of Julius Caesar's view of the Germanic tribes who "lay waste as much as possible of the land around them and to keep it uninhabited." Guns N' Roses would never see the checkered flag. They had laid waste to the more glam-driven hair bands and like a true Nietzschean warriors, they had nothing to replace them with.

Fast-forward to 2006, when Guns N' Roses were scheduled to play KROQ's Inland Invasion, when Axl was the only original member left. This is when a 44-year-old Axl Rose is said to have been provided a police escort to get him from Malibu to the Hyundai Pavilion in San Bernardino. The escort was provided by promoters, who feared Axl would arrive late. One source from Live Nation says that a beefed-up Axl emerged from his nearly three-acre mansion in Malibu's Latigo Canyon, which he purchased in 1992 for $3.9 million (according to the *L.A. Times*), and got behind the wheel of his Ferrari (probably a silver Ferrari Enzo), and punched past the escort, leading police on a chase through the winding hills of Latigo Canyon and down into the Pacific Coast Highway. It's an incredible visual, almost as thrilling as Phil Collins scoring a nighttime montage of a pearl-white Ferrari in *Miami Vice*. Axl was speeding to make his first Southern California gig in 14 years. The details of the story can't be verified as a *fact*, but we know he emerged onto the stage around 1 a.m., with artificially enhanced cornrows, Gucci sunglasses, and a leather motorcycle jacket. He was also an hour late. The *L.A. Times* said he "reclaimed his mojo." They also said his costume changes were as frequent as Mariah Carey's. Immediately after the performance, Axl jumped into his Ferrari and zoomed back to his mansion in Malibu. It sounds cinematic. He was Cole Trickle having a midlife crisis. By the mid-aughts, with his cornrows and steroidal physique, the antithesis of an emaciated Kurt Cobain coloring his unkempt hair with Kool-Aid packets, Axl had become one with the machine. The outlaw had been replaced with a titanium laminated enforcer who rarely exposed his eyes to sunlight. The process to transform Guns N' Roses into what writer Eric Weisbard described as "Terminator rock" began on the Use Your Illusion Tour.

The backdrop of *Days of Thunder* is artfully illustrated like a Hollywood Western, where smoky sunsets look polluted by the exhaust emitted from the roaring stock cars of Daytona. Cole Trickle is NASCAR's Billy the Kid, a hyper-cocky version of the Kid as translated through the MTV-tinged retelling of *Young Guns*. Film critic Michael Wilmington described the film's depiction of Billy the Kid as a "baby-faced Nietzschean warrior," which was Axl Rose before he became a hard-rock cyborg. Emilio Estevez's Billy the Kid is playful, psychotic, sardonic, and a symbol of the Old West as the last stronghold of American culture. He's Axl Rose whistling a version of "When Johnny Comes Marching Home," which is romantic, like Joan Baez covering "The Night They Drove Old Dixie Down," but because he does it with a twinkle in his eye wearing a Confederate flag jacket, it's also slightly terrifying. A lot of Axl's primitivism was grounded in his connection to the Old West, or more precisely, a distorted view rooted in what David Brion Davis described as Southern ideology that wanted a "purified and regenerated" frontier, "casting off apologies for slavery" and returning to its "proper ideal." This is the Axl Rose of "One in a Million," which we'll get to.

Like Tom Cruise's masochistic daredevil in a stock car or in the cockpit of an F-14 Tomcat, the Billy the Kid of *Young Guns* makes the concept of a death drive seem like *rock and roll*. It's an image Guns N' Roses evoked with a frozen outlaw in the video for "Don't Cry," stumbling into the snow with a revolver in his grip. It should remind the reader of John Jeremiah Sullivan discovering the name "William Rose" on a memorial to the sons of Lafayette, who were killed in the Civil War. In the same video, we see Slash's 1966 Shelby Mustang flying off a cliff and exploding, as Slash emerges at the edge of the cliff like the unkillable Wile E. Coyote. "Don't Cry" ends with Axl visiting his own gravestone, which may have several meanings: one that expresses his denial of Morrison's "death drive," perhaps talking back to Danny Sugerman, his well-documented fascination with reincarnation, or more immediately, to "bury Appetite [for Destruction]." "Don't Cry" is also the first time a rock star has played one of his own demons (covered in green body paint, like an Orion from *Star Trek* blended with Gollum).

The video for "Don't Cry" could have easily been the video for their cover of Dylan's "Knockin' on Heaven's Door." The cover itself is included in the soundtrack, but not a single shot of *Days of Thunder*. We would not be gifted with a Tom Cruise–Axl Rose collaboration until *Rock of Ages* (2012). In his preparation to play the role of hair-metal singer Stacee Jaxx, Tom Cruise not only studied Axl Rose, he requested a meeting with him backstage during a gig on the Chinese Democracy Tour. Cruise planned to imitate Axl in his performance in *Rock of Ages*. He began using Axl's personal voice coach to prepare for his transformation (Cruise trained his voice for upwards of five hours per day). The first song in the film is Tom Cruise's cover of "Paradise City," which blasts through the headphones of an aspiring singer taking a bus from Oklahoma to L.A. (which pays homage to the first scene of "Welcome to the Jungle," where a hopelessly callow Axl Rose arrives in L.A. in a bus).

In 1991, the "Terminator Rock" Guns N' Roses would become fully formed with the release of "You Could Be Mine," the first single from *Use Your Illusion*, which was released in the summer of 1991 as part of colossal marketing campaign to promote *T2*. Unlike its more horror-tinged original, James Cameron's sequel plays like a postapocalyptic Western that's serendipitously decorated with an array of Guns N' Roses iconography. The most poetic visual appears in the shopping mall shoot-out, where the Terminator pulls a steel shotgun from a box of roses, crushing a fallen rose with the heel of his motorcycle boot, which could be symbolic of machines destroying mother earth, but also, in a more Guns N' Roses sense, the combining of "opposing elements" to symbolize death by machine.

At the end of the first verse of "You Could Be Mine," Axl sings that he's seen that movie, too, which is a reference to Elton John song titled "I've Seen That Movie Too." But if we're analyzing Guns N' Roses as good-bad cinema, the crushing of the rose in *T2* is part of the Western tradition of roses representing splattered blood on the frontier—the final scene in the Guns N' Roses epic.

The coda of the video for "November Rain" is the melancholic ending of their hard-rock Western. In that video—which continues to be their most watched on YouTube—there's a scene where Slash solos in front of an abandoned white chapel (the same chapel featured in the final duel in 1985's *Silverado*). He does this in a power posture, as a helicopter hovers overhead and films him like a fast-cutting Michael Bay sequence shot during a setting sun, i.e., "magic hour." "November Rain" was the definition of a high-concept overdose, which combines Western with gothic horror, soap, and tons of melodrama that made the summer of 1992 impossible to forget. It was dazzling beyond words, momentarily poetic, heavy-handed, and as confusingly brilliant as Bart Simpson conducting a symphony orchestra. At the MTV Video Music Awards that fall, it would win Best Cinematography for depicting what is probably the most enigmatic wedding scene in the history of American pop culture. It was the wedding scene in *The Godfather* (1972) being reimagined by Michael Bay at his most bombastic. In fact, it doesn't matter who actually directed "November Rain" (Andy Morahan), as it was a quintessential Axl Rose vanity production. But the peak of Axl's creative lunacy can be seen in his prestige picture, 1993's "Estranged," when he leaps off the deck of a jumbo crude-oil tanker in a Charles Manson T-shirt, and is then submerged by pounding ocean currents that nearly drown him. We see Slash rising from the water and soloing in the middle of the ocean. The religiousness of the scene would be mocked by Nirvana drummer Dave Grohl's Slash impersonation on MTV in 1993.

In another scene from "Estranged," Axl is a proto-Puff Daddy marching out of his Malibu mansion with an army of bodyguards, dressed in all white, as he takes a white limo from his pearly-white mansion to an airplane hangar filled with mystical dolphins. Perhaps the most historically interesting aspect of the video is that it offers the only *MTV Cribs*–like tour of the mythological Latigo Canyon mansion of Axl Rose, his Graceland, where it is rumored that he keeps a private animal zoo, Ferrari, recording studio, collection of large decorative crucifixes, and other religious artifacts. There's a rare photo of a bearded Axl Rose, taken between 1994 and 2000, known affectionately as his "Wilderness Years," where he's seated grimly next to a wooden table covered in archaic religious paintings, two crucifixion statues, and another antique depicting what looks like Madonna and child. In the 1994 lawsuit filed by Erin Everly, it was reported that Axl had told Erin that he was "in touch with spirits and extraterrestrial beings."

This is the Axl Rose who appears as a Howard Hughes–inspired illustration inside Peter Wilkinson's "Lost Years" profile in *Rolling Stone*. This is the Axl Rose who would earn the nickname, "Howard Hughes of Rock," which is a moniker with unclear origins, which might be linked to a *Spin* profile from 1999 that first described him as "rock's greatest recluse." On July 29, 1999, Steve Dollar of Greensboro *News & Record* described him as "rock's answer to Howard Hughes." Of course, the nickname had less to do with Hughes, the millionaire playboy and aviation pioneer, as much as it did with the man who spent four months inside a film screening room, ungroomed, eating chocolate bars, and deteriorating under a noxious cloud of OCDs and undiagnosed maladies. Between the middle of 1994 and the beginning of 1998, Axl Rose remained in complete isolation from his public. They saw him just twice in those four years: the first time as a meek and subdued figure inducting Elton John into the Rock and Roll Hall of Fame on January 19, 1994, and the second time was in 1998, in the now infamous Phoenix mug shot— the personification of an estranged recluse.

The "Estranged" video shows police officers arriving at a white Spanish-style mansion decorated with palm trees. There's a giant mahogany door forged with a gothic design at the entrance of a freshly painted white castle. We then see the full picture of a mansion from the viewpoint of a helicopter. There's a swimming pool surrounded by trees. Two guest houses. The front of the mansion features decorated tile with glass cubes, and there are giant ceramic pots filled with flowers. The last scene of the video is Axl smiling mischievously next to a talking dolphin cloaked in a flannel shirt. The dolphin is one symbol in a novelistic breakup letter that's scattered with Axl's depression, paranoia, random acts of juvenility, spirituality, and desperate need for closure, what he described as "showing their [as in himself] own emotional destruction, and their process of transcending that."

"Estranged" is Axl visually composing a letter to Stephanie Seymour that details his suffering. When he told Erin Everly that couldn't verbalize his feelings, he probably didn't know that for $4 million, he could visualize it into a 10-minute concept film that defies all logic. Axl would describe the confusingly expensive concept video as being his "conceptual way" of dealing with the betrayal and redemption following his breakup with Stephanie Seymour. That was the video. The inspiration for the song itself was partially cooked into a smoldering finale of Del James' "Without You," where Mayne plays a piano as a "wall-to-wall inferno" torches his home. The uncontrollable flames were symbolic of Axl Rose's inextinguishable suffering following the split with his "sweet child."

To make things even more confusing, the song "Estranged" is inspired by aspects of Axl's relationship with Erin Everly, but the video is about Stephanie Seymour. None of matters in terms of its spectacle, as the viewer, initiated in the drama or not, is mesmerized by the tangled monstrosity of watching Axl Rose's attempt to translate his emotions into a big-budget thriller. It's what *Point Break* (1991) director Kathryn Bigelow would have made had she had never gone to art school, whereas the video for "November Rain" is Michael Bay at his most elegiac.

Just like *Days of Thunder* (directed by Tony Scott), "November Rain" requires the viewer to suspend not just disbelief, but also the lingering questions that we all have in the back our heads when we watch ludicrous spectacle: was it supposed to be ridiculous? When we watch films like *Days of Thunder*, we're not hoping for philosophical depth (though we get it with Nicole Kidman's "control is an illusion" speech) or Oscar-winning performances, but we do expect, at least on some subconscious level, that the filmmakers accompany us on the good-bad rollercoaster. The moment these semi-talented madmen lack such self-awareness or the ability for any kind of self-mockery, it becomes trash, but what film critic Pauline Kael would have deduced to be crudely enjoyable trash, like a historically oblivious American Western, which relives the past and yet teaches us nothing about it.

Kael would also have asked if Axl Rose perhaps took himself too seriously. He's not thumbing his nose at "good taste," the way Tarantino does with the ear in *Reservoir Dogs*, Axl Rose believes he's going beyond the ear, like the severed ear in *Blue Velvet*. This is when his vanity collides with his insecurities in a head-on collision known as his trilogy, which begins with "Don't Cry," nearly dies with "November Rain," and ends with him estranging audience. The estimated cost of Axl Rose's three-part vanity project was over $7 million. Slash, who has a nose (or perhaps an ear) for camp, plays Axl's cynical sidekick walking onto the set, briefly reading the script, and drinking himself into a compliant stupor. He plays the video's Best Man as a drunken but loyal Knight; as his steely-eyed Prince, Axl Rose, presents the contrast that was the secret element of their chemistry: chainmail authoritarianism domesticating savage insubordination.

Watching "November Rain" produces the pleasurable anxiety of watching *Days of Thunder* and waiting, as we all died, for someone to die—

which was the psychological state of every Guns N' Roses fan from roughly 1987 to 1997—their decade-long rise and fall.

That fact that "November Rain" was overbudget (it cost $1.5 million to produce, which in 1992 made it the most expensive music video ever made), slick, dimly written, and confusing is precisely its appeal as a drugged-up summer blockbuster in the league of *Days of Thunder,* which was critically panned like "November Rain," and almost as successful. *Days of Thunder* was the 13th highest-grossing film of 1990, pulling in nearly $160 million worldwide. Not bad. "November Rain" was 1992's most requested video on MTV. "November Rain" was also the "biggest production" in the history of the MTV Video Music Awards—eclipsing Madonna's as a busty Marie Antoinette in 1990—when a rococo-metal Axl Rose performed alongside Elton John on dueling grand pianos (which was orchestrated by MTV executive John Canelli).

When I first witnessed the MTV premiere of "November Rain" on June 6, 1992, I was transfixed on the image of Axl wearing what looked like a ceremonial French military jacket that had been given a baroque makeover by Versace. He wore the same jacket, with ripped blue jeans and a blue bandana, on the stage of the MTV VMAs. He looked like a heavy-metal dignitary. He was my generation's version of Elton John fashioned into a gay disco-version of Mozart. The jacket is something Axl would wear on the Use Your Illusion Tour, when he'd play "November Rain" from behind the grand piano dressed like an emperor with no pants. In the same way that *Days of Thunder* producer Don Simpson wanted to race cars with Tom Cruise, children watching MTV in 1992 (the second-generation Guns N' Roses fans) wanted to attend Axl Rose's wedding.

Like so many Hollywood productions, the concept for "November Rain," as well as the last verse of "Estranged," were inspired by a short story written by Del James titled, "Without You," where a decaying rock star named Mayne—who can no longer recognize his own reflection—discovers the love of his life with a self-inflicted gunshot wound to the head. "Most of her head splattered on the wall behind her," James wrote. Mayne realizes he cannot live without her. He is shattered, so he proceeds to wreck his rare guitar collection (his "adopted children") and turn them into fire-wood. He injects himself with cocaine and heroin, and drowns himself with whiskey. One day he's in such a daze that he doesn't notice a lit ciga-rette has collapsed onto the rug. A fire catches. Mayne is slowly burned alive while playing a love song on a piano ("Without You") as the ivory keys melt underneath his fingertips. "As flames swallowed the apartment, Mayne never screamed and never missed a note." Del James's story reads like a rock-and-roll *Tales from the Crypt* episode. One night, Del James would call Axl Rose and tell him that he had just written his best friend's death. In his introduction to Del James's *The Language of Fear*, in which "Without You" was published, Axl described the stories as possessing a "real sense of the damage that can be done whenever an individual takes things too far." There's a prescience and humility in his words that were roped off from the deranged narcissism of the *Use Your Illusion* era. Axl Rose himself has acknowledged that some of the events that transpire in "Without You" are real. It's interesting to note that Axl Rose's romantic music video trilogy was initially inspired by so much horror, a lot of which began with "banned" snuff films from the '70s (*Snuff*, *Faces of Death*, etc.).

Days of Thunder would become producer Don Simpson's Use Your Illusion Tour. Every day on the set was a party flooded by bags of cocaine, hot tubs filled with strippers, supermodels, a ballooning budget, high-end workout equipment, tanning beds, and mechanical failures. Nightly script revisions were demanded by Tom Cruise, who was fulfilling a fantasy to be a race car driver by turning a guaranteed success (*Top Gun* on wheels) into a poorly planned test drive. Matt Sorum, the drummer used during the *Use Your Illusion* era, once said that Guns N' Roses would spend $100,000 a night on themed parties that included an Indy 500 one during a stop in Indiana. The first track Sorum recorded with Guns N' Roses was "Heaven's Door." The Indy 500 party would become symbolic of the Use Your Illusion Tour, where Axl had his own literal pit crew of masseuses, therapists, and chiropractors who would adjust him midperformance. "It's, like, I'm a car," Axl told *Life* in 1992.

"It's like people who go to watch the Indy 500," former Guns N' Roses' manager Doug Goldstein told *Life* in 1992. "They don't go to watch the race, they go to see the crash."

At a concert in Chicago on April 9, 1992, Axl Rose—who wore a leather jacket with Madonna's "Justify My Love" portrait painted on the back—would describe his damaged psyche (which he graffitied into the pages of *Rolling Stone* that year) as if it were a scene from *Days of Thunder*. His trauma was like a stock car on the verge of catastrophe, "trying to find your way out of what you thought was your life but looks more in your head like a fuckin' car wreck that no one told you about."

In 2010, the *New York Times* described *Days of Thunder* as being a "critically panned blockbuster that was largely lampooned throughout the NASCAR industry for its exaggeration and overindulgence." This was the Use Your Illusion Tour through the eyes of both the critics and their heavy-metal peers. On tour, Guns N' Roses had on-call limos, pinball machines, ice sculptures, lobster plates, bottles of iced Cristal, and "more strippers than road crew," (said Roddy Bottum of Faith No More, who opened for Guns N' Roses).

"I can see naked girls in a G-string for free," Slash told *Kerrang!* in 1996. "I don't have to pay 20 grand to have 600 of them coming over!"

Axl Rose had evolved into the visible personification of a difficult actor who was both a perfectionist and an overindulgent Nero who was exhausting his treasury (i.e., tour and legal budget).

Film critic Roger Ebert once referred to *Days of the Thunder* as a "Tom Cruise Picture," which saw Cruise's character being tamed by a taller and generally more sophisticated woman: a leggy neurosurgeon played by Nicole Kidman. By comparison, "November Rain" saw Axl Rose having his heart snatched by a similar modelesque woman, Stephanie Seymour, who was the romantic lead of "November Rain." Stephanie Seymour was a Victoria's Secret supermodel who was photographed by Herb Ritts for the cover of *Playboy* in 1990 and then again in 1993 in red lingerie with the following headline: "Victoria's Secret Supermodel Stephanie Seymour Takes Her Undies Off." She was the stoic bride in "November Rain," which shattered the heavy-metal trope of strippers being cast as objectified cartoons. While filming the video, she told the camera crew that she'd previously been asked to do videos before, but had always declined, "until Guns N' Roses asked me to do one."

"She wasn't just gonna be in a tits and ass video," Axl said in, *Guns N' Roses: Makin' F@*!ing Videos Part II*. He wanted to cast "somebody that somebody could definitely get obsessed over." Watching footage of Axl going over dailies of the bouquet tossing scene, and you start to see him glow. "November Rain" is Axl Rose auditioning someone to be his bride. His monarchial transformation is complete. But the most riveting aspect of "November Rain" isn't driven by the tragic Prince and his doomed bride, no; it was always about the relationship between the Prince and his swashbuckling Knight: Slash.

Back in 1989, before he would embrace his role as the bearded monarch of Guns N' Roses, Axl looked like an androgynous scoundrel in the music video for "Patience," where his face is lit like an old Hollywood leading man. The diffused lighting enhances Axl's facial features, which are powdered into a soft glow, like a silent-era cowboy. You can still see the flickering flame of delinquency in Axl's eyes as he serenades America the way Sinatra once did. Slash is seen laying half-naked on a luxurious bed with a slithering boa constrictor around his body, which represents his cold-blooded persona, which is lassoed by Axl's tense need for control.

For Slash, the snake would become intertwined with his star power, as it further enhanced the media perception that Slash was, as in Psalm 58, the "deaf serpent that does not hear, that does not respond to magicians, or to a skilled snake charmer." Axl is the snake-charmer. Slash is a tool for the Devil: a symbol of unconscious sinfulness that grew out of the underworld of Guns N' Roses, as venom spewed out of the neck of his guitar. In the studio shots of Nigel Dick's video for "Patience," Slash's puffy hair covers his face, as he strums the guitar with his eyes closed, inwardly removed from the experience, while Axl reads from a lyric sheet and focuses on every motion, like a professional dancer. Slash's image in "Patience" is that of an exotic Spanish stallion who cannot be tamed by Axl's lasso.

The dichotomy of Slash and Axl would turn Guns N' Roses into a

Western, where two differing rogues linking spurs in the pursuit of the same train. Slash and Axl were the Butch Cassidy and the Sundance Kid of MTV. Their relationship was further complicated by the fact that Axl Rose was an inflexible perfectionist who seemed as temperamental as Madonna, while Slash was a daft sort of scoundrel who blended the lethargic coolness of a pirate with the anti-socialness of a Gen-X skater. Axl had Scottish-red hair that was soft and bouncy, while Slash had a curly black forest that was rigid and tough like spiderwebs. Slash was born in England, while Axl Rose looked like the Hollywood depiction of William Wallace as a hotheaded Scot who revolted against the English Crown. In "November Rain," Axl seems to be chasing domestic bliss, while Slash drunkenly fumbles around like a sloshed pirate, before appearing to us like an image out of an Italian Western. On the cover of a *Kerrang!* issue dated January 14, 1995, there's a cartoon caricature of the two that depicts Axl as a hotheaded Scottish brawler, while Slash, who is being strangled by Axl, looks like a scallywag from another time. The contrast of burning green eyes with calming brown skin further illuminates the animated contrast between the two. Slash grew up in a nurturing household, where he would draw and listen to Led Zeppelin records supplied by his mother. Axl Rose grew up in a fundamentalist household, where he was beaten and forbidden to listen to Led Zeppelin. One day during a drive, "Mandy" by Barry Manilow came on the car radio, and when young Axl started to sing along to it, his step-father smacked him in the mouth and declared the song to be "evil." Like filmmaker Wes Craven, who was told as a child that films were sinful, Axl would channel his childhood trauma by creating art that would crucify parents, schoolteachers, cops, and authority, in toto. Axl Rose's music video trilogy is complicated by the fact that its creator was an anti-intellectual populist trying to create something that would appeal to a liberal bourgeois audience. Axl was trying to bury his childhood under the heaviness of his rock star persona. You can almost picture him screaming back at the world like Brando in *The Wild One* saying, "My old man used to hit harder than that." Slash seemed to romanticize his past. His childhood was a fantasy that Cameron Crowe could have turned into a coming-of-age film.

Axl Rose's childhood was *Carrie* (1976). They were like gunfighters from two different sides of the frontier. Slash was Doc Holliday in *Tombstone* (1992): a diseased aristocrat with a black hat and spurs dangling over a grave. Axl was what poet Michael Ondaatje would describe the more working-class Billy the Kid as a "mirror in which to represent a time or a place or a feeling, or some part of yourself that you want to explore." For the MTV generation, Axl Rose was as close to a reincarnated Billy the Kid as Morrisey was the reincarnation of a sunflower-adorned Oscar Wilde. Morrisey was the gateway to the works of Wilde, while Axl was a gateway to the MTV depiction of the Old West in *Young Guns*, which, like Guns N' Roses, is both classic and modern.

Axl, like the Kid in Gore Vidal's version of a "killer and the all-American boy," was the by-product of a Bible-thumping culture and an Anglo-Saxon certitude. He sang in his church, while the Kid sang in Sunday school. Both Axl and the Kid were short, Scotch-Irish, temperamental, and consumed by prejudice, and both used the name William. The Kid used the name William H. Bonney (though his real name was Henry McCarty). William Bruce Bailey (or Bill Bailey) was Axl Rose's name for most of his childhood, a name that sounds like something out of a 19th-century dime novel. *Spin* once mocked Axl Rose for having such a Middle American name, but the name Bill Bailey brings us closer to America's murderous past, and one particular gunfighter, William "Billy" Bailey, who died from a gunshot to the chest outside Red Front Saloon in Newton, Kansas, on August 11, 1871. Even William Rose, his birth name, has a Western allure attached to it. Both Axl and the Kid changed their names and proceeded to violently write their own biography by melding innocence with vengeance. The Kid killed eight men before his death at age 21, while Axl Rose, by his own accounts, was arrested at least 20 times before migrating from Indiana to L.A. in 1982, before the age of 21. I suppose we can argue that Bill Bailey died when Axl turned 21. Once he arrived in L.A., Axl understood the importance of developing a myth. He began to write his own "wanted" poster, while Slash illustrated its details. They're dueling dichotomy lasted a little over a decade. On September 30, 1996, Slash in sunglasses and a

"Got Milk?" T-shirt appeared in MTV's studios and announced the band was working on new material and "reacquainting with each other." He wasn't being entirety forthright. Slash had spent most of 1995 and 1996 been publicly critical of Axl in the media, particular his decision to use Paul Tobias (Paul Huge) as a third guitar player in Guns N' Roses.

In a fax issued to MTV on October 30, 1996, Axl said that Slash hadn't been a part of Guns N' Roses "OFFICIALLY and LEGALLY" since December 31, 1995. The fax was sent from "Burning Hills, California," which were the fire-friendly canyons of Malibu, California. In a statement to MTV News in November, Slash responded to Axl's fax. "Axl and I have not been capable of seeing eye to eye on Guns N' Roses for some time. We recently tried to collaborate, but at this point, I'm no longer in the band. I'd like to think we could work together in the future if we were able to work out our differences."

Around 1994, Axl Rose had begun expanding their recording studio with orchestral instruments, beat machines, computers, and a collection of synthesizers that felt like an act of treason in the eyes of Slash. In his effort to "bury *Appetite*," Axl had turned Guns N' Roses into a production on the scale of Pink Floyd during the recording of the *The Wall*. But according to Axl, none of this happened. Like dueling politicians vying for the support of their constituents, Slash and Axl spent the next two decades fighting over the narrative of why Guns N' Roses didn't last. Slash would repeatedly claim that Axl's power play to make Guns N' Roses more "Las Vegas," along with his desire for multiple guitar players, orchestral piano ballads, and electronic arrangements, had extinguished any hope of a collaborative effort. Slash wanted more blues-based rock and roll. As part of a series of messages posted in the MyGNRForum in 2008, Axl Rose stated the following: "I have the rehearsal tapes. There's nothing but Slash-based blues rock and he stopped it to both go solo and try to completely take over Guns. I read all this *if Axl would've put words and melodies on it could've* . . . I was specifically told no lyrics, no melodies, no changes to anything and to sing what I was told or fuck off." The last sentence seems like an exaggeration, but Axl was still wrestling with the feeling of being betrayed by Slash. They would do this for the next two decades. The two sides remained stalemated between two impossible-to-reconcile perspectives, where each one claimed the other had essentially become a tyrant. Both of them would stew in egocentric pools of persecution and guilt. In an interview with MTV on January 30, 1997, Slash insisted that, "Axl's whole visionary style, as far as his input in Guns N' Roses, is completely different from mine. I just like to play guitar, write a good riff, go out there and play, as opposed to presenting an image."

What we know is that by 1993, Axl Rose had firmly secured ownership of the Guns N' Roses trademark if, and when, Slash and Duff exited the partnership. According to several sources, at some point in 1990, Axl was informed that manager Alan Niven had booked the dates for the Use Your Illusion Tour. Niven booked the tour without consulting Axl, who was mentally unfit to lead a 194-date arena-rock tour across 27 countries. In retrospect, this is almost undeniably true, but whether Niven actually booked an entire tour without approval from the band's lead singer seems apocryphal. Axl allegedly did not want to commit to the tour, for a variety of reasons, including his crumbling mental state and belief that at any moment, one or more of his bandmembers were going to OD. According to Tom Zutaut, attorney Peter Paterno drafted a sophisticated contract as a bargaining chip: Axl would be transferred the trademark of Guns N' Roses the moment the Guns N' Roses partnership was dissolved, which seemed inevitable. According to Axl Rose, this happened in 1995. But to get Slash and Duff to sign the deal in 1990, Paterno would have to give them something in exchange: control over the Guns N' Roses' legacy, which is a vague point, but just one of the many threads of the spiderweb that constitute perhaps the biggest unsolved mystery in the history of Guns N' Roses: How exactly did Axl Rose convince Slash and Duff to relinquish their rights to the Guns N' Roses trademark?

According to Zutaut, Paterno, manager Doug Goldstein, and co-manager John Reese persuaded Slash and Duff to sign the contract to give Axl Rose full control of the Guns N' Roses trademark. Slash would later claim that in 1992 (which was later corrected to 1993), at a show in

Barcelona, Axl refused to take the stage unless he and Duff signed over the rights to the band. Axl held them at gunpoint, according to Slash. "Before a gig one night in '92, [Axl Rose] hands us a contract saying that if the band breaks up, he's taking the name," Slash told *Entertainment Weekly* in 2002. "Unfortunately, we signed it. I didn't think he'd go on stage otherwise."

Duff McKagan's autobiography claims that in Barcelona, on July 5, 1993, Goldstein asked to meet with Duff and Slash. The two were then presented with a "legal document giving Axl the right to continue to play as Guns N' Roses even if either Slash or I—or both of us—were not part of it." According to Duff, the documents did not have any kind of clause or point relating to death or incapacitation. "Axl wouldn't go onstage that night unless we signed the documents." Duff and Slash signed over the rights to use the name "Guns N' Roses." Doug Goldstein, their manager in 1993, insists that he wasn't in Barcelona at the time. He also adds that by 1990, Peter Paterno was no longer the band's attorney. This would mean that attorney Laurie Soriano drew the paperwork and that tour manager John Reese presented it to the band in Barcelona.

In the same MyGNRForum post, Axl would deny the showdown in Barcelona: "Never happened, all made up, fallacy and fantasy. Not one single solitary thread of truth to it. Had that been the case, I would've have been cremated years ago legally, could've cleaned me out for the name and damages. It's called under duress with extenuating circumstances. In fact, the time that was mentioned, the attorneys were all in Europe with us dealing with Adler."

By 1991, Slash and Duff were zonked-out zombies. "We gave up the name and all that kind of stuff because no one really gave a shit," Slash told Howard Stern in 2012. According to Axl, Slash's exact words were that he simply didn't "give a shit" about the legal rights to the Guns N' Roses name. From Axl's point-of-view, he wasn't stealing the name, he was *salvaging* it in the scenario that the rest of bandmates would either OD or exit the partnership. He was Mick Jagger in the '70s, who would become the Rolling Stones' CEO when it was clear that Keith Richards was too inebriated to make prudent business decisions.

"When GUNS renegotiated our contract with Geffen," Axl continued in his MyGNRForum post, "I had the bit about the name added in as protection for myself as I had come up with the name and then originally started the band with it. It had more to do with management than the band, as our then-manager [Alan Niven] was always tryin' to convince someone [Slash] they should fire me . . . It was added to the contract and everyone signed off on it. It wasn't hidden in fine print."

According to Goldstein, one of the key reasons for the breakup was Axl's desire to have two lead guitarists. Paul Tobias, Axl Rose's childhood friend from Indiana, was going to be the third guitar player (behind Slash and Izzy Stradlin's replacement, Gilby Clarke). Drummer Matt Sorum would refer to Tobias as the "Yoko Ono of Guns N' Roses." While Tobias has never gone on the record, he did email me one evening as a response to an inquiry I had sent regarding the production of *Chinese Democracy*:

> I would love to set the record straight on my role in regard to GnR. I will say that I am epically misunderstood by most of the public and press. The truth of my role and abilities flys [sic] in the face of the gospel according Slash, Matt and Duff. I cannot be accepted by many fans without their willingness to question the word of their idols/demigods and my contract prevents me from publicly defending myself (doing so would mean telling the story of *Chinese Democracy*). I do have a story to tell that hasn't been told and I would like to tell it.

Axl's position as the gang leader of Guns N' Roses seemed destined to end in a shootout. Like Axl, Tom Cruise's beautifully ignorant stock car driver as well as Emilio Estevez's brash gunfighter represented what Western scholar Martin Nussbaum described as "a vanishing symbol of individualism in an age of togetherness and conformity." For teenagers in the late '80s, the causeless rebel with a death wish was as trendy as the now-famous black-and-white James Dean publicity photo from *Rebel Without a Cause*

(1955). Like Brando's Triumph motorcycle and James Dean's silver Porsche 550 Spyder, Guns N' Roses were never "built to last." When Mick Jagger told writer Danny Sugerman that Guns N' Roses had a "built-in obsolescence," he was communicating the feeling that Guns N' Roses had been engineered with faulty boosters; like a stock car spinning out of control and screeching towards the pearly gates. "They're set on self-destruct," Jagger said, with what Sugerman described as a "devilish grin."

In the band's first appearance in *Rolling Stone* in November 1988, Slash compared Guns N' Roses to an actor who did their own stunts. At the time, it was a colorful metaphor that meant very little, but Slash was exploiting the medium to advertise his band's death drive. Slash was like Tom Cruise dropping the hammer on a blistering stock car to prove he wasn't just a poseur, but a wild desperado who treated his instrument like a Colt pistol. Titles of early Guns N' Roses songs like "Reckless Life," "Out Ta Get Me," and "Anything Goes" reveal a band that knew how to promote themselves as Nietzschean warriors, rather than actors playing the part. They were selling impending doom the way *Playboy* was selling sex. They were *living on the edge*. Guns N' Roses wanted to let the world know they were as unscripted as a deadly car crash.

In his interview with Steve Harris, Axl was asked how he felt about Guns N' Roses being compared to metal bands like Mötley Crüe. "They have their more theatrical thing," said Axl. "Like they do a planned show every night. We don't do that stuff. It's not what we believe in."

Of course, that would change over the years, when Guns N' Roses became more "Las Vegas." But from about 1985–88, they were a beautiful and morbid Pre-Raphaelite statement in the genre of heavy metal, which, in their minds, was an act of realism. Like Morrison and Hendrix, who climbed the stairway to heaven as quickly as they climbed the ladder of success, Guns N' Roses didn't just cover "Knockin' on Heaven's Door," they lived it. Every day we watched, panicked when MTV News' typewriter stamped our TV screens, as Kurt Loder or Tabitha Soren broke the latest news, as we bit the skin off the edges of our fingers, chewed through our nails, and prayed nobody had died. It's almost tragicomic to think that Kurt Loder's MTV interview show was titled *Famous Last Words*. He interviewed Axl Rose in the garden of his home in the Hollywood hills on August 31, 1990. Loder had a very dark sense of humor, as he giggled maniacally before Axl calmly explained how he overdosed in 1986, after swallowing an entire bottle of painkillers. "27 was definitely my hardest year," said Axl, as he stared off into the Hollywood hills knowing that he was nearly joined the same "live fast, die young" club as Janis Joplin, Jimi Hendrix, Jim Morrison, Brian Jones, and Robert Johnson.

Dylan's "Knockin' on Heaven's Door" originally appeared on the soundtrack of 1973's *Pat Garrett and Billy the Kid*. All 10 songs were written by Dylan. He wrote "Heaven's Door" from the perspective of a dying sheriff. In the hands of Guns N' Roses, "Heaven's Door" seemed to be forecasting doom, like Lynyrd Skynyrd's "Free Bird," which became the memorial song of Ronnie Van Zant (who died in a plane crash on October 20, 1977). For a band that did their own stunts, "Heaven's Door" seemed like a cinematic requiem that was detached from the spirituality of the Dylan original. The first time most Americans heard the Guns N' Roses cover of "Knockin' on Heaven's Door" was on terrestrial radio or on MTV between 1990 and 1992, a two-year period when Slash seemed to be on the verge of becoming a very beautiful corpse. Axl had OD'd at least once, which became the basis of his lyrics for *Use Your Illusion I* closer "Coma," which is an elegy Slash wrote during a hallucinatory heroin trip. If the Guns N' Roses cover of Paul McCartney's "Live and Let Die" felt "custom-made," as Danny Sugerman had said, then "Knockin' on Heaven's Door" seemed like a fireworks display closing their Use Your Illusion Tour—their "last note of freedom."

In the early '90s, Slash was the personification of a rock star who was dangling on the edge of a cliff. He was struggling with a serious heroin addiction, which he would occasionally fornicate with his cocaine habit and his intense drinking problem. Slash would get so wasted that he would urinate on himself in public, which is a story Axl shared with a fan in a 2011 YouTube video. "It was great, because he would pass out and piss his pants, and then I would get to be with the girl," said Axl. "So I always followed

Slash because I knew he would pass out and I would get the girl." Slash in a 1991 interview with *Rolling Stone* said that he "OD'd so many times. I've woken up in the hospital so many fucking times."

In 2011, Slash revealed to *Us Weekly* that he "flat-lined three times (that I know of)." Guns N' Roses' cover of "Heaven's Door" includes the sound of a hammer being cocked, along with a soaring guitar solo by Slash that lifts you above the clouds, which makes it feel less like a cover, and more like a Guns N' Roses song written about their drive towards death. In Stephen Davis's biography, there's a story of Slash's unresponsive body being found in front of an elevator on the fifth floor of a hotel, which happened during their tour with Metallica. It was discovered by tour manager John Reese, who would describe Slash as if he were in a coma. Slash didn't have a pulse when the paramedics showed up and stabbed his heart with adrenaline needle. Later, as Slash claimed in his own words, his heart had stopped for eight minutes. Another version of the story appears in Mick Wall's *Last of the Giants: The True Story of Guns N' Roses*, where it says manager Doug Goldstein claimed he carried a needle with him on tour, and that it was he who rushed to Slash's body and stabbed his heart with a syringe filled with naloxone (a drug used to counter the effects of an opioid overdose).

For kids in the '90s, before Shazam or YouTube, the Guns N' Roses cover of "Heaven's Door" was their song. How could it not be? It felt like their signature tune. "Heaven's Door" remains the band's most popular cover. It rapturously moved 72,000 people at Wembley Stadium on April 20, 1992, which began as a tribute to Freddie Mercury, and ended as a Guns N' Roses revival. Like Hendrix's cover of Dylan's "All Along The Watchtower," the cover had ostensibly replaced the original; Guns N' Roses had transmogrified someone else's elegy into what felt like their closing credits song. Duff would say in his autobiography that, "somehow our feelings found a vessel in this Bob Dylan song." Tragically, their cover never actually appeared in *Days of Thunder*. But when David Denby reviewed the film in *New York Magazine*, he sounded like he was writing the opening line of an Axl Rose bio: "He is cute and he's great at something . . . But he's also cocky, and he shows off. He is reckless, callow, stupid. He is out for himself, and he goes too far."

They were all driving too fast in those days. But somehow, as if they weren't even real, nobody in Guns N' Roses died. Slash nearly died on three different occasions. Steven Adler attempted to take his life on at least two different occasions and suffered a cocaine-influenced stroke in 1996. In 1994, Duff McKagan's pancreas exploded. The pain was so bad that he begged the ER nurse to kill him. In 1989, when he was 27 years old, a smashed Izzy Stradlin unzipped his trousers and relieved himself in the galley of a passenger plane. He was arrested soon after at the Phoenix Sky Harbor airport, the same airport where Axl Rose was arrested in 1998. Izzy Stradlin became sober at 27. "[Mick Jagger] should have died after *Some Girls*, when he was still cool," Slash told *Rolling Stone*. Mick Jagger was 35 when *Some Girls* was released, the same age Slash probably should have died, but the Devil never collected his soul; Death never challenged him to a game of chess, and Dionysus never got his more "substantial demonstration of loyalty."

No band in American history has managed to evade Death's checkmate as many times as Guns N' Roses has. Those around them were never quite as lucky. They began playing "Heaven's Door" live in 1987 at the Marquee, and later as a tribute to Jetboy bassist Todd Crew, who overdosed on heroin while working as a roadie for Slash; another corpse buried underneath their Celtic cross.

In 1988, with his right hand swollen and cut from slamming it on his guitar strings, Slash was writing the tagline of his band's thunderous coda: "Our attitude epitomizes what rock & roll is all about. We fuckin' bleed and sweat for it, you know? We do a lot of things where other bands will be, like, 'get the stunt guy to do it.'"

7

ONE IN A MILLION

"HATE IS BAGGAGE. LIFE'S TOO SHORT TO BE PISSED OFF
ALL THE TIME. IT'S JUST NOT WORTH IT."

—*AMERICAN HISTORY X* (1998)

Their first *Rolling Stone* interview was dated November 17, 1988, but the actual interview took place months earlier, around the time Guns N' Roses would debut on the stage of the 1988 MTV Video Music Awards. It was two months before the volcanic scandal of "One in a Million" would leave Axl Rose's image with third-degree burns. The 1988 VMAs were the last time Guns N' Roses seemed to possess the invulnerability of "Iron Mike" Tyson. Soon after that the world would *watch them bleed*. The unlikely connection between VMAs and "One in a Million" would turn out to be a punchline. Guns N' Roses' high-octane performance of "Welcome to the Jungle" was somehow overshadowed by the comedian who introduced them: Sam Kinison, known as "Bad Sam," a coked-up former Pentecostal preacher who belligerently faced down audiences in a beggar's overcoat and beret, who unleashed a heavy-metal growl that released flames towards women, homosexuals, Iranians, and the media. He was the rhetorical bedrock of "One in a Million." What Blake, Burroughs, and Camus offered Jim Morrison, shock comics like Kinison offered a much less bookish Axl Rose: a language that he could use to verbalize his unholy impressions, which included unscrambling his bigotry with such vivid revulsion that it nearly flushed Guns N' Roses down the toilet.

"It ["One in a Million"] was originally written as comedy," he told *Interview* magazine. "It was written watching Sam Kinison during one of his first specials."

Once you've glued the collage together and viewed it as whole—which includes a disorienting stack of defensive magazine interviews—Axl Rose's justification of the lyrics in "One in a Million" disappears [that is, the explanation disappears . . .] into a glossy blur. His polygraph results are inconclusive, but if you were looking at his file, you'd see that Axl Rose was too damaged—legally insane, perhaps—to be tried for his crimes.

In a *Rolling Stone* interview from 1989, he sounded like Eminem a decade later:

"I used words like police and niggers because you're not allowed to use the word nigger. Why can black people go up to each other and say, 'Nigger,' but when a white guy does it all of a sudden it's a big putdown?"

Kinison's audacious comedy was one of the ghostwriters of "One in a Million." It liberated Axl Rose's cocaine tongue. It's been suggested that Axl wrote his reflections in "One in a Million" to jostle his friend and songwriting partner, West Arkeen, as the two belly-laughed along with Kinison's special *Breaking the Rules (1987).* Arkeen and Axl were working on demos together, and occasionally they would get stoned and watch TV. The Kinison special was highlighted by a bit about homosexual necrophiliacs. "I feel sorry for these corpses, man . . . what can be worse than fucking death?" said Kinison, as he laid down on his stomach and impersonated a corpse being penetrated from behind. "Hey, hey, what's this shit? There's a guy's dick in my ass! You mean life is fucking you in the ass even after you're dead?" The crowd cheered. This was Axl's philosopher king. Axl himself was known for having a sharp ear for impersonation and shock-jock humor. Privately, he was seen telling jokes and long stories that ended in punch lines. His friends would jokingly refer to him as "Twain-y," after writer Mark Twain. To some extent, Axl Rose was always in on the joke. But for some peculiar reason, he never sounded like he was, or at least he never had the skills to deliver his mordant humor without immense collateral damage. If there's any sense of humor in "One in a Million"—an allusion perhaps to *Midnight Cowboy*—it is as detectable as the urbanity in Sam Kinison's voice.

In 1985, the *New York Times* would describe Kinison as if they were reviewing Axl Rose: "The most interesting of the other eight comedians is the savagely misogynistic Sam Kinison. Mr. Kinison specializes in a grotesque animalist howl that might be described as the primal scream of the married man."

At the VMAs, with neon lights glowing over the stage and the screeching sounds of teenage girls flooding his microphone, Kinison, wearing a black suit with a black pendant hanging over his neck, introduced Guns N' Roses with the full force of his personality. "These guys are personal friends of mine," he said, as he increased the volume of his voice to match the screeching voices at the front of the stage. Kinison's face began to turn into the color of strawberry ice cream. He looked like a cartoon bomb that was about to explode in a comic from the funny pages. "They said nobody could bring them on but me. They're gonna rock you into *hell* . . . GUNS N' ROSES!!!!!"

"One in a Million" had still not dented their glimmering, cold-hard steel. Wearing a white leather jacket, reflective aviator glasses, and a reversed-baseball-cap look he would later claim he popularized, Axl Rose calmly walked onto the stage and grabbed the microphone. For the next 14 seconds, he released a sustained guttural howl that sounded like a fleet of stock cars igniting their engines. He exploded at the sound of Steven Adler's crashing drums and began to pound his cowboy boots like he was dancing around bullets aimed at his feet, spinning and sliding around the stage as if he were in a psychedelic rain trance. Writer Eve Babitz once wrote that Jim Morrison knew how to stand. Morrison had made an art form out of holding a microphone and wrapping himself around it like a python around a tree limb. When Morrison would finally yell into the microphone, it produced orgiastic relief from the tension. Axl was assaulting his audience and raising his fist to God; he was breaching the clouds above him with the power of his atomic lungs, which sounded like a space shuttle breaking the sound barrier. There was no junk flowing through his veins. His body was in peak condition. He looked semi-divine as he looked up at the sky with eyes closed so tight it looked like he was going to hover above the crowd and explode into a white light. It was a magnificent display of triumphalism. He had paced around the stage like Mike Tyson on pay-per-view, pivoting in different directions and looking for an angle to throw his uppercut. How could one man fluidly unleash so much suffering, angst, and intensity while being able to control his body? It was a testament to his natural-born proprioception and lung capacity. In 1988, it felt like we were watching a well-trained athlete dazzle us with their gifts. Axl's kinesthetic control was found in his ability to maintain his falsetto on the run, with his instrument projected from deep within his stomach—stopping, going, then sprinting from one side of the stage to the other. It was remarkable to watch. The physicality of Axl Rose made it seem like his voice was a well-engineered weapon of mass destruction—internal and external—his boxing glove, and his stock car. In high school, Axl had been on the cross-country team. "He had a real smart mouth on him," his former coach told *People* magazine. Axl's abs were chiseled, hairless, and sculpted for the purposes of war. His dance moves were completely foreign on MTV. He could travel between six octaves while *sprinting*. The fact that Axl Rose never ran out of breath until the 2002 MTV Video Music Awards is one of the great accomplishments in the history of rock. He would keep this up for four years, and then, just as beauty faded, so did his voice.

He was in God mode at the 1992 Freddie Mercury Tribute Concert at Wembley Stadium. This was Axl Rose as Achilles pursuing immortal glory in bright bronze armor. The rugged Nietzschean warrior who had waged war, fallen, and now achieved apotheosis as a superhuman version of himself. He was also strangely disconnected from the politics of the moment. His blindness needs to be studied, as his mere presence that day was protested by AIDS activist group ACT UP due to his use of "faggot" in "One in a Million," but also the suggestion that "faggots" were spreading diseases around Los Angeles. He was about to break all the rules. For Axl Rose to have been present that day, to some degree, he also needed to be absent. Like an athlete heading into a championship game after an immense personal tragedy, Axl Rose was in a state of steely inwardness, like Achilles, determined, and in a trance. MTV's John Norris told us to set our VCRs.

His entrance could fill the pages of myth. With 72,000 fans listening to the operatic section of "Bohemian Rhapsody," when Elton John stood to the side of the stage in a red suit, there was a feeling that something was going to happen; perhaps a dazzling pyrotechnics display. Backstage, Axl was preparing to bombard his naysayers (everyone from gay activists to feminists). Two months earlier, "Bohemian Rhapsody" had re-entered the zeitgeist when Wayne inserted a cassette into Garth's tape deck. The head-banging scene from *Wayne's World* had amplified "Bohemian Rhapsody" for the *Headbangers Ball* demo. The song was electrifying the airwaves by the time Axl Rose decided to become its conduit. It was April 20, 1992, and Axl had on a mesh crop top, which exposed his ripped core; a leather battle kilt; a red bandana, and combat boots. Everything was back except his bandana. From behind the stage, Axl blasted out like a cannonball. Seven different pyrotechnic displays simultaneously lit up the stage as he came spinning through them like the Ultimate Warrior. The leather kilt was his battle armor. This is the look that would inspire the aesthetic of Jonathan Davis of Korn; this is the Axl Rose who appears roaring into the microphone on a Guns N' Roses pinball machine, which has a Colt pistol–designed plunger. Holding a removable mic stand with both hands as if it were an aluminum baseball bat, which was Freddie Mercury–esque, Axl would complete five full spins before planting his feet in a pose that was as deliberate as a baseball player preparing to swing. He sang the head-banging coda of "Bohemian Rhapsody" with a piercing and abrasive falsetto that sounded aged to perfection. He'd then climb on top of an encased monitor with 72,000 bouncing to his voice and emancipate what sounded like lyrics he'd written about his own turmoiled childhood.

It was the finale of a future movie about Guns N' Roses—their version of Queen's flawless set at Live Aid 1985, which Axl had first watched at

West Arkeen's place. Fast-forward to Wembley Stadium, 1992, and it was Axl Rose's version of Live Aid 1985.

"I mean, Freddie Mercury and Elton John are, like, two of the biggest influences in my whole life," he told *Interview* magazine.

Axl's unwillingness to bow to his critics, especially the gay community, was Kinisonian. Axl was not simply a fan of Sam Kinison, he was a parishioner in his unapologetic church of misanthropy. Both Kinison and Axl had a background in the Pentecostal faith. Kinison, like Axl, would paint targets on audience members and mow them down with his semiautomatic punch lines. Kinison would anxiously pace around the stage and look for any excuse to turn a punch line into a verbal assault. It was often hard to tell if his audience was being entertained, or simply pumped with so much anxiety that they had no choice but to grip the handlebars on the drop— screaming for mercy.

Going to a Guns N' Roses concert was like sitting on a theme park ride that had recently produced a fatality. In 1991, when an *Entertainment Weekly* reporter asked if they were built to last, he seemed to be asking a question that Mick Jagger had already answered in 1989, when he said that Guns N' Roses were "set on self-destruct." It seems that "One in a Million" would commence the countdown. From the end of 1988 on, media headlines would describe Axl Rose as a homophobe and a racist. It was relentless; it dwarfs the intensity of today's self-pitying victims of "cancel culture." He was being publicly shamed out of existence. After Mick Wall's interview in *Kerrang!*, in which an apoplectic Axl threatened to crush Vince Neil's face, and after being manipulated by Danny Sugerman's determinism in *Spin*, Guns N' Roses' management did something unprecedented. In 1991, Guns N' Roses issued a media contract that was in part designed to make Axl feel like he was back in control, but also mitigate damages. The contract required journalists to give Guns N' Roses final approval, which *Spin* described as "giving the band final okay on every single word." *Spin* would impishly protest the contract by publishing it in full in a June issue, which ran with a headline that was both incendiary and prescient:

"No Appetite for Criticism."

The *L.A. Times* would publish the contract's details:

"The two-page document gives Guns N' Roses copyright owner-ship and approval rights over any 'article, story, transcript or recording connected with the interview,' control over any advertising or promotion involving the story and indemnifies the band from any damages or liabili-ties in connection with the story."

Any media outlet who breached the contract would be fined $100,000 in damages. *Rolling Stone*, *Spin*, and the *L.A. Times*, just to name a few, refused to sign it. Guns N' Roses' management was desperately trying to prevent another scandal. But a scold's bridle couldn't keep Axl Rose from chewing through the First Amendment. At the of end of May 1991, at a gig in Noblesville, Indiana, Axl described his home state as being like Auschwitz, the concentration camp where at least a million Jews were killed. Axl Rose was losing his ability to contain the shards of his broken psyche. "He just seemed that he [Axl Rose] really needed some mothering or something," Sinead O'Connor told *Rolling Stone* in 1991. *Rolling Stone* would provide a report from the Use Your Illusion Tour on September 5, 1991: "Guns n' Roses are very much a band teetering on the brink, and America is watching. Will they survive? Do they even want to survive?" It sounded like CNN reporting on a nation being besieged from every direc-tion. This was printed in the aftermath of several disastrous concerts that summer, including the now infamous "Riverport Riot," which was a crime scene that had Axl Rose's fingerprints all over it.

It was July 2, 1991, about 83 minutes into their set at the Riverport Amphitheater in St. Louis, Missouri, and Axl began to stalk a member of the audience who was holding a camera, which was banned by the venue. The camera presented some kind of irrational threat to Axl, as he paced around like "Bad Sam" during a fit. "Hey, take that! Take that! Now, get that guy and take that!" he yelled to security. When security was slow to respond, Axl dove off the stage in a black fur coat, which was a stage dive that would be played on MTV as often as Gulf War footage on CNN. Axl flew over a row of chairs, collided with a fan named Bill "Stump" Stephenson, who was holding the camera, and began ripping through a

St. Louis biker gang called the "Saddle Tramps." He was quickly pushed back on stage. It was a comically outrageous scene, and uncomfortable to watch, as Axl was wearing skintight cycling shorts that made it look like he was facing down a biker gang in his underwear. He was like Kurt Russell in *Big Trouble in Little China* (1986) confidently impersonating John Wayne without realizing he had lipstick smeared across his face.

Once back on stage, Axl told the crowd, "Well! Thanks to the lame-ass security, I'm going home!" Like Sam Kinison, Axl would spike the mic with such indignance that it sounded like a pipe bomb. He proceeded to march out of the arena like a diva going to their trailer. Axl was *breaking the rules*, again, but this time there were consequences. Fans began to throw beer at the stage. Then chairs began to fly. The tour buses had begun firing up their engines. Axl had already left the building when the lights came on and revealed millions of dollars of equipment on the stage. Fans began to chant "bullshit!" as they marched towards the stage. Civilization had crumbled beneath the tyrannical boots of the redheaded Caligula. Bill "Stump" Stephenson was being carried off in a stretcher as half-empty cups flew over his body. There was a fan wielding a knife on stage (this was caught on camera). Another fan had blood pouring down the back of his head after being struck with a flying wooden chair. One fan pulled his blue jeans down and exposed himself to the cops. As a fire hose began to spray the crowd with pressured water, a 60-ton sound-and-light rig began to swing over the crowd. "If that rig comes down, there will be massive death," one tech said, as a Guns N' Roses roadie was struck in the head with a bottle of beer while trying to retrieve Slash's guitar. Nearly three thousand fans were tearing the amphitheater into pieces. Every cop in St. Louis was radioed in, as helicopters beamed their spotlights down on a scene the media would describe as the Riverport Riot. "It was some sort of white-trash Fellini film," one fan described it to *The A.V. Club*. A Houston news anchor in 1992 would observe that Guns N' Roses had "quite a different crowd than the Republican convention." The news first broke on MTV with host Tabitha Soren, who had a restrained giggle tickling her face as she shared the absurd story with viewers. "Rose announced that he would get the guy himself and then jumped into the crowd and allegedly pummeled the fan. Venue security jumped in to pull Rose off the fan, and then Guns N' Roses' security jumped in to pull them off Rose." Soren delivered the breaking news standing in front of what looked like an antique map of Missouri, with a black-and-white picture of Axl Rose in a cowboy hat placed over the map. It was MTV's version of *America's Most Wanted*. Two months after the riot, Axl Rose wore a vintage St. Louis baseball hat in the video for "Don't Cry." Axl was drawing fire when he wore a "St. Louis Sucks" T-shirt and cursed the city in the liner notes of *Use Your Illusion*. His provocations were needlessly juvenile and shock-jock.

It wasn't until a year later, days before embarking on a tour with Metallica (which began July 17, 1992), that Axl Rose would be arrested for an outstanding warrant relating to the Riverport Riot. Axl Rose can be seen smiling in the back of a squad car in New York, after he was arrested upon landing in Kennedy Airport. He was charged with four counts of misdemeanor assault and one count of property damage.

MTV's Kurt Loder broke the news with Ray-Bans and a black sports coat, standing outside the courtroom in New York where Axl was being processed. "Hi, I'm Kurt Loder with an MTV News special report . . . " which he delivered with the kind of cool detachment that always made his reporting feel like a something out of a Bret Easton Ellis novel—as there was a subtle tone of mockery in his voice—suggesting he never took Axl as seriously as the "rockist" music press. He was the anti-Mick Wall.

Before his arrest, just six days after the Riverport Riot, in front of a crowd of nearly twenty thousand screaming fans inside the Starplex Amphitheater in Dallas, Axl Rose began to wave his middle finger at his critics. With reports of $200,000 in property damage, 60 reported injuries, lawsuits from every direction, and a warrant out for his arrest, Axl spoke directly to the same demographic of malcontents who were being indoctrinated by Sam Kinison, the most dangerous comedian in world. "Thank you, Dallas, fuck you, St. Louis, and God bless America."

Axl Rose would ignite riots in St. Louis, Philadelphia, and Montreal, which would transform into a multifaceted tragedy where Axl walked away physically unscathed, but his image was permanently injured. Montreal ended Guns N's Roses' nonaggression pact with Metallica. In the summer of 1992, Metallica toured with Guns N' Roses in what was billed as the stadium tour of the century. Tickets were $27.50, which in retrospect was absurdly low for a concert featuring 140-minute sets by both Metallica and Guns N' Roses. It was a double feature that would travel the country with an orchestral horn section, backup soul singers, Lars Ulrich's rotating drum set, a mirrored stage, complicated sound-and-lighting rigs for each band, an oxygen tank for Axl Rose (including an "ego ramp" as James Hetfield once described it, which split the stage into two catwalks that extended into the audience), colorful Versace suits for Duff and Axl, and the sort of pyrotechnic display you'd associate with professional wrestling. It would take nearly two hours to switch between Metallica and Guns N' Roses stage, who would close the shows. In 1992, for anyone with even a vague interest in rock music, the coupling of Guns N' Roses with Metallica was a spectator experience on par with Magic Johnson facing off with Michael Jordan in the NBA Finals.

On August 8, 1992, during Metallica's performance of "Fade to Black," singer James Hetfield stepped onto a vent that would release a chemical fireball that would wrap itself around his skin. The crowd in Montreal was unaware of the situation, but the fire had cooked his skin like cheese melting off the edge of a slice of pizza. A pyrotechnic misfire had engulfed Hetfield's body in a greenish fountain of flame. He had second- and third-degree burns to his hands and face; his strings burned right off his asymmetrical-shaped ESP Explorer guitar. Guitarist Kirk Hammett later said that he could see the skin melting off his hands. A bucket of water was poured over Hetfield, as smoke began to rise off his body like a scene from Backdraft (1991). The Metallica set was cut short, and Guns N' Roses were asked to go on early. Achilles was being called into battle. He was in his tent. "Wild Thing" was being asked to close. Air Jordan had the ball with the clock winding down. 10, 9, 8 . . .

It took Axl Rose 135 minutes to arrive on stage. When he did, he looked visibly annoyed that he was pinch-hitting for Metallica. "He could have been the hero of the day," Hetfield said on VH1's *Behind the Music* in 1998. Instead "he threw a fit," as Axl was having issues with his monitor and strained vocals. "That's when all hell broke loose," said Kurt Hammett. Axl's injured voice was his escape clause.

The increasingly Hollywood transformation of Axl Rose is best understood in a scene from Metallica's 1992 documentary, *A Year and a Half in the Life of Metallica*, where James Hetfield reads from Axl's tour rider: "Axl Pose," said Hetfield, as he derided Axl for demanding "absolutely no substitutions" be made to the items on his rider, which included, "one cup of cubed ham . . . it's gotta be cubed fuckin' right, so it'll get down his little neck. One rib-eye steak dinner . . . didn't even know the guy ate meat, he looked like a fuckin' vegemitarian," said Hetfield. "One gourmet *cheese* tray; pepperoni pizza, fresh; cans of assorted Pringles chips; greasy shit to grease his hair back; Sue Bee honey, which makes him *sing like this* [impersonating Axl's falsetto]."

"In case anybody here is interested," Axl told the crowd in Montreal, "this will be our last show for a long time." He would slam the microphone on stage and walk off, which became the battle horn that would cue the rioters. It was happening again. When the smoke cleared, Axl would refuse to apologize for igniting an event that caused $400,000 in damage to Montreal's Olympic Stadium—where Guns N' Roses were subsequently banned. During the rioting, the two bands were sequestered in their dressing rooms, and Axl is said to have been sipping on champagne and smoking a cigarette using a cigarette holder, complaining about his voice. "It reminded me of when Rome burned and Nero played his fiddle," said Hammett. Metallica's episode of VH1's *Behind the Music*, which aired a year after Guns N' Roses had essentially dissolved, circa 1998, would forever secure Axl the title of hard rock's biggest heel. He was permanently branded as a prima donna with the temperament of an amoral Roman dictator with daddy issues.

In a 1993 interview with *Rolling Stone*, Hetfield closed the iron door on Axl Rose like John Barrymore in *Twentieth Century* (1934). "They're a different type of band," he said. "And I use the word *band* loosely. It's a guy and some other guys. We were out to show people that there was something a little more progressive and hard core than Guns N' Roses. And to go about it our way. But it was hard going on, dealing with Axl and his attitude. It's not something we'd want to do again."

A Guns N' Roses concert could either be a good day on the set (where the only drama was a salad with too much dressing), or the kind of the day where you needed to call the paramedics and have someone committed. They weren't the "most dangerous band in the world" because of a romantic connection to Darby Crash crushing a beer bottle over his face, or Izzy Pop cutting himself on stage and flinging bits of flesh into the audience. Guns N' Roses were dangerous because they had a singer who would trigger a fan base filled with testosterone-pumping jocks, rednecks, metal-shop bullies, and the so-called "forgotten American" who viewed the Confederate flag as a symbol of rebellion, as opposed to treason. There were bomb scares, riots, gang members, and almost no minorities (though touring helped them recruit a strong following in South America, Japan, and Mexico). Guns N' Roses fans were the same headbanging meatheads that Kurt Cobain would criticize on "In Bloom" as well as the liner notes of *Incesticide*: "At this point I have a request for our fans. If any of you in any way hate homosexuals, people of different color, or women, please do this one favor for us—leave us the fuck alone! Don't come to our shows and don't buy our records."

Pontificating in Chicago in 1992, Axl grew frustrated with the gaucheness of the audience: "Shut the fuck up: 'yo Axl, cool, metal, dude! Rock 'n' roll, party, do cocaine, yeah!' I ain't here for that." But those were the exact same arena-rock fans who would become Axl Rose's base. In 1992, Axl Rose was a celebrity on the verge of a mental health crisis, like Kanye West in a MAGA hat, or Britney Spears shaving her head and impaling an SUV with an umbrella. A Guns N' Roses show in 1992 was what Slash would describe as a "typhoon of chaos" in the *Montreal Gazette*.

But the rivets holding together Axl's psyche had begun to loosen as early as 1988, at the Monsters of Rock Festival. Guns N' Roses were heading into the festival at Castle Donington with what writer Danny

Sugerman would describe as a "self-fulfilling doom philosophy." It had rained the night before in the village. With the sun still out, Guns N' Roses took to the stage as a wave of fans began to surge their way towards the pit. It looked like a battle scene from *Braveheart* (1995), where armies were colliding in a sea of mud. About 15 fans suddenly collapsed into a patch of mud about 20 feet from the pit. Axl was requested to stop performing, which he did, as security began untangling the sticky heap of humanity. Before playing "Welcome to the Jungle," the promoters asked Axl to remind the crowd to step back. "We got some people unconscious still," said Axl, as he stood on mud that had been flung onto the stage. In the process of pulling a few kids out of the mud and pushing them towards the pit, Guns N' Roses began to play. Flags began to wave as if someone had scored a goal. Suddenly, a riptide of bodies pulled about 30 kids down into four inches of thick mud. They began to suffocate. Towards the end of the set, Axl would tell the crowd, "Don't fucking kill yourselves." After the show was over, two limp bodies were discovered face down, plastered into the mud. There were about 107,000 people at Donington that day, with metal bands such as Iron Maiden and Megadeath feeding their need for decibel therapy, and it was Guns N' Roses—the least metal band on the bill—who would have two dead bodies on their record. The Devil was always a few steps behind Guns N' Roses, ready to collect a soul.

The press condemned Axl Rose for the Donington tragedy. Two fans were dead under the thumping boots of Axl Rose. That was the perception. They were, after all, "the most dangerous band in the world." The "self-fulfilling doom philosophy" had led to two dead fans—that was the film they wanted to write. "The media blamed the band, fueling our notorious bad-boy image," Steven Adler wrote in his book. Axl would discuss the incident in their *Rolling Stone* cover story from 1988, which took place a month after the death scene.

"I don't know really what to think about it," said Axl, who began to feel the tingle of his persecution complex. "We didn't tell people to smash each other," Axl says. "We didn't tell people, 'Drink so much alcohol that you can't fucking stand up.' I don't feel responsible in those ways."

Guns N' Roses were a fatalistic band that remarkably managed to continuously dodge Death, while those around them were sacrificed. As I've said before, there are a lot of bodies buried under the Celtic cross of *Appetite for Destruction*, including the charred remains of West Arkeen, who died in 1997, along with Guns N' Roses, in toto. Arkeen was buried with his deeply underappreciated legacy, as he co-wrote a number of Guns N' Roses' most memorable tracks, including "It's So Easy" and "Patience." His death reads like the plot of a Del James horror story. In the *LA Weekly*, journalist Matt Wake described Arkeen's painful entry into the world: "As an infant, he suffered from craniosynostosis, a birth defect in which the skull grows irregularly, often constricting brain growth. It required an operation that left an ear-to-ear scar over the crown of his head."

He died suddenly at age 36, when found lifeless inside his Fruitland Drive residence in Studio City, dead of an accidental overdose. Cocaine, heroin, and morphine were found in his system. His body was covered in burns connected to a horrific barbecue accident that occurred 11 days before his death. Wake reported that in the immediate aftermath of Arkeen's death, some of his friends stole his guitars, home recordings, and lyric books. His gravestone in Lancaster reads: "PEACE, PARTY, C-YA." West Arkeen never commented on "One in a Million."

On April 10, 1992, Sam Kinison's 1989 pearl-white Trans Am was crushed in a head-on crash with a truck. Kinison died at the scene. He was 38 years old and his "embarrassing heavy-metal sycophancy"—as the *L.A Times* would describe it in 1988—would continue to rumble and crackle under Axl Rose's vocal cords. But whether you're crashing into the pavement going 80 miles per hour like a tragically overconfident daredevil, twisting into the wind, or finding yourself staring into the headlights of oncoming traffic—the most immediate question is: "What drives someone towards a death wish?" Guns N' Roses were a band that turned fistfights, lawsuits, riots, lawlessness, hate speech, and impending doom into populist theater. MTV was their *Wide World of Sports*. Were Guns N' Roses driven by the same sort of unhealthy machismo that fueled Evel Knievel's star-spangled death wish? Were they being led into the jungle by a war-mad nihilist who would commit genocide to secure a beach? Were they poisoned with the kind of contempt for vulnerable groups that seemed to be Sam Kinison's drug of choice? Axl Rose certainly gambled with his reputation the way Evel Knievel gambled with his body.

Eve Babitz once described Jim Morrison as "Bing Crosby from hell." Following the logic of Babitz, Axl Rose is Jim Morrison from the stagnated frontier of Lafayette, Indiana, or as John Jeremiah Sullivan described it: "Nowhere." In a photo from an April 1989 issue of *RIP*, Axl is seen holding a pump-action shotgun between his legs with a thick beard and the stone-cold stare of a convict. He looked sponsored by the NRA. The headline was bleeding with puns: "Axl Shoots from the Hip: The First Truly Honest Interview with GN'R's Controversial Frontman Will Blow You Away!" A contrasting portrait appears on the cover of *Rolling Stone* in August of the same year, where Axl Rose has his sleeves rolled up on a gray flannel coat, with his hands on his hips. He had the laser-focused determination of Tom Cruise in *Rain Man* (1988).

But who was the real Axl Rose? In one interview, he looked and talked like he was *law and order*, in another, he was Kiefer Sutherland on a lavish sushi date. This was the Axl Rose who had sold nearly seven million copies of *Appetite for Destruction* and had transformed from a feral street-urchin into the Lester Bangs's definition of Mick Jagger as a "moneybags revolutionary . . . for acting smarter and hipper and like more of a cultural and fashion arbitrator than he really was." This was the Axl Rose with softly brushed ginger hair, diets, reconstructed teeth, dyed eyebrows, cigarette holders, designer vitamins, tinted sunglasses, and colorful suits he'd wear like a rapper.

But really, who was the *real* Axl Rose? Was he the blue-collar redneck in *RIP*, or the more ambitious "moneybags revolutionary" in *Rolling Stone*? We don't have an answer because in 1989, Axl Rose's personality began to fracture into several different forms. In 1989, Axl lived in a dimly lit condo in West Hollywood, his "illusion city," which is how Kenneth Anger described Hollywood in *Hollywood Babylon*. His condo had a broken mirror that reflected his chromophobe post-hair-metal aesthetic; a black-leather couch with a black Uzi submachine machine tucked behind it, like the one from the first *Terminator* (1984); a black piano; black curtains; a black pair of heels sitting atop a black speaker; a black rug; a rotary phone he'd launched into his mirrored wall, and platinum records hanging on the wall as meticulously arranged as his handwriting. He looked like a malnourished vampire styled by fashion designer Thierry Mugler. He lived like this for two years, as he demonstrated his dedication to burying his past with a chic upgrade that never could camouflage his "nowhere" roots. He was now a modern pop star, a bestial version of the George Michael–types he wanted to annihilate in 1987. He was preparing for his close-up, as photographer Robert John zoomed in and snapped a photo of Axl at the apex of boho-chicness, with glassy eyes to match. John snapped the photo that appears on the cover of *Rolling Stone* from 1989, when Axl began telling kids to take business courses. A year later he'd start wearing his baggy designer suits to court. That same year, 1990, he would confirm to Kurt Loder that 27, the year of backlash from "One in a Million," was the hardest year of his life.

"I'm like the president of a company worth between $125 million and a quarter billion dollars," he told *Rolling Stone.* Both the *RIP* and *Rolling Stone* shots were photographed by John, while the interviews were conducted by his confidant and close friend, writer Del James, who Axl met in the summer of 1985. Axl gained the editorial control he was seeking in 1986. By this point, Axl had grown distrusting of the media and began stockpiling weapons in his condo, including a riot-grade shotgun, while struggling to diffuse the bomb inside his head. His interviews were now orchestrated productions using his own in-house team. Axl could not get the media to sign his restrictive contract, so he decided to create his press agency: Robert John and Del James. During the apogee of his fame, he was beginning to shape-shift into the "Howard Hughes of Rock." The glaringly right-wing photo in *RIP* appeared just as his record label was trying to make Axl Rose seem less xenophobic.

Every interview Axl Rose did between 1989 and 1992 was an opportunity to bandage the shotgun wounds afflicted by "One in a Million."

And in every interview, with very little exception, Axl sounded like the lunatic trying to assert control of the looney bin inside his own mind, like Nicholson in *One Flew Over the Cuckoo's Nest* (1975). He sounded like a serial killer justifying his need to kill, the politician doubling-down on their political miscalculations. The real Axl Rose may have been the *right-wing hippie*, or a backwoods Jim Morrison, but that was not how he wanted the public to view him. In his "tiny skull-sized kingdom," as David Foster Wallace would have described it, Axl Rose was the working-class Mick Jagger.

One of the more absorbing interviews with Axl Rose took place in a May 1992 issue of Andy Warhol's *Interview*, which ran a sensual Bruce Weber photo spread that included a close-up of Stephanie Seymour's colorfully painted toes dangling over a glass table. The discursive interview took place in March, when Axl's infatuation with seeming more bourgeoise was at its peak. Axl would begin to display a microscopic amount of regret for his past crimes. When the interviewer asked him about the backlash to feminism in the early '90s, where "men have felt as though it were O.K. to become pigs again," Axl looked back at "It's So Easy" and shook his head at the trivialization of rape and battery. He seemed to be having an awakening, which was molded by Seymour's gentle political calculations, Kurt Cobain, the humiliation of "One in a Million," and years of intense psychotherapy. "Yes. We, Guns N' Roses, did [think it was okay to be pigs] for a while," Axl replied. "Or I did, because it was the only way to deal with it—it was O.K. to be obnoxious and rude like that for a while. It's not O.K. for me personally to be that way anymore. It was accepted for us."

The last sentence could have been "expected of us." The interview is noteworthy for a couple of reasons. First, there's a voyeuristic batch of photos of Axl and Stephanie French kissing, where she looks like a lush European actress, like Elsa Martinelli or Claudia Cardinale. You can nearly smell the French perfume wafting off her long neck, as she stretches back into Axl's arms and exudes the dangerous confidence of a femme fatale with a plan. It was reported that Stephanie consoled him like a mother when Axl got the phone call that Izzy Stradlin was quitting the band. She was a mother to him. She was also grooming him into her rock star pet. "She manipulated Axl, and constantly went behind his back," says one source regarding the swan-necked beauty, who appeared on several *Vogue* covers. She was also on covers for *Sports Illustrated* and *Playboy*, including one from March 1991, which included photographs by Herb Ritts. On the *Playboy* cover, Seymour looks like Ursula Andress posing inside a photographer's naturally lit studio. Her sharply defined jawline, ale-colored skin, and thick brownish-gold hair makes her look like a more ferocious Cindy Crawford.

Axl allegedly told his assistant at the time, Colleen Combs, that he had been "hit by a Mack truck . . . the license plate said, 'Seymour.'" Axl Rose wanted to create the family he never had with Stephanie Seymour; he viewed her as his vehicle to domestic happiness and more acceptance in high-society circles. She could have been his political spouse. Her presence would help him grow into the "sonic statesman" that had always eluded him. She would be his pathway to the luxuriating life of a middle-aged Mick Jagger, who would attend Elton John's White Tie and Tiara Summer Ball in a rose garden surrounded by marble statues and the faint sound of a violin playing The Verve's "Bittersweet Sympathy." This was the life Axl Rose was chasing. Stephanie was his "one in a million." With her by his side, he began to look more like a star. He wore colorful blazers, drank Cristal champagne, began wearing designer jeans (the leather tights were out), smoked using a cigarette holder, and seemed to become obsessive about straightening his hair. Axl had begun to look like the damaged but opulent child of Hollywood royalty—Kiefer Sutherland dating Julia Roberts.

The Herb Ritts spread in *Playboy* depicts Seymour as a mermaid with grains of sand attached to her wavy hair. Seaweed, seashells, and fishnets are the only wardrobe items that dare cover her majestic body, as water dances around her tanned skin in that musical sort of way Ritts composed with Madonna's video for "Cherish" (which included a mermaid). He would do it again with a soaked Tom Cruise on the cover of *Rolling Stone* in 1990. "Her eyes," Ritts would say of Seymour, "in different lights, they change color, from blue to green." The green in Axl Rose's eyes would radiate when his mood began to swing, according to Vicky Hamilton.

In the music video for "Don't Cry," we see Seymour in a tasseled black dress, cradling Axl Rose as they descend into the bottom of the ocean, as we see a flashing glimpse of the floral brand tattooed around his ankle. It's devastatingly romantic. It's also an image taken from a thousand different aquatic-themed pulp magazine covers. The rest of the video includes shots of Seymour and Axl in a series of domestic disputes, which were reenactments of his relationship with Erin Everly.

"This scene is somewhat of a dramatized reenactment of something that really happened," Axl told a cameraman on the set of "Don't Cry." The scene depicts a suicidal Axl Rose raising a Glock towards his temple, as Seymour wrestles it away from him. Axl finally shoves her into a wall, as the Glock in her hand points towards a photo of the two at a picnic. Seymour is wearing a skintight tank top with blue jeans. She has brown lipstick. It was the first time she had acted. "I like to see that side of him," a smiling Seymour said during hair and makeup on the set. The illusion would become their reality on December 25, 1992, when Seymour arranged a Christmas party for Axl in his Malibu estate.

There are reports of the kind of Christmas party it was. It seems to either have been an opulent display of excess, where cocaine was the most popular hors d'oeuvre—or something a bit more intimate. Either way, Axl was not in the mood for a party when he arrived home that night and slammed the door shut. Axl had gone upstairs in a petulant rage, but eventually, the two began to fight, with various stories alleging that Seymour struck Axl with a chair and punched him the groin. Seymour countered by saying that Axl slapped and punched her down a flight of stairs, claiming that she had grabbed his testicles in order to defend herself. There are other sordid details that allege that Axl erupted and threw a glass bottle against the wall and violently dragged a barefooted Seymour over it—which permanently alters the reflection from the Bruce Weber photos. She would scream in agony, we're told. This was also reported in a 2000 *Rolling Stone* profile on Axl Rose. In a sworn declaration, Seymour claimed that Axl was "out of control." Axl would later claim that they were engaged to be married on February 4, 1992. Seymour denied this claim. He could no longer cast her as his bride. The two separated three weeks later, when Seymour was allegedly unfaithful to Axl. It wasn't the first time. In August 1993, Axl sued Seymour by claiming she had "kicked and grabbed" him and had refused to return more than $100,000 worth of jewelry. Seymour would countersue, claiming Axl had given her a black eye and a bloody nose. Then something bizarre happened: Stephanie Seymour's Brazilian nanny and housekeeper, Beta Lebeis, stopped working for Seymour and became Axl's assistant. In an issue of *Classic Rock* from 2002, Beta is described as Axl's "cook" and "personal assistant." Sources close to Axl Rose have suggested that Beta was the one who informed him that Seymour was being unfaithful with names that included Warren Beatty. When their relationship began deteriorating in 1992, Axl would begin losing grip of his already slippery relationship with normalcy. He would cover Charles Manson's "Look at Your Game, Girl," claiming that Manson's song about a damaged lover captured his last days with Stephanie Seymour. That same year, he would begin penning a love song about her titled "This I Love," which he would describe as the "heaviest" song he had ever written. In April 1995, speaking to a Canadian radio station, Slash would complain that Guns N' Roses were turning into an Axl Rose solo project. Slash said he refused to be a part of anymore "Stephanie Seymour ballads." Axl Rose never completely recovered from Stephanie Seymour, who became his Delilah—who has snipped off the source of Axl's power.

In 2014, Stephanie Seymour was the subject of a photoshoot by *Harper's Bazaar*. At one point during the shoot, "November Rain" came on the radio. Seymour was being captured in a black corset with thigh-high lace Tom Ford boots. "Is this a practical joke?" she asked, as she rolled her eyes. "Getting involved with Axl Rose? Clearly a mistake," she said. "It taught me a lot, though. He was a violent person, and I realized I never wanted to be around that again. The thrill of the whole rock 'n' roll thing wore off. I saw the worst of that world and it soured me."

Axl was absolutely hypnotized by Seymour's elusiveness and upper-class sensibilities, as he had been by past-life regression therapy (which begins with a form of hypnosis). *Rolling Stone* reported that Axl believed that Seymour and he were together in 15 or 16 past lives. The interview in Andy Warhol's *Interview* was conducted by Ingrid Sischy, who is gay. For about half the interview, Axl is not aware that Sischy is gay, which becomes clear when she brings up Axl's use of "faggot" in "One in a Million." Without knowing Sischy's sexuality, Axl proclaims that he's "pro-hetero." When Sischy surprises him by announcing her sexuality, he responds with another sloppy explanation: "I don't make any judgement, you know. Sometimes we can be stupid, like somebody rooting for their team and just going, 'Oh, our team's the best.' That song sounds like I am, because when we went to the studio it came out very forceful. I played it on guitar and it was done very humorously."

This is the interview where Axl would give his most detailed explanation of "One in a Million." Perhaps Sischy intimidated him. She may have been the first member of the gay community to interrogate him in person. In the early '90s, Axl was being pummeled by a Greek chorus of criticism by the gay community. A few months after the release of "One in a Million," Guns N' Roses were pulled from a David Geffen–affiliated AIDS benefit in New York. All of this becomes tragically ironic when you rewind the tape and recall that in the '70s, it was Axl who was being called a "faggot" by the homophobic rednecks in Lafayette, Indiana.

"I want you to talk to me about this thing where people say, 'Axl Rose is homophobic,'" said Sischy. "Well, a lot of people use the word 'faggot,'" Axl responded. "And they're not getting told they're homophobic. But, homophobia? OK, I'll repeat myself—this is something I said in *Rolling Stone*. I don't know, maybe I have a problem with homophobia. Maybe I was two years old and got fucked in the ass by my dad and it's caused a problem ever since, but other than that, I don't know if I have any homophobia. How was that?"

Axl Rose would tell *Rolling Stone* in August 1989 that he "had some very bad experiences with homosexuals." In the presence of Sischy, Axl proceeded to explain that the "One in a Million" lyric was inspired by a news story about a homosexual prostitute who was working on Santa Monica Boulevard. The prostitute had AIDS, which outraged Axl, who was protesting USA for Africa's "We Are the World" charity song for glossing over the reality of what was happening on the streets, which Axl was exposing on "One in a Million" like a West Coast gangster rapper— at least that's how Axl saw it. It was then framed as a "joke" inspired by Sam Kinison. And yet, Axl had spent much of the past five years arguing that his band was a rejection of frivolity, bubblegum, phoniness, and that they were more "reality-based." While there's obvious (and pleasurable) satire in a song like "Used to Love Her," there's no hint of that in "One in a Million." It felt more like a disgruntled confession of a member of the white working class arriving in LA and becoming repulsed by the multi-culturalism. It lacked the deceptive sarcasm and playful theatrics of Randy Newman's *Good Old Boys*. "One in a Million" was the redneck without the filter of a bourgeois liberal satirist.

By the time he sat down with *Interview* in 1992, Axl seemed to be suffering from post-traumatic stress linked to his confession. "One in a Million" become his scarlet letter. He could never again be adored by *every* American. "One in a Million" began the process of transforming Axl Rose into a cult figure, as opposed to a pop star. "I didn't realize it then—but, I know there's people in, say, Louisiana, where giving them that song is like giving them a gun and telling them, 'It's O.K., go shoot those you're preju-diced against.' It's a rough one," Axl said.

Axl has reportedly only performed "One in a Million" on two or three different occasions, and only one of those performances is captured on film. On October 30, 1987, Guns N' Roses performed an acoustic set at legendary punk club CBGB, as the audience laughed along to the unsavory lyrics. I suppose the black comedy was better recieved in front of Axl's base. Once the song was over, they cheered. Slash was probably the only Black person in the room.

Former manager Alan Niven provided his take on "One in a Million" to me in an email:

> I first heard it when Axl sat on his bed and played it for me.
> In that moment, he shapeshifted into a person he was in the

past moment, and instead of someone abrasive, he seemed only vulnerable to me. He was the young soul from Indiana somewhat intimidated by his initial urban experience in L.A. There was nothing gratuitous about his intent or performance in that moment and consequently I backed the band doing it. In the moment I didn't think through the effect on Slash and Ola [Slash's mother]. We don't always make perfect decisions. But then I never really thought of Slash as 'black,' per say [sic]. We used to be less racially divided in England and peoples were just peoples—not African American or otherwise. Slash was born in Hampstead, for heaven's sake. He was more English to me than colored.

"One in a Million" was released on November 30, 1988, when Guns N' Roses were coming off a summer that had transformed them from an exploitation film into the pre-production of "Terminator Rock." It was the eighth song on *G N'R Lies*, a follow-up to *Appetite for Destruction* (an EP), where the wide-eyed romantic from *Midnight Cowboy* had grown horns and returned to the city that had obliterated his sense of small-town normalcy. As payback, he delivered a reactionary ode for the white working class, which was two years before Axl would have the audacity to wear an N.W.A. hat on tour. He wore it in two different music videos, perhaps as an homage to a band whose second album, *Niggaz4Life*, was released in 1991. He also wore it to send a message. Axl, like a lot of other white kids from Middle America, seems to have connected with the abrasiveness and nihilism of West Coast gangster rap. The most memorable photograph of Axl in an N.W.A. hat shows him in a red sports coat, floral tights, and black sunglasses, with a stone-cold expression on his face—every bit the wannabe gangster. At one point, Axl had expressed a vague interest in producing a rap-rock cover of "Welcome to the Jungle" with Ice-T. Rappers, like comedians, offered Axl Rose the grammar to express himself. He chose the wrong source material for his lowbrow expressionism. *The Guardian's* Mark Cooper said in 1989 that, "Like hard rockers Guns N' Roses or such emerging stand-up comedians as Andrew 'Dice' Clay and Sam Kinison, N.W.A. make no attempt to blunt or transcend the savagery of their milieu or to change it. In fact, they appear to revel in it."

"We thought we were so badass," Axl told *New York* magazine in 2006. "N.W.A. came out rapping about this world where you walk out of your house and you get shot. It was just so clear what stupid little white-boy poseurs we were. It was like, 'All right, we can give up the act.' If you're talking about which lifestyle is more hardcore, the one where you get shot always wins." In a 2008 Q&A, Axl said that N.W.A.'s Eazy-E "really wanted to attack the media over attacking me for 'One in a Million.'"

In hindsight, "One in a Million" was a creative miscalculation. It was unquestionably the most counterproductive artistic decision that he had ever made. "The very people he was making fun of loved it," said Doug Goldstein. Axl also lacked the urban authenticity of Ice Cube in 1990's *AmeriKKKa's Most Wanted*. Axl's street poetry didn't have the same proletariat struggle informing it. It was an issue of timing. It felt "studio gangster" for a world-famous celebrity to rage against minorities and homosexuals. Even though he was writing from the perspective of Axl Rose from "nowhere," he recorded it as Axl Rose from the hills of Hollywood. From a storytelling perspective, Axl, as Oscar Wilde had once warned, did not seem to appreciate the dangers of unfiltered sincerity. He was also a millionaire, the CEO of a brand, not a meth-addled gas station attendant.

"One in a Million" cavalierly described Black street hustlers by using the N-word and homosexual sex workers with a homophobic slur (during the peak of AIDS hysteria), which unleashed swift condemnation from the music press. At the same time, Madonna—the most famous woman in the world in 1989—was giving Black artists and gay aesthetes top billing. "When I was a little girl, I wished I was black," she told *Rolling Stone* in 1989. Axl Rose would say that immigrants were transforming American cities into a mini-Iran—that their Persian, for example, sounded like Arabic, which sounded like Hindi, which all sounded like Greek to him. In six minutes, Axl had managed to turn Guns N' Roses into a hate group.

The noteworthy *RIP* photo from 1989 seemed intentionally designed to provoke his progressive critics.

"One in a Million" haunted Axl Rose. It followed him to Los Angeles Memorial Coliseum on October 18, 1989, when Guns N' Roses would open for the Rolling Stones (with Living Colour, an all-Black rock band from New York, as the opener). They would do this for another three nights. The *L.A. Times* described it as a "Showdown at the Coliseum," where the Rolling Stones would pass the torch to Guns N' Roses in a ceremony that would take place in a coliseum seating over seventy thousand plebeians. In his preview in the *L.A. Times* dated October 15, 1989, Robert Hillburn would refer to Guns N' Roses as the "bastard offspring" of the Rolling Stones, "L.A.'s own." The Stones would be described in equally sporting terms as the "defending champions from London."

It seems the media wanted it to be some kind of sporting spectacle. Axl Rose had become a continuous replay of a failed Evel Knievel jump. For nearly a year, "One in a Million" had defecated all over his reputation. Slash and Izzy were zombified junkies. A month earlier, backstage at the 1989 MTV Video Music Awards, Izzy was slugged so hard in the face by Mötley Crüe singer Vince Neil, that Neil's gold bracelet flew off his wrist. The cause of Neil's flying fist has been debated for years, but it seems it had something to do with Izzy either assaulting, sleeping with, or simply flirting with Neil's wife, Sharise Ruddell, an ex–mud wrestler who would nearly charge Izzy with rape. Neil would claim in Mötley Crüe's autobiography, *The Dirt*, that Izzy just collapsed, like a "tipped cow." At the same time, back in L.A., Slash was shooting smack with Mötley Crüe bassist Nikki Sixx. Days before the "Showdown at the Coliseum," Vernon Reid, the guitarist for Living Colour and a member of the Black Rock Coalition, had expressed his discomfort with "One in a Million" during a radio interview. On the first night, after manager Alan Niven had to drag a reluctant Axl out of his apartment with an LAPD escort, Axl stormed the stage with a reversed ball cap and a gaudily visible chip on his shoulder. It was later said that Axl feared a sniper's bullet that day. Moments earlier, he had confronted Reid backstage. "I heard on the radio that you guys got a problem with some of the things I got to say," said Axl, according to writer Danny Sugerman, who was there that night. Axl would then defend himself by saying that he didn't view "you guys as niggers," pointing to the members of Living Colour. The N-word's use in the arts has a complicated history. In 1996, Def Jam founder Russell Simmons said that, "When we say 'nigger' now, it's very positive. Now all white kids who buy into hip-hop culture call each other 'nigger' because they have no history with the word other than something positive . . . When black kids call each other 'a real nigger' or 'my nigger,' it means you walk a certain way . . . have your own culture that you invent so you don't have to buy into the US culture that you're not really a part of. It means we're special. We have our own language." Ice Cube once claimed the word was a "badge of honor."

In *Pryor Convictions*, Richard Pryor said, "Nigger. I decided to take the sting out of it. Nigger. As if saying it over and over again would numb me and everybody else to its wretchedness. Nigger. Said it over and over like a preacher singing hallelujah." Pryor later regretted using the word in his comedy: "To this day I wish I'd never said the word. I felt its lameness. It was misunderstood by people. They didn't get what I was talking about. Neither did I . . . So I vowed never to say it again."

Before one note was played at the Coliseum on October 18, Axl would grab the mic and tell the crowd to "calm down." He was fuming. He also sounded drunk, as he slurred his words into the microphone. "I'm sick and fuckin' tired of this publicity bullshit about our fuckin' song 'One in a Million' with police and niggers and niggers and faggots and radicals and racists . . . "

With uncomfortable levels of aplomb, Axl went on to say that, "I don't give a goddamn fuck what fuckin' color you fuckin' are," he told the massive crowd, who seemed like they were ready to explode in applause, "as long as you ain't no goddamn thief, drug-using, fuckin' crack-selling piece of shit." The crowd roared as if Sam Kinisin had just nailed a punch line on one of his most vociferous rants. He was saying what they were too afraid to.

" . . . [the audio can't be heard in this section] use the word fuckin' nigger but that don't mean every Black man's a fuckin' nigger, that means if you go downtown and some fuckin' asshole's tryin' to sell you free parking for $15 bucks, kick him in the fuckin' nuts." At this point the crowd is becoming unglued, wild, screaming in euphoric unison. It's a group spectacle, and Axl Rose himself is amused. The anger subsides. "I don't give a shit about gay people, either, but I don't need some faggot trying to rape me." We'd heard all this before, of course, but all the negative press had driven Axl further into his "Victory or Death" armor. "Immigrants? I don't care what fuckin' goddam country you're from, you're here in America, just act like it, that's all."

Over 70,000 people were at each show. Axl Rose, for all his bravado and defiance, never performed "One in a Million." The comedian had edited one the most provocative jokes out of his set. Minutes later, before playing "Mr. Brownstone," Axl called out his bandmates in an unprecedented act of public shaming.

"I hate to do this on stage, but I've tried every other fuckin' way. And unless certain people in this band get their shit together [someone in the crowd bursts out in laughter], these will be the last Guns N' Roses shows you'll fuckin' ever see." There was no reaction from the crowd, who was senselessly cheering the whole evening. "Cuz I'm tired of too many people in this organization *dancing with Mr. goddam Brownstone*." His anti-drug, racist, homophobic, right-wing transformation didn't lead to jeers or aghast silence—everyone cheered.

During the performance of "Out Ta Get Me," Axl would walk off the dimly lit stage and collapse onto the floor. It looked like a 10-foot tumble into the photographer's pit. He continued to sing. During the encore of "Paradise City," Axl would add, "There's no need to look for a fuckin' paradise city, cuz none exists."

In their review, the *L.A. Times* would compare Axl to Jim Morrison. "The most striking of the similarities with Morrison . . . is Rose's tendency on stage to act on raw impulse and emotion. He is someone you can't take your eyes off. There is a sense of genuine involvement." The comparison had become so clichéd that Axl, on the third night, would tear into the newspaper. Part of Axl's frustration was that he had begun running Guns N' Roses like Mick Jagger; he was their CEO, and not a single member of the media saw it this way. They viewed Axl like an impulsive junkie, or a redneck cliché, not a business mogul. Axl wanted to be seen like his fashionable *Rolling Stone* cover, while everyone saw the shotgun-wielding "Forgotten American."

On the second night, October 19, a demoralized Slash would appear on stage alone wearing a Betty Ford Clinic T-shirt. He was commanded by Axl to issue a short anti-drug PSA about rock-and-roll excess:

"A lot attention's been brought to this band about some of the excesses that we get into . . . Anyways, last night almost saw the very fuckin' last gig of this band." Slash sounded noticeably nervous and self-disgusted, as if he was tasting his own vomit erupting into his mouth. It felt completely false. It was a confession delivered under forced intimidation and duress. "Smack and all the crap, is just not what it's all about, and Guns N' Roses isn't gonna' be one of those weak fuckin' bands that falls apart over it." The Ayatollah had commanded a "Just Say No" edict, and Slash complied, with his veins likely flowing with smack.

Danny Sugerman's account claims that Axl was backstage telling David Lee Roth that he refused to go on stage until Slash had completed his message. "Three out of four musicians in the band were smacked out of their minds for the show, and everyone thinks *I'm* the junkie," Axl said to Roth. The junkies in his band, the negative press, the flood of accusations of racism and homophobia, the roller-coaster romance with Erin Everly; Axl Rose was watching his world crumble like the city walls that once surrounded Rome. He was screaming at the world to help him. His cries for help were a series of monumentally self-destructive career moves. Axl Rose was yelling into the abyss.

On the night of Slash's self-flagellation, Vernon Reid, the Black guitarist of Living Colour, would criticize Axl's comments from the night before. "If you don't have a problem with gay people, don't call them faggots. If you don't have a problem with Black people, don't call them niggers. I haven't met a nigger in my life."

"I had supported Ax with 'One [in a Million],'" said Niven. "He first played it for me on an acoustic sitting on his bed. In front of my eyes he shape-shifted into the terrified little lad from Lafayette, scared of the Angelino underbelly, and I did not think him of being gratuitous. I thought he had gone to an artistic edge and represented a genuine moment of his experience. It spoke to how we develop our fear of others."

8

STAR-SPANGLED DANGER

"MASTURBATION. REREADING OF LETTERS FROM
UNFAITHFUL WIVES AND GIRLFRIENDS. CLEANING YOUR RIFLE.
FURTHER MASTURBATION. REWIRING WALKMAN."

— *JARHEAD* (2005)

By the summer of 1990, Americans were preparing for a conflict in the Middle East. "This will not be another Vietnam," President Bush promised. Guns N' Roses, as a brand, had been transformed into a lifted pickup truck with a Confederate flag on its hood, and nationalism was suddenly back in vogue. 15 years after Vietnam, CNN was broadcasting footage of air strikes over their targets like video game cutscenes. Just as Guns N' Roses were entering the Use Your Illusion era, American troops had entered the scorching deserts of Saudi Arabia and Kuwait, where they would spend their downtime hydrating and listening to heavy metal. A *New York Times* report from February 21, 1991, would illustrate the converging borders of heavy metal and war: " . . . the night is far from quiet. There is the constant booms of artillery fire and the screeches of fighter planes . . . And on the very border, heavy-metal rock music plays out toward Kuwait through concert-size loudspeakers."

On Christmas Day 1989, when Panamanian dictator Manuel Noriega found refuge in the Vatican's embassy in Panama, US forces strategically placed speakers around the building. It was part of an operation to use heavy-metal music to psychologically torture Noriega (who was an opera lover). He surrendered after three days. The playlist included "Welcome to the Jungle." It sounded like Americans at war.

The music supervisor of Black Hawk Down (2001), Kathy Nelson, told a reporter in 2002 that "Welcome to the Jungle" was requested to be used in the film because it was actually played during the Battle of Mogadishu. In Iraq, circa 2003, giant speakers would blare Metallica in order to Americanize the locals. Were Appetite of Destruction tapes floating around the Saudi Arabia–Kuwait border from 1990-91? One fan told me that their older brother, who served in the Gulf War, would listen to Appetite for Destruction and Metallica's Metallica (The Black Album) on his Walkman; especially Metallica, as parts of the Black Album were being produced during the escalating tensions between the US and Saddam Hussein. "Don't Tread on Me" sounded like Metallica firing tracers at Saddam Hussein's garish palace.

The Gulf War was Generation X's TV war, in prime time, which amounted to a filmic experience of war that was devoid of any serious threat. No film captures the tone of such a suspiciously anticlimactic war better than 2005's Jarhead, which produced an outstanding soundtrack that includes Nirvana's "Something in the Way." But one of the tragedies of Jarhead was the absence of the machine-gun intensity of Appetite for Destruction—which would have beautifully juxtaposed the film's slow-burning landscape shots of burning oil fields and bronze-colored malaise. One can only imagine the adrenaline and terror of hearing "Welcome to the Jungle" (or "Civil War") scoring the postapocalyptic scene of a ripped Jake Gyllenhaal sticking his tongue out to taste the burning oil raining down from above. It was supposed to be used in the pre-battle preparation scene in Black Hawk Down. But due to diplomatic tensions between ex-bandmates Slash and Axl, the song never appeared in the theatrical release of the film, and instead "Falling to Pieces" by Faith No More was used. Unlike Queen, Guns N' Roses never had one of their hits repopularized by Hollywood. The use of "Paradise City" in the party scene of Can't Hardly Wait (1998)— one the best uses of a Guns N' Roses song on film—was originally supposed to be a Van Halen song.

Jarhead gifted us with a Christmas sing-along to Naughty by Nature and a machine-gun bonfire to Public Enemy. As documentary filmmaker Ken Burns put it in a 1991 *New York Times* op-ed, the Gulf War was a "war of talking heads" and a "subsidiary of television." The most memorable visuals included the eerie sight of Baghdad's skyline being lit up by tracer fire, and glossy magazine photos that demonstrated America's need to reclaim its confidence with a conclusive victory after Vietnam. One picture I remember vividly was taken in Denver on February 3, 1991, and depicts a woman named Faith Ramsey in white leggings and a baggy American flag sweater, victoriously waving the American flag on West Colfax Avenue. This was the end of the war. I remember a tanned Hulk Hogan appearing at WrestleMania VII in camo pants and a stars-and-stripes bandana (which took place a month after the ceasefire). I especially recall Axl Rose in concert in 1991, as he leaned back on one leg and screamed into a detached mic stand wearing nothing but combat boots and skintight stars-and-stripes cycling shorts he found in Rio. Axl's soft mane dangled behind him under a blue banana, as colorful stage lights glowed around him like the scattered sparks of a fireworks display. Axl looked like a surrealistic American Gladiator. It remains one of the most spectacular concert photographs of its generation. The credit belongs to photographer Kevin Mazur, who captured it at Rock in Rio II on January 15, 1991. While the photo wasn't taken at their show in Dallas on July 8, 1991, it might as well have been. "Guns N' Roses is just a prime fucking example of freedom of expression," Axl told the Dallas crowd. He could not escape the First Amendment fundamentalism of "One in a Million." By 1991, Axl Rose was in a firefight with the press. He was their Saddam Hussein. *Spin* would report on the wartime state of Guns N' Roses in 1991: "In the midst of wild success, they have been variously drug addicted, paranoid, homophobic, racist, xenophobic, ruthless, violent, a threat to the liberty of the press, and a pain in the ass to almost everyone."

Another Gulf War–era image I recall was taken by Robert John in the Tokyo Dome, as Axl is seen with his legs spread open in a power pose and pointing his fingers towards the sky in his American flag jacket. Except for Christy Turlington saluting us in a Perry Ellis ad, and Madonna being spanked half-naked under an American flag in a 1990 "Rock the Vote" PSA, singing "freedom of speech is as good as sex," rarely has a pop icon sexualized patriotism like Axl did on the Use Your Illusion Tour—where he was transformed into a masculine pinup model. This is the period when gay men began to fawn over images of Axl Rose in patriotic tights. He looked like a masculine Piper Laurie ringing the Liberty Bell in a skimpy Uncle Sam number. Axl even had designer legs, which he honed with daily workouts on his StairMaster. Had the Gulf War extended to the point where the State Department was releasing the names of bombs, one can safely assume that at least one bomb would have been named "Axl," a phallic representation of Axl's hard-on for war (i.e., "Victory or Death").

The year 1991 turned out to be the most pro-wrestling period in the history of Guns N' Roses. This was when Axl Rose should have produced his own workout tape. The period would have a lasting effect on second-generation fans. For one, it pushed Guns N' Roses further away from alienated teenagers who were revolted by Reagan-era jingoism. Even though Axl wasn't intentionally transforming himself into a right-wing avatar, I do think his aesthetic made him appealing to the same demographic that wanted to see America carpet-bomb the Middle East. You won't see very many photos, if any, of Kurt Cobain wrapped in an American flag. Between 1990 and 1993 in particular, Axl looked like he was working for the State Department in an effort to boost morale. While Axl never commented on the Gulf War in any serious way, except for saying cheekily that he "didn't know shit about Iraq" at a concert in Deer Creek, Indiana, in the aftermath of Bush's liberation of Kuwait, he was very clearly waving the flag with the gusto of Faith Ramsey. The collateral damage of Axl Rose's patriotic embrace is complicated, but it did produce some very evocative, star-spangled imagery. It metastasized into popular culture far more aggressively than, for example, Axl Rose in his gray blazer or his riot-grade shotgun. Pouty-lipped singer Lana Del Rey, who was six years old in 1991, would describe Axl in her 2008 demo "Axl Rose Husband" in terms of the masculinity she associated with Axl Rose as a ripped pinup doll (the opposite of Laura Jane Grace, who was attracted to Axl's androgyny). She wanted to pledge her allegiance to him. By the mid-aughts, Axl Rose had become an unfashionable sex symbol for millennial hipsters, who were occasionally rejecting the quirky male leads of the period in favor of hyper-masculinity. It was ironic. A middle-aged Axl Rose had become a sex symbol because of how absurd he looked. He was no longer fashionable, which made him weirdly sexy; he had the brash confidence of an aging MMA fighter on the Vegas Strip. We see this version of Axl on the cover of *Billboard* from February 14, 2009, with his fingers covered in two colossal black stones, and his face is pulled back by thick braids that look like stretched bungee cords. He had begun to look sci-fi. This was the Axl Rose who introduced The Killers at the 2006 MTV VMAs, when he wore a black velvet jacket, bell-bottoms, and a striped shirt that was unbuttoned down to his belly. He looked like what AXE Body Spray smelled like: pungent and toxically unnatural. This is the hyper-masculine cyborg that seduced the interest of Lana Del Rey. She had transformed herself into one of the most alluring faces of her generation. She was a Lynchian expression of manicured beauty combined with the kind of lustful melancholy that oozed off Priscilla Presley's youthful face. Axl Rose was Del Rey's Elvis. She was 27 when they met.

Lana Del Rey was born in New York on June 21, 1985, two weeks after Guns N' Roses played their first show together at the Troubadour. Lana Del Rey wrote and released "Axl Rose Husband" on her customized MySpace page in 2009, under the project name "Sparkle Jump Rope Queen." *Chinese Democracy* premiered on MySpace a year earlier at midnight on November 19, 2008. This is where the obsession grew. It's possible that Lana Del Rey was listening to Guns N' Roses on MySpace. Four years later, the tabloids ran photos of Del Rey and Axl leaving the Chateau Marmont together (on her left arm, Del Rey has a tattoo of "Chateau Marmont" in cursive handwriting). Axl wore bell-bottom designer jeans and a fedora that seemed to go out of style the minute he put it on. We wondered, all of us, if it was a dalliance with Lana Del Rey or a publicity arrangement to reinvigorate Axl's fading sex appeal? Was Del Rey exploiting her lascivious allure like

Elizabeth Taylor's tabloid run in the early '60s? This was Axl Rose's last gallop as an American sex symbol.

Rumors swirled that that two were dating. There are photos from 2012 of Del Ray seen leaving two back-to-back Guns N' Roses shows in L.A. There's another of her backstage at a Guns N' Roses show wearing a Frank Sinatra T-shirt. In 2017, when *Pitchfork* asked her about TMZ dating rumors, she responded that "they're usually true. Maybe where there's smoke there's fire." According to Del Rey herself, she had a fetish for older and slightly more masculine men. She had to go back in time to find such a rock star. Over the years, she would be photographed in various vintage Guns N' Roses T-shirts. Her 2012 EP *Paradise* could be interpreted as a homage to "Paradise City," which is sprinkled with the Americana found in practically every Lana Del Rey record. In the 2017 track "Groupie Love," she describes being the worshipper of a figure who may very well have been Axl Rose.

Del Rey's interest in Axl Rose seemed to grow over the years, as it was reported that she was one of the exclusive few who saw the band reunite on April 1, 2016, at the Troubadour in Los Angeles. On her 2014 album *Ultraviolence*, Lana had a romantic ballad titled "Guns and Roses," where she sings about an elusive heavy-metal love with commitment problems who listens to Guns N' Roses. In her music video for "Born to Die," she would dress her aesthetic using the *star-spangled danger* she had discovered in concert photos of Axl Rose in the '90s. Like Axl, *Born to Die*–era Lana Del Rey seemed to blend both beauty and crime together into a postmodern expression of her influences. Her interpretation of the American dream is tragically decadent. It is doomed and filled with faded photos of vintage cars, JFK assassinations, flags as blankets, Midwestern skies, slow dances, death wishes, guns, and roses. On "Ride," where she is seen in the video wearing a Native American headdress, it is as if she's describing the feeling of speeding down the Pacific Coast Highway and turning up the volume on the First Amendment lunacy of Guns N' Roses. You feel it, like Axl Rose on "One in a Million" or "Back Off Bitch," but without the steely-eyed xenophobia, as she reminds us that she believes in the "country America used to be." She's sentimental, "blessed with beauty and rage," heartfelt, and free—like a postmodern hippie. She was interpreting Americana as a second-generation Guns N' Roses fan, not a first-generation one. The patriotic photo of Axl Rose at Rock in Rio II; his triumphant pose at Wembley Stadium; the Charles Manson T-shirt, and the skintight bicycle shorts had transformed her generation.

Del Ray was from New York but drawn to Hollywood glamour, as if she had lived there in a past life. It seduced her like Charles Manson's psychedelic whispers. When she describes Axl as her "daddy," she sounds like she's asking him to look into her eyes, to see the thunder and rain glimmering in her pupils, and accept her as his *sweet child*. She does it all with a sense of irony that suggests that she appreciated Axl Rose as a serious artist and surreal leftover from the era of "sex, drugs, and rock and roll." Her eyes were like the color of emeralds that burned with the intensity of a "hard, gemlike flame," which is what art critic Walter Pater once described as the secret to an artist's life. For Lana Del Rey, *Use Your Illusion*–era Axl Rose was a poster on her wall when she was coming of age. Axl was the starter who would ignite her "gemlike flame." Axl was Del Rey's Charles Manson, and she was his psychedelic muse who was drawn to his aura and wicked manipulations. Del Ray's fascination with Manson is well-documented. She has a video where she plays a floral Manson girl. She later claimed that she was nearly cast to play Sharon Tate in a James Franco project about the Manson murders. On 2019's *Norman Fucking Rockwell!*, she sings about writing on her walls using blood. Lana Del Rey was the last time anyone cared about who Axl Rose was (or was not) dating.

The connective tissue linking Axl Rose to Manson is best explained in a statement Marilyn Manson made to *Rolling Stone* in 1999:

"From Jesse James to Charles Manson, the media, since their inception, have turned criminals into folk heroes."

In 1969, a few months before the stabbing of a fan at a Rolling Stones concert, Charles Manson had orchestrated the slaying of nine people in L.A.—which would end the "peace and love" illusion of the '60s. Politically, it was the quagmire in Vietnam, but culturally, two events signaled the cultural genocide of the Woodstock generation. First, it was the free Rolling Stones concert at the Altamont Speedway, where a member of the Oakland chapter of the Hells Angels drove a knife into Meredith Hunter as dreamy hippies on LSD goggled at Jagger, who was trying to reason with the lost children: "Brothers and sisters . . . everybody just cool out." Jagger, the voice of reason, was higher than the flower children who were hypnotized by his velvet pants. *Gimme Shelter* (1970) depicted the drug-addicted arrogance and detachment of the Stones at Altamont, which Axl Rose is said to have watched, constantly, learning very little from it.

The Manson murders hadn't simply sprayed blood over the carnations of the '60s; they had planted the seeds that would grow into the darker and more polluted landscape of the '70s. Writer Joan Didion described the feeling of imminent terror that had begun to pollute the sterlized suburbs of Los Angeles: "This mystical flirtation with the idea of 'sin'—this sense that it was possible to go 'too far,' and that many people were doing it— was very much with us in Los Angeles in 1968 and 1969. A demented and seductive vorticial tension was building in the community. The jitters were setting in." Didion remembered receiving a phone call informing her about the murders at Cielo Drive and immediately feeling that "no one was surprised." "The world is getting crazy," said a woman leaving an L.A. courtroom during the 1971 Manson Family trial.

The Use Your Illusion Tour exploded across MTV News the way the Manson Murders bled across newspapers in 1969. It was the "demented and seductive vorticial tension" for those of us who watched and waited for someone to die. It felt like Manson's L.A. being turned into a traveling circus. When the '70s began, there was a pall in the atmosphere (and it wasn't just the thick smog), as the national economy was heading towards a recession. In L.A., the homicide rate was rising at a record rate, while the Bronx began to look like the dystopian prison colony depicted in John Carpenter's *Escape from New York* (1981), which Axl Rose was traveling through in 1980, at 18, in blue jeans and cowboy boots—and where he was accosted by a Black man. In 1980, New York City experienced 1,814 homicides, which was a ridiculously high number. As a comparison, there were just 289 in 2018. Gun ownership in America was rising in the post-Manson era (roughly 47 percent of Americans owned a gun in the '70s).

The year 1980 began as the most violent year in the history of L.A.; it was a city still struggling to wipe Charles Manson's feral stench off its doormats. The Manson murders were one of the ingredients in our *appetite for destruction*. Thirteen years later, Axl Rose would become Generation X's gateway to Manson, covering Manson's psych-folk song "Look at Your Game, Girl" as a hidden track (or "unlisted bonus track") on 1993's punk covers album *The Spaghetti Incident?* Geffen's preemptive damage control included denying that the track even existed (as reported by the *L.A. Times* on November 21, 1993). The track was not included in advances sent out to reviewers. When the album dropped a few days later, it was confirmed that Axl had covered Manson, who was 59 at the time and serving a life sentence in Corcoran State Prison. Manson had bummed around the fringes of the L.A. music scene as early as 1967, when he was a minimally talented hobo with a dark cloud hanging over his sunny propaganda. In 1993, he had finally made it: the biggest arena-rock band on the planet had covered his music and promoted his likeness to millions of teens. Lana Del Rey was watching. We all watched as Charles Manson's face became the most infamous rock T-shirt of the era. Concern mounted that the cover could earn Manson hundreds of thousands of dollars in royalties, as Manson, incredibly, was reported to have secured the copyrights to "Look at Your Game, Girl." According to the California Board of Corrections, for every million copies sold, Manson would have received $62,000 in royalties. "I would hope that if Axl Rose had realized how offensive people would find this, he would not ever have recorded the song in the first place," David Geffen told the *L.A. Times* in 1993. "The fact that Charles Manson would be earning money based on the fame he derived committing one of the most horrific crimes of the 20th century is unthinkable to me." Charles Manson would not earn royalties from Axl Rose covering "Look at Your Game, Girl," though it was rumored that he had written to the band expressing his disappointment that they hadn't asked his permission to cover the song. Geffen Records announced that it would pay $62,000 for every million copies of the album sold to the son of aspiring writer Wojciech Frykowski, one of Manson's victims at the Cielo Drive murders. Bartek Frykowski, Wojciech's 35-year-old son, had children who were Guns N' Roses fans.

Responding to the controversy in the *Chicago Sun-Times*, Richard Roeper described Axl Rose as "no different from Madonna . . . another performer who substitutes various shock-poses for true versatility."

The other members of Guns N' Roses don't officially play on the track, which features a clean acoustic guitar and bongos (apparently someone named "Carlos" or someone using that name as a pseudonym played the acoustic guitar you hear). Some have even suggested that Axl's bandmates were shocked to find out it was even included on the album. In his 2008 autobiography, Slash mentions Charles Manson, but doesn't directly make the connection between Axl and the most famous psychopath of the 20th century. "L.A. was innocent before that [the Manson murders]," Slash wrote in his autobiography. "Those murders signified the end of the utopian ideals of the sixties Flower Power era." Slash's horror fetish was born out of the blood the Manson murders splatted across America's psyche.

But Axl had been drawn to the lyrics and melody of "Look at Your Game, Girl," which is about a woman engaging in self-deception and manipulation, which Axl connected to during his breakup with Stephanie Seymour. Axl would later claim he thought "Look at Your Game, Girl" was originally written by Beach Boys' drummer Dennis Wilson, which was a poorly crafted lie, as the end of the track includes Axl whispering in a low voice, "Thanks, Chas."

"Manson is a part of American culture and history," Axl said in a statement, where he claimed he wore the Manson T-shirt to "make a statement because a lot of people enjoy playing me as the bad guy." Axl was using fashion to protest his sanctimonious critics like Madonna, who would use costumes and religious iconography to antagonize everyone from the Catholic Church to MTV censors. Like Marilyn Manson and to some degree Lana Del Rey after him, Axl Rose was provoking his critics by doubling-down on the scandalousness of his image.

At a concert in 1988, Axl referred to a heckler in the crowd as a "faggot" and then invited him to first, *suck his dick*, and then to fight him in a front of a cheering crowd of fans. In Paris in 1992, he described actor Warren Beatty as a parasite who lived vicariously through young women. After the 53-year-old Beatty dallied around with a 32-year-old Madonna during the filming of *Dick Tracy* (1990), he briefly dated a then-23-year-old glamour model named Stephanie Seymour.

Axl would use the microphone to verbally obliterate Metallica, Kurt Cobain, security guards, air-conditioning repair men, Nirvana hats (which he set on fire), drugs, "alternative" music, "pussies," "psycho bitches," his own mother (who he refers to as a "cunt" in the *Use Your Illusion I* track "Bad Obsession"), his record label (who he invited to also *suck his dick*), the press, and other mainstream rock stars. On the Use Your Illusion Tour, Axl Rose would occasionally end shows by bowing in silky Everlast boxing trunks and a boxing robe. On the *Use Your Illusion* diss track "Get in the Ring," Axl threatened to crush the skulls of female critics, or *bitches*, as he'd describe them, before unleashing a tirade on Bob Guccione Jr., the founder of *Spin* magazine, who he'd invite to "get in the ring" so he could kick his "bitchy little ass." He was a more amplified version of Charles Manson, who sat behind bulletproof glass and told Tom Snyder that he was the reflection of America's dark side. On March 17, 2018, Axl's cover of "Look at Your Game, Girl" was allegedly played at Charles Manson's funeral.

In the way that violent plane crashes and head trauma had deteriorated Howard Hughes's mental health, it seemed the avalanche of bad press, as well as his own obsessive-compulsive need for control, had increased the volume of the civil war raging inside his head. Whatever his actual intentions, by covering Charles Manson and wearing a T-shirt with his face on it, Axl had turned the image of Manson into iconography for Gen X and older millennials, a second generation of Guns N' Roses' fans. An entire generation discovered Axl Rose during a period where he seemed like the visual personification of a crumbling American society, from the Old West to Charles Manson. Lana Del Rey was part of a generation who watched MTV News break the news that Axl Rose had caused riots in several cities, assaulted a neighbor with a bottle of wine (and a piece of chicken), quit, rejoined, and quit his band, again, covered Charles Manson, and wrote a song where he said "nigger" and "faggot"—refused to apologize for it— strutted around the stage in a Confederate flag jacket, and did it all while waving his middle-finger at his critics. "What a guy," said Kurt Loder.

"Mr. and Mrs. America—you are wrong. I am not the King of the Jews nor am I a hippie cult leader," Charles Manson would tell a courtroom on January 26, 1971. "I am what you have made me and the mad dog devil killer fiend leper is a reflection of your society."

9

PUMP UP THE VOLUME

"RISE UP IN THE CAFETERIA AND STAB THEM
WITH YOUR PLASTIC FORKS."

—*PUMP UP THE VOLUME* (1990)

Few films capture the anger of the '90s better than *Pump Up the Volume* (1990). Hard Harry's opening monologue is a testament to how frustrated teens felt during the boom of Gulf War propaganda, suburban malaise, and MTV's corporate version of "rebellion," which was still narcotized by the mood-enhancement, "greed is good" propaganda of the Reagan-era. They were confused, lonely, and alienated by glossy advertising campaigns and Kurt Loder's detached Ray-Bans. They weren't seeing themselves on MTV. There weren't any voices channeling their feelings. "I felt like something was happening," Samantha Mathis—one of the stars of *Pump Up the Volume*—told *The Ringer* in 2020.

We forget that in 1990 all of culture was transmitted through a handful of TV networks, corporate magazines, and film studios. MTV was the Mecca of teen culture. Teenagers felt imprisoned by the gaze of middle-aged, mostly conservative and white TV and studio executives. The early '90s were the hangover from the corporate heavy-metal fantasy of the '80s. Teens wanted their own culture. Hard Harry, played by Christian Slater, was a filmic representation of the frustrated teenager of Gen X; a chronic masturbator who wants to start a revolution from the basement of his parents' house. He can't share his feelings, or connect with his parents, so he talks to his high school through a shortwave pirate radio broadcast. Then he begins to realize he has power. He's a rebel *with a cause*—not Brando rebelling as a form of "psychic masturbation," the antecedent of Axl Rose. The bride in "November Rain" was his "sellout" dad's fantasy—one of Donald Trump's favorite music videos. He wanted to play board games with Clarissa Darling, or get a vanilla milkshake with Brenda Walsh. He didn't want to snort cocaine and roast pigs; he wanted to revolt.

"After all, it's a jungle out there," Hard Harry tells his listeners, as he feeds a cricket to a lizard that crunches on it like a peanut-filled candy bar. "I have no friends, no money, no car . . . there's nothing to do anymore," Harry says.

Teens had begun flicking snot-rockets at the flags that lined suburban streets during the Gulf War. MTV wasn't going to broadcast such dissidence. Axl Rose had become a representation of the status quo. His hyper-American persona and Metallica's right-wing turn on "Don't Tread On Me" had turned the rebels into the fascists. "I am the system," Harry's square dad laments at the kitchen table, worrying that he'd suffocated his radicalism with his necktie.

In the summer of 1990, when *Pump Up the Volume* was released, the biggest music videos were still superficial remnants of MTV amusement park rides. Madonna's "Vogue" paid tribute to glamorous Hollywood publicity photos and bohemian New York City dance culture. Detached from her gaze, suburban kids were doing kickflips on their skateboards and struggling with anxiety disorders. They needed something to see themselves in. MTV videos by Bon Jovi, Poison, Skid Row, Mötley Crüe, and Warrant's innuendo-laden "Cherry Pie" video felt like replays of '80s male fantasies that seemed to never come true for pimple-faced suburban teens. Everything felt like it was a part of the replay culture born in the Reagan era. It felt like MTV was selling an outdated culture. "Society is mutating so rapidly that anybody over the age of 20 really has no idea!" Harry says.

These were the screwed-up and exhausted teens who would never be invited to prom (or opulent rock star weddings). They were looking into the gutters of underground culture, which had begun to leak into the bedrooms of suburbia through hand-drawn lo-fi cassette tape-trading culture. Compilations such as *NME*'s *C86*, the "twee" aesthetic of K Records bands, stapled together fanzines, fashion shows at Evergreen State College, and a DIY (Do It Yourself) ethos had begun to alter the brain chemistry of suburbanites who needed a new sound. Young girls were done being Axl Rose's whipped, gagged, and handcuffed subs.

By 1994, MTV was addressing issues like homophobia, racism, feminism, and AIDS in the San Francisco season of the *Real World*. But between 1980 and 1991, popular culture was ignoring the angry and socially conscious nerd who would become the punks of the *exhausted decade*. They were desperate for something more "reality-based," and Guns N' Roses were now promoting an illusion. They couldn't broadcast their feelings without being crucified, like Hard Harry, so they wanted someone to communicate it for them. This was a generation of malcontents who would eventually mow down their classmates at Columbine High School on April 20, 1999. While Axl Rose was Johnny Lawrence in *Karate Kid* (1984), Kurt Cobain was the bullied outsider seeking revenge. "I always felt that they would vote me 'Most Likely to Kill Everyone at a High School Dance,'" Kurt Cobain told writer Jon Savage in 1993.

This was an American teenager who had begun to vocalize their grievances in scribbled journals and demo tapes that included Liz Phair's *Girly-Sound* recordings, which included the track "Flower," where Phair fantasizes about sexually dominating a male body (the anti-"It's So Easy"). They were finally seeing themselves in unearthed underground tapes by Sonic Youth, Dinosaur Jr., the violent screams of Babes in Toyland, Pixies, and melodic punk records like *Milo Goes to College* (1982), where Milo Aukerman's avatar would become the symbol of the frustrated nerd that Rivers Cuomo would reimagine on 1994's *Weezer* (aka *Blue Album*). Weezer's brattish librarian aesthetic was decorated by in-jokes, cardigan sweaters, queerness, thick horn-rimmed glasses, and an undramatic sense of irony that Guns N' Roses seemed allergic to. They were a big-budget Hollywood film that had suddenly begun to seem as cool as Dee Snider comparing heavy metal to weightlifting. This created a schism between Guns N' Roses and the teenager who wanted something that was "Young Adult"—not just something written for them, but in their voice. By 1991, the volume on teen ghetto-blasters were turned up so loud that corner offices at MTV could hear them. By 1993, when Kurt Cobain sang that he wasn't like them (i.e., popular kids), but that he could pretend, on the verse of "Dumb," he was unleashing the teenage voice that MTV didn't recognize until "Smells Like Teen Spirit" mowed them down like an AR-15.

These were teenage boys (and girls) who were bullied, sexually assaulted, and terrified of men who talked like Axl Rose on "One in a Million." Third-wave feminism, which was as foreign a concept to Axl as Middle Eastern foreign policy, had begun to translate a language that young girls would use to free themselves from the bondage of "It's So Easy." It was too late for Erin Everly, but it wasn't too late for the micro-generation that emerged between Erin Everly being tied and gagged in "It's So Easy," to Bikini Kill arming suburban girls with weapons to defend themselves.

In 1989, Kathleen Hanna (the founder of Bikini Kill) would likely have heard Axl Rose using the N-word on "One in a Million," or at least knew he was the MTV generation's poster boy of misogyny. In 1989, a woman was beaten every 15 seconds. *The Washington Post* wrote about the "invisibility" of the problem, which was hidden behind the pyrotechnics and exploding cum shots of '90s arena-rock, which were denying the brilliance of the Go-Go's in favor of "Terminator Rock." Rockist music critics would never mention the Go-Go's in the same breath as Led Zeppelin and Guns N' Roses (and yet, *Beauty and the Beat* is certainly superior to *Use Your Illusion*). Such prejudice was either undeliberate bad taste or a deliberately chauvinistic attempt to control taste. MTV was offering no alternative to rockist dogma. The feminist insubordination of the "riot grrrl" movement began to metastasize out of smart fanzines like *Jigsaw*, which infected the consciousness of the raped, beaten, and silenced girls who were told they could never start a rock band or mosh in the same circles as the boys. These were the pits that Axl Rose had threatened with the cast-iron edge of his mic stand. Bikini Kill was swinging back. They weren't being muted by MTV, they were being gagged, tied, and strangled by the *entire* music industry; personified in a famous photo of Liz Phair with a strip of duct-tape over her mouth, with smeared eyeliner and tied hands (which was exploring S&M). They viewed Axl Rose the way revolutionaries view monarchs. "I want to scream because no matter how much I scream, no one will listen," which is line from a xeroxed Bikini Kill zine included in Sara Marcus's history of the riot grrrl movement. The high-pitched squawk of Axl Rose was no longer liberating for anyone except his fans.

For young women, the vainglorious image of a libidinous rocker firing pressured water at a blonde bombshell began to symbolize their disgust with the heavy-metal patriarchy. These feelings were coming through on cassette tapes and spoken-word performances by emboldened riot grrrl pioneers like Kathleen Hanna, who was screaming murderous rage from the apartment units of Olympia, Washington. "I'm gonna tell everyone!" Hanna screamed back at the male-dominated same system that had kept Erin Everly subservient. Axl Rose could not put her in bondage or shove a red ball gag in her mouth. She was the vengeful woman in *I Spit on Your Grave (1978)* disemboweling her rapist with a boat propeller and delivering the one-liner: "Suck it, bitch!"

"I hear the revolution . . . the revolution's coming . . . I taste the revolution," Hanna screamed on "Rebel Girl." For a silent majority of teens, Guns N' Roses weren't just "Terminator Rock," they were the machine they wanted to rage against. It was an image firmly based in the gaze of the jocks and headbanging meatheads who were punching their muscle cars and yelling "faggot" at art students wearing Smiths' T-shirts. Punks like Kathleen Hanna felt like political revolutionaries who were subverting the corporate rock monopoly that was entirely dominated by men like Axl Rose. Riot grrrl was egalitarian, free, uncopyrighted, and a movement designed to appeal to the voiceless minority who were being stomped on by popular culture. It wasn't a rejection of eroticism or sexuality; it was a rejection of the way it was being used to handcuff, rather than liberate the female gaze. Axl was the abusive ex-boyfriend whom riot grrrl was exposing.

Bikini Kill was marketed on a local label called Kill Rock Stars, which released a 1991 compilation that included Nirvana, Bratmobile, and Melvins. The name itself, Bikini Kill, sounds even more *anti-glam* than Guns N' Roses in 1987. If reminds you of the experience of Erin Everly in bathing suit, tied up, thrown into a closet, then forcefully penetrated from behind. It was a forceful assault on the wet T-shirts contest of *Slippery When Wet*. By forming Bikini Kill, Kathleen Hanna was allowing women to freely mock Axl Rose, and guys like him, who were still hiring pumped-up models in tiny G-string bikinis to serve them band beer on stage. Bands like Bikini Kill and Hole were furiously trying to be heard through all the "tits and ass" (though Kathleen Hanna and Courtney Love were advertising two very different versions of feminism).

When Nirvana played Seattle's Paramount Theater on Halloween 1991, Kurt picked Bikini Kill to be their opening act. "I sometimes feel that no one's taking the time to write about certain things in rock," Courtney Love told *Melody Maker* in 1991. "There's a certain female point of view that's never been given a chance."

In the early '90s, the pioneers of the sound were producing pop that blended schoolboy innocence with a sandbox of toy instruments that felt inviting to everyone, not just virtuosos molding themselves after Slash. It was the difference between a sloppily arranged stick-and-poke tattoo and intricately designed Ed Hardy sleeve. Bands like Beat Happening, Talulah Gosh, and K Records' Tiger Trap were nontraditional punk that seemed to be mocking the insincerity of masculine arena-rock stars. The kids who weren't cool enough to be in rock bands in the '80s were now rejecting the very definition of cool as something queer, irresponsible, esoteric, unambitious, and fractured. This was the generation of Richard Linklater's *Slacker* (1990).

This was the culture Kurt Cobain emerged from. This was the aesthetic and attitude that would inspire him to wear a yellow ball gown on his first appearance on MTV's *Headbangers Ball*, which ran on November 2, 1991, where he looked like a giant lily flower. He was reimagining androgyny through the gaze of Pacific Northwest feminism and his own slackerism.

The sexual persona of rock was drifting towards the feminine persuasion, and Guns N' Roses, in the most Darwinian sense, could not adapt. With his delicate, glimmering blue eyes and self-emasculated persona, Kurt Cobain would become the poster boy of a culture that felt more comfortable with queerness. When Axl Rose forcefully rejected the gay community as "pro-hetero" rock star, Kurt proclaimed "God is gay" and told a journalist that he once thought he was gay (this was when Guns N' Roses began its transition to "dad rock"). Axl was dating a Victoria's Secret supermodel who wanted to domesticate as his bride, while Kurt Cobain was being dominated by a woman who didn't wear lingerie—a woman who had chipped fingernail polish, acne, and more masculine aggression than most men; Kurt was Courtney's "flower." "I definitely feel closer to the feminine side of the human being than I do the male," Kurt told *Rolling Stone* in 1992. "Or the American idea of what a male is supposed to be. Just watch a beer commercial and you'll see what I mean."

For Kurt Cobain, Guns N' Roses were the beer commercial. By 1993, the Use Your Illusion Tour was decorated with strippers and steel vanity ramps, while Kurt Cobain essentially refused to sexualize women and shunned his own celebrity. His androgyny (he wore a dress in the video for "In Bloom") was a fashionable protest of phallocentric hard rock. He wanted the cheerleaders in the video for "Smells Like Teen Spirit" to look overweight and asexual, while Axl Rose cast a glamour model in "November Rain" to inspire male obsession.

"The only person who believed me was my friend Kurt," Kathleen Hanna said 2013's *The Punk Singer*, as she discussed her experience of being raped. With a can of black spray paint, Kathleen Hanna would spray "Kurt smells like Teen Spirit" on the wall of Cobain's dilapidated apartment (it was the brand of deodorant Kurt wore). Kurt sprayed "God is gay" across walls and pickup trucks; he would go on to graffiti "queer" and "abort Christ" across local four-by-four trucks and abortion clinics. There's a 1986 mug shot of Kurt Cobain, who was arrested for spraying graffiti across the side of a building. It was a form of protest. It was a cruder version of Hard Harry being obnoxiously punk on a pirate radio broadcast.

Kurt and Kathleen's generation were rock's version of *revenge of the nerds*. Bands like Babes in Toyland were screaming at benefit gigs for domestic abuse, while Axl Rose was allegedly abusing Erin Everly. Kurt was writing anti-rape songs like "Polly" as a way of channeling his disgust with misogyny, while Axl was releasing "Back Off Bitch" on *Use Your Illusion I* during the rise of third-wave feminism. Axl had gone from being the bullied redhead at his high school who was called a "faggot" into Ace Merrill from *Stand By Me* (1986).

In a *Rolling Stone* profile on Nirvana in 1991, a friend of Kurt's joked that *Nevermind* sold one copy to every abused child in America. Kurt was one of them. In a February 1993 interview with the *Advocate*, Kurt was asked if Axl reminded him of guys he went to high school with. "Absolutely. Really confused, fucked-up guys. There's not much hope for them." Teenagers were no longer seeing themselves in Guns N' Roses.

Pump Up the Volume was the angry teen unloading on the "confused, fucked-up guys" of his generation. The film begins with the sound of a radio transmitter being powered up, as we float over the unchanging and compact suburbs of Arizona, which represents an America that was becoming what *The New York Times* described in 2001 as a "sprawl beyond sprawl" that had begun to wrap itself around urban jungles. Even the geography was evolving away from the urban jungle that Guns N' Roses had written about. It was Darwinian. It was change happening inside America's very DNA. "You ever get the feeling that everything in America is completely fucked up?" Hard Harry asks his listeners. "You know that feeling? That the whole country is, like, one inch away from saying, 'That's it! Forget it!' Think about it, everything is polluted: the environment, the government, the schools, you name it. Speaking of schools, I was walking the hallowed halls yesterday and I was asking myself . . . is there life after high school?"

High schoolers were asking questions that Axl Rose did not have the emotional intelligence to answer. Nirvana captured why being a Gen-X teenager was such an emotionally draining experience. Punk made them feel less alone. Sonic Youth's "Teenage Riot" would embody the kind of frustration that spoke directly to teens who felt that the rigidity and corporatism of Bush's America were leading them towards a suburban gulag. The Gulf War image of Axl Rose wearing stars-and-stripe shorts, like Slash's Uncle Sam top hat, was their indirect reminder of Bush-era propaganda. Progressive teens were no longer hearing what Guns N' Roses had to say; their fan base was getting older and more rigid in their views. In *Terminator 2* (released on July 3, 1991), when 10-year-old John Connor is working on his dirt bike and listening to Guns N' Roses, it wasn't dishonest. They had become what writer Eric Weisbard described as "fascistic right-wing entertainment."

In *1991: The Year Punk Broke,* Thurston Moore of Sonic Youth documented a scene of thrashing irresponsibility and irreverence that was filled with burnouts and women who refused to be objectified in their sunflower-pattered fabrics, torn tea dresses, and combat boots. The punks were producing a sound that was intentionally unpleasant, noisy, disorienting, and completely allergic to the cinematic high-concept machismo that had become the empire of Guns N' Roses in 1991, which was led by a Julius Caesar reboot, who would roast pigs with his friends and demand "Victory or Death" in his interactions with his bandmates. The emerging punk wave was, as Thurston Moore put it, a way of connecting with disillusioned kids who no longer wanted to compete in the capitalistic illusion of Guns N' Roses. "There's kids out there, and they have the same feelings," said Moore. "It's us and Nirvana, and all the other bands we're going to be playing with. To us, it's like a dare to our parents; it's a dare to the Bush administration; it's a dare to the KGB who have overthrown Gorbachev this morning as we speak. God knows what it's going to be like in the future, and the future for us . . . is a dare. To us, I mean, fuck 'em. Fuck 'em all."

Teens felt hopeless. There was an acidic hole inside them that was also boiling inside Kurt Cobain's stomach when he expressed his teen-angst on songs like "School." In 1991, Sonic Youth's Kim Gordon wore an "I Hate

School" pin on her denim jacket. The last time Guns N' Roses would talk about high school was in the liner notes of *Appetite for Destruction*. The paradox of Axl Rose was that, while he was uncomfortably frank for his views about the women and minorities, he seemed to self-censor when it came to his teenage years. We know very little about it, because it is absent from his work. Kurt allowed his past to rip his guts open and to spill into the stage. The ungraspable beauty of his pain felt literary—which teenagers would consume like novels or lines of prose poetry. As Axl entered his thirties, every teenager in America wanted him to say something, anything, rather than pillorying them with his petulant need to address the scandals of his celebrity.

Axl never wrote a song about his sexually abusive father. Axl's childhood had become his Vietnam (a memory he wanted to erase or rewrite with machine guns). He never fully revealed himself in his music, which burnished his mystique, but also made him an imperceptible figure who felt like a an action star, not a real person. The moment Kurt Cobain felt like he was becoming Axl Rose, when he failed his own purity test, he shot himself up with a toxic amount of heroin and placed a 20-gauge Remington rifle into his maw and blew his brains out. He had become a martyr for emotionally distraught teens, while Axl Rose had begun to age into a reclusive millionaire who seemed eccentric and detached, like Greta Garbo and Howard Hughes. He would become an antique reminder of the last rock stars. Kurt Cobain would become a fashion symbol of *kill rock stars*. Rock was dead-ish.

The colors and fabrics of '90s fashion would translate into "heroin chic" ads by Calvin Klein and photographers like Davide Sorrenti and Corinne Day who seemed to subvert the tanned and voluptuous look of the '80s. The sex appeal of malnourished bodies and racoon eyes would begin to populate the magazine ads of youth culture. By the time Slash quit Guns N' Roses, the heroin chic aesthetic was exploding on MTV with the wood-paneled apartment of Fiona Apple's "Criminal," where the singer looked smacked out and vulnerable like a Nan Goldin snapshot of a "Heart Shaped Bruise."

The changes in the look and smell of popular culture came from the *grunging* of rock and roll. The fragrances were becoming more androgynous, as bathroom shelves began to smell fresher, more feminine, like Calvin Klein's One and Eternity, Armani's Acqua di Gio, and drugstore perfumes like Liz Claiborne's Curve. If there were a perfume that captured what Guns N' Roses smelled like, it was Christian Dior's Poison, which had a very heavy smell that was overwhelming, loud, and as dizzyingly old-fashioned as the makeup counter at a department store. Teen spirit, if you will, smelled like an arrangement of sunflowers over the moth-holed threads of thrifted flannel shirts.

America was going back to the '60s, as Guns N' Roses were trapped in the California house parties of the '80s: orgies, sparkling champagne baths, and full-breasted Domino's pizza delivery girls ("Dominos and tits," Axl would describe it on stage). The youth fashion had begun to bloom underground inside thrift shops that would eventually decorate high-fashion runways with ripped jeans, wool sweaters, untucked flannels, unwashed hair, working boots, and a lumberjack aesthetic that was a lot of things, but it was also very anti-metal.

Axl was at least semi-aware of the fact that his world was being drowned by a tsunami of denim and bleach. He made slight modifications to surf the wave. He had begun to toy with grunge in the video for "Don't Cry," where he wore a Nirvana hat and untucked flannel shirt. He also wore a Nirvana hat at Dublin Airport on May 14, 1992. He stopped shaving and began wearing combat boots, and at the Rock and Roll Hall of Fame ceremony in January 1994, Axl would perform alongside Bruce Springsteen in a baggy flannel shirt and light blue jeans. He even switched his custom basketball shoes for brown working boots. He looked like Bridget Fonda as the coffee barista from *Singles* (1992). But in 1992, when he was hypnotized by the high-fashion aura of Stephanie Seymour, Axl was photographed in tinted glasses and smart Versace suits, and attending red carpet events in designer jeans. He even agreed to be photographed by Herb Ritts, who portrayed him as a sexual object in black-and-white photos that were featured in *Rolling Stone* in April 1992 (which ran in near conjunction with Nirvana gracing the cover with a sloppy and raw-looking Kurt Cobain wearing a "Corporate Magazines Still Suck" T-shirt). While Nirvana were mocking *Rolling Stone* on its own cover, which felt sarcastic and absurdist, Axl Rose was being unnecessarily blunt in songs like "Get in the Ring," where he sounded like smoke was exiting his ears. Kurt Cobain's "war against the media" was more subversive and cunning. It felt like something Andy Kaufman would have done. Axl Rose was a rerun of Morton Downey Jr.

On his *Rolling Stone* cover dated April 2, 1992, Axl looked like an airbrushed supermodel with sculpted features and designer hair. The image looked diffused and sophisticated. For Ritts, he was translating the image of a rock star into something idealized and modern. In a series of black-and-white photos, Axl is shirtless, ripped like the factory workers in Madonna's "Express Yourself." He's also pictured in unbuttoned jeans or floral leggings, and his legs rivaled the flawless beauty of Michelangelo's "David." Like a shirtless Jim Morrison being captured by Joel Brodsky in 1967, the eroticism of Axl Rose had been eternally preserved in the photographs of Herb Ritts. The stylish images seemed creatively inspired by the more refined eye of Stephanie Seymour (a close friend of Ritts), who wanted to transform Axl through the lens of Ritts's stylish portraiture, where Axl is seen as an Adonis, the way Basil fawned over every detail of Dorian Gray's natural face in Wilde's novel. Axl's hair looks conditioned and straightened into a soft, but immovable mold. He looks like a lonely sculpture sitting inside an artist's studio. Where is his band? British journalist Bryan Appleyard wrote of Ritts: "It is difficult to say which came first—Ritts or the gym cult—but they are the same thing." Ritts's photos of Axl looked like a Calvin Klein advertisement, where Axl glows under Ritts's studio lights, where you can almost hear the sound of his muscles crunching in a synchronized dance with Ritts's camera. The fact that Ritts was using his camera to objectify a self-confessed "pro-hetero" male made the photos of Axl even more provocative (particular after a majority of the public knew Ritts was gay). I don't think Axl would have sat for him if he had known that Ritts was not only gay but also HIV positive.

On his cover, dated April 16, 1992, Kurt Cobain looked like he'd styled his strawberry-blond bedhead with petroleum jelly. He's surrounded by his bandmates—never alone, like Axl—standing in a pastoral landscape from a forgotten part of America (it was snapped near Melbourne, Australia). He looks like a feral junkie who hitched a train into Layette, Indiana. The photo was taken by Mark Seliger, who said that Kurt was experiencing stomach pains that day.

Just as Axl Rose was being refashioned into a hairless and ripped glamour model, which felt inspired by Stephanie Seymour, Courtney Love was actively using the press to present supermodels as the arm candy of dim hair-metal bros. In a now-notorious 1992 *Vanity Fair* profile by journalist Lynn Hirschberg, it seemed Kurt took pleasure being the submissive beau to Courtney Love. Their relationship was the reverse of Axl and Erin's, where Axl was forcefully in the dominant position. Kurt looked fragile and tired in the presence of a taller and more verbally gregarious Courtney. He also seemed comforted by her boldness and Madonna-esque desire for fame, which he lacked.

By 1992, Courtney had begun to use the press to outmuscle the careerist rock stars of the patriarchy. They had what she wanted, and Courtney would turn her ambition into a primal vendetta that was either shared by Kurt or imposed upon him. We'll never know for sure. But the cultural war between Guns N' Roses and Nirvana had begun to bloom in the fall of 1991, with Courtney Love engineering her fame machine by channeling the pre-code sexpot. If Erin Everly was the popular prom queen, then Courtney Love was the exotic vamp with blood dripping down her bottom lip.

The disturbed beauty queen who appears on the cover of *Live Through This*, with her eyeliner dipping down her face—this is how Courtney Love wanted the world to interpret her aggressively sloppy form of feminism. In a 1996 *New York Magazine* feature titled "Feminism Rocks," writer Kim France wrote that, "While our culture admires the angry young man, who is perceived as heroic and sexy, it can't find anything but scorn for the angry young woman, who is seen as emasculating and bitter." For Courtney

Love, Axl Rose was a symbol of a culture that viewed angry women—certainly those fronting rock bands—as "psycho bitches." Courtney Love put on her symbolic Charles Manson T-shirt and doubled-down on the prejudice. She was the female Axl Rose with a much more astute grasp of the Warholian fame game. Hole wasn't simply competing to produce a record that was comparable to *Nevermind*, it was caustically screaming at the kinds of rock stars who had suggested that women could not be rock stars. By the mid-1990s, a grieving Courtney had performed at the VMAs in a pink satin dress and barefooted. She had thrown her compact at Madonna on live television. She was climbing the ladder of success with the ruthless guile and gutter-sniping allure of Barbara Stanwyck in *Baby Face* (1933). As a pop star, Courtney Love outshone both Kurt Cobain and Axl Rose.

Kurt and Courtney would proceed to portray Axl as a kind of racist P.E. teacher, while Kurt was the introvert who didn't like to play sports. It was a deliciously cinematic contrast. Kurt and Courtney were using the blowback of the racist and homophobic lyrics of "One in a Million" to troll Axl Rose. He was incapable of a counterpunch that didn't make him seem even more like the racist P.E. teacher. It was tragicomic watching the bully get bullied. On stage, Kurt would often be seen wearing torn blue jeans, dresses, cardigan sweaters, drugstore sunglasses, oversized flannel shirts, and striped wool sweaters. His aesthetic would capture his relationship with his record label, where Kurt would play the part of damaged adolescent with a mogul for a "daddy." At the *Unplugged* taping, Kurt sarcastically tells a story of how he'd asked David Geffen to buy him Lead Belly's half-million-dollar guitar, but that daddy had said no. Kurt's desire to buy the guitar would come up in a 1993 interview with *Spin*, where he seemed as if he was alluding to Axl: "I just wish there was some really rich rock star I could borrow the cash from."

The thrifted *populism* ensured that the whole world viewed Axl Rose as the "really rich rock star," which would turn their feud in class warfare. Convincing the world that he was still part of the proletariat was both a PR strategy and a defense mechanism for Kurt. When Courtney bought the couple a Lexus, Kurt asked her to return it. At the peak of his celebrity, Kurt would buy a 1965 Dodge Dart for $2,500, while Axl would buy a Ferrari and a convertible BMW. For Kurt, it was a conscious move to remove himself from the corporate rock image that had begun to weigh heavily on him. For Axl, everything from his mansion in Malibu, the supermodels at his disposal, sports cars, the expensive workout equipment, private gym, private zoo, costly jewelry, custom-tailored jackets, designer sunglasses—all of it was a display of power and his acceptance of his role as America's biggest corporate rock star.

Axl viewed himself like an athlete who would use his wealth to reflect his physical prowess. When Kurt asked Geffen for an unusually high budget to produce the full-spectrum technicolor video for the "Heart-Shaped Box" video, he was, at least in his mind, using corporate money to create subversive art. Axl Rose was using corporate money to produce action movies, themed parties, Versace suits, lawsuits, and a traveling psychic who would analyze auras for him.

Kurt felt that in order to deodorize the stench of his own celebrity, he needed to present himself as the antithesis of the corporate-rock sellouts. In the same way that Guns N' Roses had used Poison's aesthetic to portray themselves as "anti-glam," Kurt and Courtney had used Axl's arena-rock persona to portray themselves as more punk. Axl's response would make him look both guilty and desperately unfashionable. He wasn't in on the joke. He was being roasted and could not find a way to work through the embarrassment of feeling uncool. Axl did not have a talent for self-mockery; his sensitivity made him incapable of possessing the sly irreverence required to outwit Kurt and Courtney on the schoolyard. It was *Revenge of the Nerds* (1984), and Axl Rose was Ogre in a spelling bee. He was being dismantled by their witticism, which made him feel both unmanly and unintellectual. Axl responded by literally burning a Nirvana hat on stage and referring to them as a "bunch of pussies." For teenagers who were being called "pussies" by jocks and metalheads, Axl had become their oppressors. He had become Kevin's older brother from *Home Alone*

(1990), Buzz McCallister, who would refer to his alienated younger brother as a "phlegm-wad" and threaten to feed him to his tarantula.

One of Courtney's most underappreciated contributions to the rise of grunge as a fashion statement was her unofficial role as the image-maker of Kurt Cobain. Courtney understood, as Axl and Slash had in 1987, that the only way to become the dominant force in music was to control the narrative. In September 1991, the same month that Nirvana would release *Nevermind* and Guns N' Roses would release *Use Your Illusion*, Hole released *Pretty on the Inside*. Courtney Love knew that the only way for Hole to have their scream heard was to penetrate the ruling class that was muting it. What better way to promote *Pretty on the Inside* to abused *teenage whores* ("Teenage Whore" is the first track on *Pretty on the Inside*) than to feud with their symbolic abusers, Axl Rose and his supermodel girlfriend, Stephanie Seymour, who looked so infuriatingly perfect in the Bruce Weber photos.

"That guy has on a Nirvana T-shirt," a grossed-out Kurt is quoted as saying in *Vanity Fair*, after seeing a guy in heavy-metal regalia getting out of a van. "I'm used to it now," he said. When Kurt found out that men in Reno were listening to "Polly," while raping a young girl—the song was written about the abduction and rape of a 14-year-old Tacoma girl in 1987—he addressed it in the liner notes of 1992's *Incesticide*: "Last year, a girl was raped by two wastes of sperm and eggs while they sang the lyrics to our song 'Polly.' I have a hard time carrying on knowing there are plankton like that in our audience. Sorry to be so anally P.C. but that's the way I feel." Being "anally P.C." was a future that Kurt Cobain was shaping. Axl Rose's political-incorrectness on "One in a Million" seemed comically outdated by 1991. Kurt's music was driven by his protest of the patriarchy and racism he witnessed in his hometown of Aberdeen, Washington. If, at any moment, he felt like his music was being appropriated by the people he was protesting, Kurt would consider ending Nirvana, while Axl only vaguely cared—as per *Interview*, 1992—that "One in a Million" had become an anthem for white nationalists. Axl Rose's activism was to use the First Amendment like a baseball bat. Privately, Kurt Cobain thought

Axl Rose was a joke; publicly he used him to score political points. "We're not your typical Guns N' Roses type of band that has absolutely nothing to say," Kurt told *Seconds* at some point between 1991 and 1992.

Hirschberg's *Vanity Fair* profile revealed that Nirvana refused to play Axl's 30th birthday. By the fall of 1992, the feud between Nirvana and Guns N' Roses had become mainstream gossip. Hirschberg would describe Courtney Love as possessing a "train-wreck personality" that was ambitiously chasing fame like the rock stars she would mock for being overly Hollywood. This grand hypocrisy would eventually transform Courtney into the villain of this story. Courtney was portrayed as a grabby fame monster who was recklessly shooting up heroin while she was pregnant. At a show in 1992, Axl would use the *Vanity Fair* profile to humiliate Kurt and Courtney. But jousting with such insolent punks required a level of social intelligence that Axl Rose lacked. He could not camouflage his inferiority complex. He was being targeted by a new kind of bully in horn-rimmed glasses and a Daniel Johnston T-shirt. They were forcing Axl Rose to engage in unintentional self-mockery. He became the dad ranting from his kitchen table with a can of Miller Lite clenched firmly in his fist: "Kurt Cobain is a fucking junkie with a junkie wife. And if the baby's born deformed, I think they both ought to go to prison." He sounded vaguely pro life. He would echo these statements in a *Metallix* interview where he said, "They [Nirvana] would rather sit at home and shoot heroin with their bitch wives than tour with us."

His anti-drug rants would backfire in a hundred different directions. By 1993, Quentin Tarantino was considering casting Kurt and Courtney as a drug-dealing couple in *Pulp Fiction* (1994). Tarantino is thanked in the liner notes of *In Utero*. By 1993, Axl Rose had no appeal in the eyes of hipsters or aesthetes. The cultural civil war between Nirvana and Guns N' Roses helped turn Kurt and Courtney into an identity-marker for the culturati. The more Axl criticized Nirvana for being druggies and used "alternative" as a pejorative, the more he seemed like the P.E. teacher with mesh shorts and sculpted calves.

In a *Rolling Stone* interview from 1994, Kurt would describe a specific kind of rock fan, which would represent the Guns N' Roses audience as a "Neanderthal with a mustache, out of his mind, drunk." In the *Advocate*, this is how Kurt responded when asked about Guns N' Roses fans coming to Nirvana shows:

> When we played that No on 9 benefit in Portland . . . some kid jumped onstage and said, "Hey, man, Guns N' Roses plays awesome music, and Nirvana plays awesome music. Let's just get along and work things out, man!" And I just couldn't help but say, "No, kid, you're really wrong. Those people are total sexist jerks, and the reason we're playing this show is to fight homophobia in a real small way. The guy [Axl Rose] is a fucking sexist and a racist and a homophobe, and you can't be on his side and be on our side. I'm sorry that I have to divide this up like this, but it's something you can't ignore. And besides, they can't write good music.

In a 1990 interview with Kurt Loder, Axl Rose, seemingly at his most relaxed and self-reflective, sounded pensive about how his music was being received by his more "neanderthal" fans.

"It was real hard knowing some of these kids go, 'yeah! I drink and drive, and everything's in sight,' said Axl, who was commenting on the lyrics of "It's So Easy." "It's hard when you know you're doing your material, and a majority of your audience isn't getting what you meant."

Axl didn't necessarily want Kurt's moral approval. But he *desperately* wanted Kurt to acknowledge him as an artist. The closest Axl ever got to this was in Kurt's 1994 suicide note: "When we're back stage and the lights go out and the manic roar of the crowds begins, it doesn't affect me the way in which it did for Freddie Mercury, who seemed to love, relish in the the love and adoration from the crowd which is something I totally admire and envy." After Axl heard an early copy of *Nevermind* in 1991, he expressed an interest in meeting the person behind an album that was selling 1.2 million copies per month less than four months after its release.

Kurt Cobain, who was described by music journalist Jessica Hopper as the "anointed grunge Buddha," declined the meeting. When Axl asked Nirvana to open for them, Kurt declined and followed by deriding Axl in the media just to make sure America knew that Nirvana was nothing like Guns N' Roses. Kurt's contempt for heavy metal had been projected onto Axl, partially because of "One in a Million," but also his personal connection to riot grrrl. Kurt wasn't simply presenting a philosophical difference between Nirvana and Guns N' Roses, he was advancing a socioeconomic argument, too. He'd use the interview in the *Advocate* to paint the portrait that he lived in a modest home and shopped at secondhand shops; that his annual expenses were "definitely not what Axl spends a year." Kurt's class warfare was devastating, and Axl was paralyzed by rage. And so, he called Kurt a "pussy," set a Nirvana hat on fire, and became the angry ex-boyfriend of MTV. Kurt made Axl lose his confidence. He would retreat further into his skin. Speaking privately to friends in 2016, Axl Rose said that all the bands that he adored, never liked him back. It was very tragic. I believe Axl Rose wanted to be loved by Kurt Cobain. I don't believe Axl Rose ever recovered from the cultural abandonment. Kurt Cobain had ghosted him for all of eternity.

Then again, Axl Rose had put his art in a subordinate position to his ego. Every night on the Use Your Illusion Tour, Axl's brother and sister would produce garishly themed parties that had dismantled all the anti-glam PR the band had orchestrated between 1986 and 1988. There were parties themed around fashion designer Gianni Versace and Roman orgies, where oiled hardbodies would deliver a roasted pig that Axl would feast on. The Use Your Illusion Tour crew in 1992 is said to have been composed of 80 people, including four bodyguards, a masseuse, strippers, a psychic, therapist, and one "thoroughbred horse" named Axl Rose, who was taking 60 vitamins a day and working with a chiropractor who would cranially adjust him during shows. It was a traveling pro-wrestling promotion that was designed with a steel stage covered in a jumbo Guns N' Roses logo, which was framed by two blown-up banners covered with Mark Kostabi's "art." The aesthetic of the Use Your Illusion Tour was like a high-end music festival blended with an industrialized stunt show at Universal Studios. The volume was being turned up on the effects, not that *heartfelt feeling* that had taken Guns N' Roses from the streets to the top of the charts in 1988. The merger of "opposing elements" that had made Guns N' Roses so intoxicating had been consolidated into a single dictator's vision.

During his MTV *Unplugged* performance in 1993, Kurt would ask that set be dressed in black candles, stargazer lilies, and red velvet curtains. It looked like a vanitas painting of someone foreshadowing their decay. In his own diary, there's a treatment for the video "Rape Me," where Kurt notes his desire to see "vaginal flowers" like orchids and lilies blooming and withering in a time-lapse effect. By this point in his career, Kurt had the aura of a punk martyr who was going to die for the sins of arena-rockers like Axl Rose. In response, perhaps subconsciously, Axl would wear a "Kill Your Idols" T-shirt that depicted Christ in a crown of thorns. He was also expressing his indignation with the media, like Sonic Youth before him, who wrote "Kill Yr. Idols" in 1983 after *Village Voice* critic Robert Christgau gave them a negative review. Axl wasn't simply asking his audience to think for themselves (his version of Charles Barkley's "I Am Not a Role Model" ad); he was providing a comment on the sanctification of figures like Kurt Cobain. Axl didn't want to be worshipped, but I believe he wanted to be appreciated, held, mothered, and when he felt abandoned, he would crawl deeper into his own compulsions and paranoia—his persecution complex became a mask.

The decline of Guns N' Roses has been credited to a number of watershed moments, which include the negative press generated by "One in a Million," Axl's meltdown at the Coliseum, his mental health problems, poor management, legal disputes, and creative differences in the follow-up to *Use Your Illusion*. But the 1992 MTV Video Music Awards foreshadowed their cultural downfall in a vivid, multi-colored trailer-park showdown in Los Angeles. The VMAs took place on September 9 at UCLA's Pauley Pavilion. It was a night that would honor Guns N' Roses with the Michael Jackson Video Vanguard Award, which Nirvana mocked by having a Michael Jackson impersonator accept their award for "Best Alternative" video.

The VMAs that year were highlighted by the two contrasting performances, where Guns N' Roses wore elaborate outfits, and Nirvana wore the same exact clothes they were wearing the night before. Standing next to the trailer in an adorably brattish photo by Kevin Mazur, Nirvana look like tourists; bassist Krist Novoselic wore a broken camera over his shoulder. There are almost no photos of Guns N' Roses standing together backstage. Axl was separated from his band for most of the night. But there was a grand performance in the works, where Axl sat behind a piano in an antique-looking military jacket, rising from underneath the stage on a hydraulic lift connected to a custom Harley-Davidson piano seat. Axl played the role of a stoic monarch, as he sat across from Elton John, whom he would cover during a concert wearing a "One in a Million" T-shirt and red bandana, as he'd sing an acapella version of Elton John's 1992 hit "The One." Just as Axl was being accused of being a homophobe, he was also becoming more public about his adoration for Elton John. On the stage of the 1992 VMAs, the two grand pianos would rise onto the stage accompanied by the sound of a rumbling Harley-Davidson motor. It was the second duet between Axl Rose and Elton John. It felt as if Elton wanted America to forgive Axl for "One in a Million." Slash would end their performance of "November Rain" by soloing on top of a piano.

It was orchestrated and beautifully costumed, like an opera. It even had an Elton John PSA: Axl Rose doesn't hate gay people. Axl was combining grandiosity with a kind of theatrical panache that Kurt would defy on the same stage, when he ended Nirvana's shambolic performance by impaling the neck of his guitar into a stage amp. Nirvana played by first improvising with a few chords of "Rape Me," which startled the producers at MTV. They continued to play a messy version of "Lithium," which ended with bassist Kurt Novoselic concussing himself with his own tossed bass guitar. Drummer Dave Grohl ran over the microphone and taunted Axl: "Hi, Axl! Hi, Axl! Where's Axl? Hi, Axl! Hi, Axl!" They were being purposefully gauche. By knocking Michael Jackson's *Dangerous* off the top of *Billboard*'s pop charts, Kurt had become consumed by the burden of responsibility associated with criticizing corporate rock. Any artist whom he perceived to be a corporate product, he would immediately skewer in order to live up to his unofficial mandate as savior of punk—the leader of an anti-glam insurgency. Michael Azerrad described Nirvana in 1992 as, "no glamour . . . no glamour at all, in fact." There were, like Guns N' Roses in 1987, an *anti-glam* band

One of the important aesthetic differences between Nirvana and Guns N' Roses can be seen in the photos of Kurt Cobain's smashed Stratocasters and Epiphones (his favorite was a Fender Mustang), as compared to Slash, who viewed his guitars his beautifully maintained automobiles, as opposed to toys. "We're just musically and rhythmically retarded," Kurt Cobain told *Guitar World* in 1992. "We play so hard that we can't tune our guitars fast enough. People can relate to that."

MTV's Kurt Loder would later describe the cultural importance of the 1992 VMAs as "two worlds colliding," where the establishment was being publicity challenged by the new wave. It was an intensely political clash between two artists, their bands, and America's two warring factions. "In my dreams," Kurt Cobain told *Spin* in 1993, "there's always this apoca-lyptic war going on between the right and left wing."

On September 17, 1991, Guns N' Roses released *Use Your Illusion I* and *II* on the same day, as two separate albums (a blue and yellow CD, 75 minutes and $15.98 each). "No, I've never really looked at it as two separate albums," Axl told *Musician* in 1992. "That was Geffen Records' marketing plan. I've always looked at it as an entire package. For me it fits together perfectly for the 30 songs in a row. Everything that we decided to record for the album made it."

By 1991, Izzy Stradlin would begin to protest Axl's increasingly tyran-nical behavior in an issue of *Details*: "Nowadays, we just let Axl do pretty much what he feels he has to do, 'cause he'll only do it anyway. And if it doesn't work, maybe he might learn something. Then maybe we can fix it." Two years later, Izzy would be touring with Rastafarian dreadlocks in a loose and completely anti-commercial band called the Ju Ju Hounds. He had divorced himself completely of the arena-rock persona. The Ju Ju Hounds were a band that Kurt Cobain might have liked.

Axl Rose had lost Izzy Stradlin's endorsement, too. Izzy officially exited Guns N' Roses on November 7, 1991. He would go on to compose 11 solo albums that seemed pathologically minimalistic. "Because the album reached such gargantuan proportions as far as the production and complexity and the massive expectations," Slash told *Music Radar* in 2011 that "Izzy started to bow out. He was harder to find, because that was against his rock & roll philosophy, which I totally agree with." His childhood best friend was abandoning him at roughly the same time that Kurt Cobain was refusing to have anything to do with him. "Bolting is Izzy's defense mechanism," Slash wrote in his autobiography. "It just got to the point that Axl, he was going to run the show," Izzy told the Lafayette *Journal & Courier* in 1993. "He was going to run Guns N' Roses. I just decided I wasn't going to be a part of it." Izzy Stradlin became sober at age 27, which is the age Kurt Cobain would take his life. "That was my low point. Around '89, I had bottomed out," Izzy told TuneCore in 2006. By 1991, Guns N' Roses had evolved into Axl Rose's vanity project. The cover art he would choose for *Use Your Illusion* didn't present a protest or subversive statement. It did not depict images of violence, rape, or lowbrow art. It was a misguided attempt at appealing to a nose-pinching culturati that had as much interest in Guns N' Roses as NASCAR.

The cover art for *Use Your Illusion I* and *II* was a Mark Kostabi enigmatic painting of Raphael's *School of Athens*, while Nirvana's *Nevermind* portrayed the minimalistic image of a baby floating under water. Kostabli's cover would make *Use Your Illusion I* and *II* seem like the world's most expensive use of clip art. Kostabi was a student of Warhol who used an acrylic-on-canvas method to produce paintings that would sell for an average of $30,000. He had perfected a kind of assembly-line process of painting that would allow to him to buy a million-dollar condo in New York and a three-floor 15,000-square-foot studio on West 38th Street called "Kostabi World," located in Manhattan's garment district, where he produced paintings of faceless figures placed into tacky settings that made political and social statements. Kostabi was also known as a commercial machine who valued commerce in ways other artists generally did not.

His artwork appeared in tabloids and an episode of *Miami Vice*. They were production-line paintings that Kostabi referred to as "trash"; some of them were even accused of being outright forgeries. This is the artist that seduced Axl Rose. It's been reported that Axl paid a small fortune for the painting, which is a copy that's been pulled from a detail of Raphael's *School of Athens* (available in the public domain).

"Modern art is a con," Kostabi once said, "and I'm the world's greatest con artist." He was rarely invited into the private halls of the contemporary art intelligentsia. His mission was to make as much money as possible by expending the least amount of effort. Each floor of Kostabi's studio was used to plan and develop his art by essentially repurposing classic works through his own gaze. He's been described as a "bad boy," a "con artist," and the "bastard child" of Andy Warhol. Kostabi even had a "think tank," where he'd brainstorm ideas for celebrity clients. One of those clients was Axl Rose, who walked into a gallery on Rodeo Drive in 1991 and discovered a painting titled "Use Your Illusion." While Guns N' Roses were dabbling in the bourgeois boho-dance of modern art, Nirvana snapped photos at the bottom of a public pool in Pasadena. They were adolescent art students; CalArts students with their hands covered in chipped paint, while Guns N' Roses were becoming art collectors who could not differentiate between a Jackson Pollock and a crime scene.

Axl would try to explain Kostabi during a *Rockline* interview in 1992: "I also wanted to use that picture because it was art. It was art that has a lot of controversy around it because of Kostabi's methods of actually doing the paintings. The background was taken from a very old painting, but it's still something really nice to look at. I don't know how I feel about the way it was done, I just know I like it . . . didn't expect that from us, did you?"

A *Details* cover from December 1991 was titled, "Guns N' Roses: The Art of Falling Apart." On the road with Guns N' Roses, drummer Matt Sorum would describe what seemed like a Penelope Spheeris mockumentary: "Every night's a fuckin' party, man" he told *Details*. "Chicks, beers, you name it . . . Take any chick you want, man. It's like being a kid in a candy store." One night at the Four Seasons Hotel in Toronto, Sorum jumped up and grabbed hold of a chandelier in his room. "It wasn't like the movies," he told *Rolling Stone* in 1991. "I fell on my ass."

Guns N' Roses were touring the globe in a luxurious chartered MGM Grand 727. They had become a big-budgeted version of one of the metal bands from *The Decline of Western Civilization Part II: The Metal Years*. Axl was listening to the new wave, but disinterested in riding it. He could hear it in the corporate offices of Geffen Records, which had signed Nirvana in 1991. In fact, Axl was one of the first mainstream rock stars to endorse grunge bands like Soundgarden. Axl promoted Nirvana in a *Musician* interview from June 1992: "I think that the world has gotten really bored, really fed up and really pent up with frustration, and that comes through in Nirvana. I think a lot of people were aware of that feeling and he happened to find the song that touched it and was able to let that feeling out in people. And I'd like to do anything I can to support it. That's why we want them to play with us."

They would never play together. During the decade-long gestation period of *Chinese Democracy*, Axl seemed like he was scrambling to regain his relevancy. Grunge had made him feel anachronistic, so he began to overcompensate. He was an artist constantly trying to define a culture that was moving past him at warp speed. Axl Rose was trying to reinvent himself as a cyberpunk studio wiz, like Trent Reznor, as opposed to the messianic rock star Kurt Cobain had mocked. In the process, he depersonalized his sound. "There is the desire definitely to do it, to get over some of the hump of the people that are trying to keep you in the past," Axl told *Rolling Stone*'s David Wild in 1999. "Axl was trying to respond to the different waves of music, and it seemed like he was trying to wait out the changes to capture something new," Wild said. "Past success weighed on him heavily," he added. Though I would argue that it wasn't simply past success, but the perception that he was outdated, which would become catalyst for his need to continuously rearrange and edit the tracks on *Chinese Democracy* through an assembly line of musicians. DJ Ashba, Bumblefoot, Buckethead, and NIN's Robin Finck were all part of the reconstruction of Axl Rose from hard-rocker into industrial-rock fetishist. A coherent version of Guns N' Roses seemed to exist only in Axl Rose's dystopian imagination. On a deeply psychological level, I believe Axl Rose wanted to create avant-garde music that would be appreciated by art critics and indie music fans the way *In Utero* had. He wanted to gain the artistic acceptance that Kurt Cobain had denied him.

After eight years of dodging the mainstream glare of MTV, Axl Rose would emerge onto the stage of the 2002 MTV Video Music Awards, and stumble to convince the world that he had become vogue again. The last time Axl had appeared on television was in the locker room of the 2001 NBA Finals, when he looked like he'd either bleached or shaved off his eyebrows. Electronic music producer Moby had met Axl in 1997, describing him as, "a little bit like a beaten dog." This appeared to be the Axl Rose who spoke to sports commentator Fred Roggin in the Lakers' locker room; one who had long brownish-red hair and a vaguely urban accent and the sort of bashfulness you'd associate with someone who had never been in front of a camera before. He seemed lobotomized by his journey into the wilderness, as if Kurt Cobain had forced him to deconstruct every inch of body, sound, and psyche. "Nothing scares Axl more than a fear of failure," former manager Doug Goldstein once told me. Axl Rose had replaced himself.

He would perform at the 2002 VMAs in front a national TV audience, with a new face (Axl Rose was so unrecognizable that he actually had trouble getting into the venue without ID). The first reaction people had to his 2002 VMAs performance was that Axl looked like he was wearing clothes that were twice his size. He looked like a southern rapper. He also had artificial-looking dreadlocks, invisible eyebrows, and a blue bandana that never seemed to sit correctly on his head. For fans, it felt like a gut punch, like the night Mike Tyson had been knocked out by Buster Douglas in a world-shattering upset. Tyson was unbeatable. But on February 11, 1990, at the Tokyo Dome, he had been knocked out by a four-punch combo from a guy nobody had heard of. Tyson looked slightly like a "beaten dog." Rumors were rampant that he hadn't trained properly. He was, as *The New York Times* reported, "off-balance."

Axl Rose would run out of breath singing his signature song, "Welcome to the Jungle." The band was so thoroughly unprepared that bassist Tommy Stinson had expressed his reservations to Axl, who decided to fly them to New York with just 24 hours to rehearse. In the process, Slash had been replaced with a "stunt guy" wearing a Michael Myers mask and a KFC bucket over his head. A lot of viewers thought Buckethead head was just Slash in a Halloween costume. Slash would later tell Howard Stern that he refused to watch the performance. The rehearsal footage from those VMAs were later sold by a former MTV staffer, who shopped it on the black market for what one collector claimed was "somewhere around $6,000."

The one thing that everyone recalls from that night is that Axl Rose looked like he was going to faint. It felt like watching a once-great prize-fighter in the final round, wobbly, and begging for air. There were glimmers of Axl Rose, but it seemed to be suffocating underneath the mask he was wearing. His raspy falsetto was muted by the loudly incongruous traveling circus that surrounded him. There was bassist Tommy Stinson, a punk who wore a red plaid suit. There was former NIN guitarist Robin Finke, who had a powdered face and lipstick with his head shaved bald, except for a ponytail on the back of his skull. Axl wore an oversized Jerry Rice football jersey, a black leather bucket hat, and baggy leather jeans. The classic bullet logo on the bass drum had been reengineered into a Communist star with "GN'R" written in a Chinese-style font. For most viewers, Guns N' Roses had seemingly been reinvented into a communist rap-rock band.

Like a North Korean rocket being launched without an engineering check, Axl would sprint across the stage, pause, fiddle with his earpiece monitor, and try to catch his breath. He began to lose his breath right at the point in "Welcome to the Jungle" where there would customarily be a guitar solo, but because it was a medley, there wasn't one. He was suffocating in space. His voice began to sound like someone trying to have a phone conversation while jogging up a hill. By the time he caught his breath, Axl was like Tyson the day after Buster Douglas: when a god was transformed into a mortal. Watching the performance felt like the sort of tense anxiety you feel when you're about to watch your favorite character get killed on an episode of *Game of Thrones*. Nirvana alone did not end the mainstream appeal of Guns N' Roses. The 2002 MTV VMAs didn't, either, but they did leave us feeling like we'd just witnessed the moment when the invisibility of youth faded from Axl Rose. The aging process had begun in 1991.

Seven days after the release of *Use Your Illusion*, Nirvana released *Nevermind*, and on September 20, 1991, the music video for "Smells like Teen Spirit" premiered on MTV depicting a sepia-tinted and haunted high school gymnasium, where Kurt looked like a member of America's miserable student body turning the volume up on their angst. Even though Kurt's beauty was that of a teen idol, his face was covered in unshampooed hair and dark shadows.

Neil Young once said that Kurt Cobain's voice sounded wolfish. The sound was the by-product of a suffering caterwaul that came from deep within his irritated stomach, which suffered from ulcers, IBS, and drug abuse. The red irritation inside the wounded lining of his stomach was where Kurt would release his sorrow. If Axl's possessed a scream that exploded out of his professionally trained abdominals, then Kurt screamed from his poisoned belly like a wounded beast. His vibrato trembled with a country twang and a diction that would turn into strained desperation. Kurt's voice would crack as if the acid in his stomach was cooking it from below. There was nothing professional or industrial about it, while Axl's voice sounded like it required a pit crew to keep it operating at peak performance.

Kurt's singing wasn't always decipherable in the days before the internet, but the lyrics that grew through the cracks of his scream felt like the journal entries of the depressed teenagers in *Pump Up the Volume*. Nobody even knew what "Smells Like Teen Spirit" actually meant in 1991, but it sounded like a blend of *Carrie* with a mélange of doom metal and punk (which would define the sound of grunge). Kurt Cobain was setting MTV on fire and locking in all the jocks and beautiful people. "Smells like Teen Spirit" was an anti-capitalist brand that every teenager wanted to wear. When Nirvana first played the song at Seattle's OK Hotel on April 17, 1991, Kurt sarcastically introduced his band as "major label corporate rock sellouts." This was self-deprecation that Axl Rose never possessed. It was Kurt's acid-spewing flower emerging from the cuff of his unwashed flannel. It was there at the 1992 MTV VMAs.

Backstage at those VMAs, Courtney Love finally saw the opportunity to confront Axl in person. When the two bands' trailers were placed in close proximity to each other, the confrontation Courtney had courted for months fell right into her lap. When their paths crossed, the two couples were drawn into a duel when Courtney screamed at Axl to be the godfather of her child (other reports suggest she was screaming obscenities at Axl). Axl was being filmed for a documentary; he was surrounded with a posse of 20 to "50 bodyguards: huge, gigantic, brain-dead oafs, ready to kill," which Kurt would later say to further sell the difference between the two couples. Axl, who was holding Stephanie Seymour's hand, ignored Courtney and piercingly gazed at Kurt, demanding that he *shut his bitch up* or he would take him "down to the pavement." You also have to take into account that at this point, Axl Rose probably believed that Courtney Love was trying to possess his soul.

"He believes people are always trying to find a window through to control his energy," a friend of Axl's told *Rolling Stone*.

Through Kurt's childlike eyes, Axl must have looked like Charles Manson twiddling the ends of his graying beard and telling Tom Snyder that the only kind of women he liked were the ones who *kept their mouths shut*. For Courtney, who would have castrated Manson and taken over his family, this was an opportunity.

She was like a splashy gossip columnist chasing a lead on a scandal. Kurt was wearing an unwashed Daniel Johnston "Hi, How Are You" T-shirt and ripped jeans. He looked like a drawing being ripped out of a cluttered third-grader's sketchbook covered in torn stickers. He had scabs forming on his face. Courtney wore red lipstick and refused to use makeup to cover her bumpy acne. Axl wore a tucked-in shirt depicting a faded image of Michelangelo's *The Creation of Adam* with a long rosary hanging over it. His hair was straightened under a blue bandana that looked as if it had been ironed onto his head. Seymour looked chic in a strapless black couture dress and an elegant gothic choker around her neck in the style of the wedding cake scene from "November Rain." Her fame was a derivative of both her stoic beauty and glammed-up red carpet look.

In a 1994 *Vanity Fair* profile, Courtney's mother and therapist Linda Carroll said that "her fame is not about being beautiful and brilliant, which she is. It's about speaking in the voice of anguish of the world." A twist in the narrative is that on the red carpet of the 1997 Academy Awards, Courtney wore a low-cut white Versace dress and a diamond necklace and looked more like Marilyn Monroe than Nancy Spungen. At a party in 1995, Courtney tried to use Quentin Tarantino's Oscar to crack Lynn Hirschberg over the head. The same year at Lollapalooza, she slugged Kathleen Hanna. "That punch was so well deserved, I wouldn't take it back for anything," she told the *LA Weekly* in 2013. Courtney Love was blending pop star ambition with the fury of a roller-derby enforcer.

With history to guide us, we can now safely assume that the feud between Nirvana and Guns N' Roses were enflamed by Courtney Love's impishness. "The biggest star in this room is Courtney Love," said Thurston Moore in *1991: The Year Punk Broke*. The one undeniable feature of Courtney's wardrobe was that she would design herself into whatever costume was required to subvert the patriarchy. This was also her genius. Betraying people, including her own fan base, was how Courtney accumulated fame. She was a fame monster. Courtney's Machiavellian power play would become the main event backstage at the 1992 MTV VMAs, which was a face-off between the professionally styled and groomed nouveau riche and two Pacific Northwest junkies who'd blown all their cash on dope. "Nothing about Courtney is an accident," wrote Lynn Hirschberg in 1992. Indeed.

Depending on which story you read, Cobain was either bouncing his infant on his knee or holding her in his arms when Axl demanded he silence his wife, a woman who had never known the meaning of silence. The VMAs had turned into high school during a particularly tense recess, and the nerds were about to exact their revenge. This was their school shooting. In response to Axl's sexist demand, Kurt would sardonically say to Courtney, "OK, bitch—shut up!" A few people in the room chuckled, and Axl grabbed Stephanie's hand and began to angrily walk away, as Stephanie turned to Courtney and asked if she was a model. "No," replied Love. "Are you a brain surgeon?" It's hard to know if Kurt even realized that a portion of Axl's torment was a projection of the anger and resentment he felt towards Slash and Izzy, who had allowed heroin to turn Guns N' Roses into a band with a "built-in obsolescence." It wasn't just the difference in style, Axl viewed Kurt as a part of the same disease that nearly robbed him of his band. Kurt was, as *Hits* in 1992 would report, "slam dancing with Mr. Brownstone."

At the 1992 MTV Video Music Awards, "November Rain" won the Michael Jackson Video Vanguard Award, and video of the year went to Van Halen's "Right Now." In 1992, at the peak of Nirvana's boom, "November Rain" was the most-watched video on MTV. While it didn't immediately hurt their box-office appeal in 1992, for Gen-X teenagers who ironed band patches on their backpacks, Kurt Cobain's dismissal of Axl began the obsolescence process of Guns N' Roses. By the mid-1990s, Axl was like Bon Jovi through the eyes of Mike Judge's nihilistic defenders of rock purity, Beavis and Butt-Head:

Beavis: "Hey, Butt-Head, remember when these guys were *cool*?"

Butt-Head: "Ahhhh, no . . . you probably like these guys, *wuss*."

In July of 1993, Guns N' Roses ended their 28-month world tour like a half-demolished stock car that had been driven into the junkyard. By December 1993, when the $4-million video for "Estranged" in heavy-rotation on MTV, the network had already shifted gears towards a mass-promotional agenda centered around grunge or grunge pop. "Estranged" was a video that had twice the budget of "November Rain" and seemed about 10 times less popular. In November 1993, MTV would tape Nirvana's now-legendary *Unplugged* performance—which ran in 1994, when Guns N' Roses had seemingly vanished from popular culture (they had refused to do *Unplugged* and were never invited to do SNL). By the end of 1993, Kurt Cobain was the most famous and talked-about rock star on the planet.

At the 1993 MTV VMAs, it seemed grunge had taken hold of popular culture. Guns N' Roses didn't perform or get nominated. At the 1994 ceremony, Guns N' Roses simply didn't exist—while the ghost of Kurt Cobain haunted MTV. That night, Aerosmith, the band Guns N' Roses had mirrored themselves after, had managed to repackage themselves into a contemporary pop-rock band with the music video for "Cryin'," which won the Moonman for both Video of the Year and Viewer's Choice. In the video, a 17-year-old Alicia Silverstone looked like a grunge-pop extra from the set of *Empire Records* (1995). Aerosmith suddenly felt more contemporary than Guns N' Roses, who seemed to have been lowered into the same lava pit as the Terminator.

Between 1993 and 1995, Axl was tangled up in a jungle of litigation that included the Steven Adler lawsuit; two different lawsuits from Stephanie Seymour and Erin Everly (both in 1994); and a lawsuit from the fan he assaulted in St. Louis. While Axl was dealing with the collateral damage of being the CEO of the declining Guns N' Roses corporation, the ghost of Kurt Cobain was being deified to the status of saint. The only numbers we have to calculate the impact of Nirvana on the market value of Guns N' Roses is the release of *The Spaghetti Incident?* In November 1993, a punk covers record seemed like penitence for the overwrought *Use Your Illusion*. Even with the publicity generated by the Charles Manson cover, *The Spaghetti Incident?* would sell about 190,000 copies in its first week—debuting at number four on *Billboard*. It was an average showing. It also felt like Guns N' Roses desperately trying to reclaim some sense of purity. Following the suicide of Kurt Cobain, *MTV Unplugged in New York* was released in November 1994 by debuting at number one and moving 310,500 units in the first week. This would be the highest first-week sales numbers of Nirvana's career. Nielsen reports that 2008's *Chinese Democracy* sold 549,000 units in the first 12 weeks of release.

By 1999, a generation of teenagers felt more in common with the emotionally damaged school shooters than Axl Rose. The teenage killers at Columbine listened to techno, Rammstein, KMFDM, Nine Inch Nails, The Prodigy, White Zombie, The Chemical Brothers, Marilyn Manson,

The Offspring, and the soundtrack from *The Doom Generation* (1995). This was the generation who went through puberty with the trauma of constantly dreaming of what the splattered skull of Kurt Cobain must have looked like. This was the generation that blended Kurt Cobain's alienation with the stylized violence of *The Matrix* (1999).

The introverts were now in control. Kurt Cobain had wanted teenagers to choose between Nirvana and Guns N' Roses, and they chose Nirvana. When *Rolling Stone* asked Henry Rollins in 1993 to describe what was so important about new rock and roll, he replied that, "Nirvana slayed the hair bands. They shot the top off the poodles. All of a sudden, all those bands like Poison, Bon Jovi and Warrant became like Rommel in the desert: overextended, bloated, no more Vaseline. And now they're just rusty tanks in the desert with no gas. It's those bands like Nirvana, that came along at that time, who are going to be remembered for changing the face of rock."

Unofficially, at least, Guns N' Roses were no longer a band in 1994. After Kurt Cobain blew his brains out, *Kerrang!* took a poll to determine the shittiest things that happened in 1994. Number one was Kurt Cobain's death. Number four was the "Guns N' Roses split." They might not have been born together (the first Nirvana show was in 1987), but they both had funerals in the same year: 1994, which is when Slash began working on a solo album, which led to Axl threatening to sue if it contained any Guns N' Roses' material. They both saw the film *Interview with the Vampire* (1994): Slash though it was trash. Axl thought it was art. The critics thought it was both art and trash.

On March 31, 1994, Duff McKagan went to LAX to board a flight to Seattle, where he had recently bought a new home. Kurt Cobain was waiting to board the same flight. The two would then sit on the flight and chat all the way from L.A. to Seattle. After landing in Seattle, Duff claims that he had wanted to invite Kurt to his house, but it was never to be. Kurt jumped into a limousine and headed towards his Lake Washington home. On April 5, 1994, just six days after running into Duff at LAX, Kurt's body was found inside the greenhouse of his waterfront property.

"Consider the life of a teenager," said Hard Harry. "You have parents, teachers telling you what to do; you have movies, magazines and TV telling you what to do; but you know what you have to do."

Even though Kurt Cobain felt completely unqualified to be the voice of a generation, his suicide transformed him into the crucified Jesus printed across Axl's "Kill Your Idols" T-shirt. Because they never made peace, Axl will always be haunted by the specter of grunge. Kurt would be sanctified for leaving behind an egalitarian wardrobe, impenetrable authenticity, and an ageless portrait. The people drank his blood like Judean wine. Axl's portrait decomposes like Matt Mahurin's tragic painting of Johnny Depp from *Rolling Stone*, 2018. His wardrobe is as preposterously unfashionable as Michael Jackson. Kurt Cobain is the inspiration for the androgynous fashion runway that styles Brad Pitt in a sequined dress in *Rolling Stone*, and Harry Styles in a gown on the cover of *Vogue*.

Axl Rose's corrupted beauty and fluctuating weight has become a bizarre obsession. Kurt Cobain died before his beauty would fade. Everyone from Weezer to Billie Eilish have fragments of Kurt's aesthethic occupying their pop personas. Other than Lana Del Rey's flirtation with the ironic appeal of Axl Rose, his influence on modern culture is as unnoticeable as Van Halen (Billie Eilish once said that she had never heard of Van Halen). Axl Rose has become a curiosity for his middle-aged fans; his eccentricities have overwhelmed his art. A trip through Axl Rose's secluded Malibu estate seems more interesting today than his music. Because of Kurt's refusal to bequeath his blessings onto Axl, the *Last Supper* of rock and roll will always place Kurt in the position of Jesus, with Axl as the leering Judas—hidden away from our eyes. In "Victory or Death," Axl Rose chose to retreat into his cult of personality, while Kurt Cobain chose death. Neither of them were victorious.

10

BETTER OFF DEAD

"THE WORLD CHANGES . . . WE DO NOT.
THEREIN LIES THE IRONY THAT FINALLY KILLS US."

—INTERVIEW WITH THE VAMPIRE (1994)

"I've learned that when certain traumas happen to you," Axl told *RIP* magazine in 1992, "your brain releases chemicals that get trapped in the muscles where the trauma occurred. They stay there for your whole life." This was Axl Rose at 30. "Then, when you're 50 years old, you've got bad legs or a bent back."

On April 1, 2016, the Troubadour marquee had turned Santa Monica's gay borough into a dazzling premiere. Fans gazed at the plastic letters that formed what looked like an illusion: "Guns N' Roses Not In This Lifetime . . ." For Guns N' Roses fans, it was going to be Elvis's triumphant '68 TV special. It was going to be the rebirth of Guns N' Roses at the same sacred spot where they played their first show on June 6, 1985. It was going to be the resurrection of Axl Rose.

Axl would strut onto the stage after nearly two decades of hasty career decisions and swoon us with his gimlet-eyed stare and six-octave vocal range. He would appear to us in an intimate light. He would be recharged as a physical specimen that looked boisterously confident in skintight jeans and vintage cowboy boots. Between songs, he'd release a cloud of sentimentality into the air, and perhaps throw a small tantrum—we wanted to see him throw one, it was part of his "greatest hits."

Axl would have a mischievous gleam in his eye, as he'd look over to Slash, engulfed in jungle of hair, as their admirers in the front row shook like they were being healed by a televangelist's bejeweled touch. It would be the first time Axl and Slash would share a stage since the Use Your Illusion Tour ended in Buenos Aires on July 17, 1993. They were reunited on the same stage where they played their first *Appetite*-era show together on June 6, 1985. But it didn't seem real. It still doesn't

In 2009, Axl described Slash as a "cancer" in an interview with Del James. "In a nutshell, personally I consider him a cancer and better removed, avoided, and the less anyone heard of him or his supporters the better." He would describe Slash as, "a whore for the limelight."

In 2010, TMZ reported that security at a Guns N' Roses show had informed fans that they could not bring their Slash top hats into the venue. Slash T-shirts were to be turned inside out or taken off. "What's clear is that one of the two of us will die before a reunion," Axl told *Billboard* in 2009. "However sad, ugly or unfortunate anyone views it, it is how it is." Even when they reunited, Axl would accuse Slash of having produced an autobiography filled with inaccuracies. He would privately accuse Slash of "ripping off" guitar solos from Pink Floyd's David Gilmour. Axl credited Slash's costly divorce with ex-wife Perla Hudson as a catalyst for the reunion. Perla, like Erin Everly before her, would auction off her ex-husband's memorabilia in an "uncoupling auction" that included Slash's MTV Moonman for "Welcome to the Jungle," which sold for $40,625.

But what led to the negotiated peace between Slash and Axl? There were no answers. The fact that we don't have a clear answer suggests the situation is as sensitive as a brokered peace between Palestine and Israel. Axl's management (i.e., "Team Brazil"), according to one source, is dedicated to sheltering Axl from emotional triggers that could derail the reunion. As of this writing, Axl Rose (or Team Brazil on behalf of him) have declined interviews by Jimmy Kimmel, Jimmy Fallon, *Rolling Stone*,

Billboard, Howard Stern, *Spin*, Eddie Trunk, *LA Weekly*, and the *L.A. Times* (just to name a few). He's being cloistered, but from what? What these are is unclear. Led by Stephanie Seymour's former nanny, Beta Lebeis, Team Brazil acts as a ministry of information that goes beyond the traditional role of "gatekeeper" for Axl Rose. When Axl and Slash met in secret to discuss the possibility of reforming Guns N' Roses, Fernando Lebeis, Beta's son, had taken a self-congratulatory selfie—with Slash and Axl in the background—and sent it around to friends. For those who've seen the photo, the message is clear: Team Brazil orchestrated the meeting.

On April 1, standing in the pit of the Troubadour, I began to dream of a coda where Axl would sit on a leather stool next to Slash, who would be strumming an acoustic number, and we could sing along to with the swaying flames from colorful plastic lighters. It would be an emotional cleanse; all the blogs would proclaim that the Las Vegas version of Guns N' Roses had been reinvented into the Guns N' Roses that blasted through MTV like a screaming submachine gun. Axl had been working with a physical trainer (we had seen photos of him on the beaches of Malibu). He had begun to tastefully edit his wardrobe to look less like Sly Stallone at a Vegas pool party (which had been his look for most of the 2010s).

In preparation for the *resurrection*, Guns N' Roses had relaunched their classic bullet logo after 16 years of Chinese propaganda art. It was like finding out MTV was playing music videos again. It was to be a rapturous night, one that would relieve any anxiety that Axl or Slash would die before they could reunite. The clock had been ticking for two decades. Axl must have felt like an aging diva booked to play Carnegie Hall; no extravagance or pomposity, just Axl delivering a comeback special that would electrify the spirit of American hard rock. Nostalgia for the Sunset Strip was momentarily back in vogue, with no dissenting opinion. Courtney Love had been demonized into obscurity. Nirvana was mostly a fashion statement on Instagram.

What actually happened on April 1 is foggy. Depending on who you ask, it was either Judy Garland at Carnegie Hall or the rock-and-roll equivalent of the space shuttle *Challenger* tragedy: Led Zeppelin at Live Aid

1985. "The machinery, like the nation itself, seemed unprepared to cope with a mission that went up and didn't come back down." This is how *Newsweek* reported on the *Challenger* explosion in 1986. What were we about to witness? Under the blue glow of sterile LED lights, Slash would play his guitar with as little emotion as possible. The poundage showed, but besides that, it was definitely Slash, not a "hired gun" (which is what Guns N' Roses had been for nearly two decades). Slash would exchange no words with Axl. He was dissociated, precise, and completely professional. Standing behind them was a stylish Asian woman with bluish-green hair; she would spend the rest of the evening bouncing behind a synthesizer and adding texture to Axl Rose's high-pitched falsetto. Her name was Melissa Reese. On the opposite side of the stage, Duff McKagan stood under a light that made his skin look like it had seen more sunrises than an Apache. I began studying about 500 mesmerized fans who looked as if they were about to witness the resurrection of Christ. They were the "bug-eyed natives confronted by a Zippo lighter" in *Infinite Jest*. The flame was Axl Rose. He was standing next to Slash. The significance of this for Guns N' Roses fans cannot be understated. No analogy will do. Jaws were detached from their skulls.

Fanboys, models, ghosts from their past, and a handpicked group of celebrities were crammed into the Troubadour for what felt like the most anticipated rock reunion of all time. Nicolas Cage peered down from the balcony like a ten-thousand-year-old vampire. He was practically hypno-tized for 17 songs. "He looked like a ghost," said an onlooker. When he walked onto the stage, Axl had on a studded leather jacket with a cowboy hat sitting over drenched and stringy hair that might or might not have been his actual hair. This is part of the many mysteries of Axl's mystifying appearance, which would go through wardrobe changes at the frequency of Lady Gaga at the Super Bowl. He went backstage six times for five different wardrobe changes. Persistent tabloid rumors of Botox, face-lifts, eyebrow dying, hair implants, and pharmaceuticals had turned his appear-ance into an attraction. Everyone has a version of Axl Rose they want to see. There's the bestial, rabid dog from "Welcome to the Jungle." There's the Gulf War pinup doll from 1991. Some of us wanted the dreadlocked cyborg from 2006. Everyone has a type.

The Axl Rose of 2016 was a postmodern blend of every previous version of Axl Rose. Dangling from Axl's chest was a diamond-encrusted crucifix you'd normally see hanging off the neck of a trap rapper. His hands looked as if they'd been decorated by a professional stylist who studied publicity photos of Liberace and Elizabeth Taylor. His eyes looked puffy when he removed his aviator sunglasses. His fragile yet sharply masculine beauty had morphed into a cosmetically complicated artifice. We weren't allowed to take any photos. All electronic devices were confiscated and then hermetically sealed. There were those who were so overwhelmed by the experience that they looked frozen into the ground; others looked like they were giddily feeding off the adrenaline like Patrick Swayze's crazy-eyed surfer in *Point Break* (1990). Like Francis Fukuyama witnessing the crumbling of the Berlin Wall in 1989, it felt like the "End of History." We were free. There was another group who felt like what we were witnessing was a *simulation*.

I hadn't slept for 24 hours. I stood in the pit and frenetically took notes in what felt like an altered state of consciousness. I was transformed by the spectacle, insomnia, and flood of nostalgia pouring over me. I had become vulnerable and childlike in my gaze. I was hooked on dopamine like an infant sucking on superhuman mother's milk. I was awash in it, which is what I've deduced to be the cause of my amnesia. I remember very little from that night. The next morning, crawling out of bed with my review already posted, all I remembered were flashes that were as imperceptible as Erin Everly in the video for "It's So Easy." I couldn't recognize what I had written. My brain had been washed by the experience. It took me nearly two years of self-interrogation to understand what had happened. When I went home that night, I wrote a review for the *LA Weekly* that seemed like the work of a Guns N' Roses' patriot. It was entirely off-balance and the product of what I would argue in a court of law as a state of "temporary insanity." The psychological effect of a yearlong publicity campaign by Guns N' Roses had essentially murdered my objective mind.

To be a journalist and have to report objectively on the fulfillment of a childhood fantasy is damn near impossible. I failed to do my job; but then again, this was a job that nobody had done before.

Standing among the Axl Rose parishioners felt like being pulled into a pilgrimage that began with a short UPROXX documentary in 2015 titled *One Man's Plan to Reunite Guns N' Roses*, and exploded at Troubadour on April Fool's Day, which was now a Guns N' Roses ride. We waited in line for 11 hours to get our wristbands at the old Tower Records, at around 4 a.m., another hour so to get into the venue the following night at about 10 p.m. By the time I walked into the Troubadour a few minutes past midnight, on April 2nd, when I felt like I was consumed by my own two-decade-long need to view Guns N' Roses through my second-generation MTV eyes. Maybe I was trying to give my uneventful, suburban existence a jolt by submitting myself to the wave of emotion, like teenagers who once melted when Elvis shook his hips or experienced orgiastic joy when Mick Jagger puckered his lips. It was the closest I would ever get to fainting into a puddle of my own childhood fantasies. Imagine being a child in their pajamas unwrapping a box containing a Super Nintendo. That was me.

A few months after the Troubadour show, I was emailed a link to high-definition recording of the "Sweet Child O' Mine" performance. It was the only footage I would ever see from that night. I quickly realized my *LA Weekly* review was the product of a form of insanity. What I was watching on my laptop could not have been what I had witnessed that night. Had I suffered from some kind of cognitive glitch? Had toxic levels of fandom wrapped a bandana around my eyes? There was something extremely troubling about the footage; every imperfection was magnified. I had reviewed Guns N' Roses at Coachella for both *LA Weekly* and *Spin*, simultaneously, with a 100-degree fever after vomiting into a toilet bowl and requiring an emergency Z-Pak. I was hallucinating when I wrote those two reviews, clinging to the rim of a toilet bowl. Yet I remember every detail. I have zero recall from the Troubadour. All I have are my notes.

Watching the footage was exhilarating, but also crushing. Axl's eyes looked vacant. He was sweating profusely. His falsetto was wobbly and inconsistent. This is what it must have felt like watching Elvis during his last days, who looked like he was going to internally combust into a pool of Quaaludes and peanut butter, and yet, especially on the coda of "Unchained Melody," his lungs would momentarily expand and unleash the heavens. That was Axl Rose at age 54, as Kate Hudson peered on from the balcony with a look of both vague amusement and mystified curiosity. Is that really Axl Rose? He looked like he'd manage to purge all of his demons (including the ones that burned the coals powering his scorching vocals). In the coming months, I would come to find out that Axl Rose was a Democrat and defender of animal rights. In January 2019, I emailed writer Chuck Klosterman to get his thoughts on the reinvention of Axl Rose:

> I find it pretty fascinating, but I don't really think it's a reinvention. I don't think this is any kind of a career move. I think that—by essentially removing himself from the public sphere for 10 years during the 1990s and early 2000s—he incrementally became a totally different person. If you look at the guy he was in 1989, his whole identity was built around expressing whatever he happened to feel within the same moment he felt it, regardless of the context or how that message was received. That's actually the same way he is now. It's just that the feelings he feels are wildly different. Now, why did that happen? I'm not certain. But my suspicion is that he spent a very long time compulsively analyzing his own personality, and the end result of that process (for him, or really for anyone) usually prompts a person to evolve in an unexpected direction. The paradox of isolation is that it usually changes someone more radically than the experience of interacting with society.

Next to Axl Rose stood a guitar player in a buttoned-down red shirt that exposed his rippled physique and designer tattoos. The hardbody in the red shirt was swinging his arms around as if he were playing in front of seventy thousand people at Wembley Stadium. His name was Richard

Fortus, and he looked like the combination of an Argentinian soccer star and playable character in *Guitar Hero*. Izzy Stradlin was home, either in Ojai or Malibu, or perhaps Lafayette, but he wasn't at the Troubadour. Izzy was the most prolific songwriter in Guns N' Roses, and yet the band had collectively decided that his deal to join the reunion would include a much smaller share of revenue than the other members. Izzy's departure in 1991, along with his mercurial nature, in general, had turned him into a liability. He would announce his side on things on Twitter on September 7, 2016: "Bullshit," he wrote. "They didn't want to split the loot equally. Simple as that. Moving right along . . ." Izzy would not appear on a stage with Guns N' Roses at Coachella, when a jumbo screen played a video of skeletons performing sex acts, which was followed by synchronized pyro explosions and bursts of confetti.

Speaking to *MuchMusic* in 1988, Axl Rose criticized KISS for being more theatrical than musical. "Our music comes first," he said. Depending on your definition of "Guns N' Roses," they haven't released new and original music since 1991 or 2008. Axl Rose has put his songwriting in a subordinate position to the business of running Guns N' Roses. Part of my review would appear in Paul Elliot's coffee table book on Guns N' Roses, in which I am quoted as saying: "Axl was all smiles. He looked reinvigorated, constantly pushing his vocals to prove that he's still got what it takes to lead this band. The only question is: how long will this new chapter last?"

During such a spectacle, the audience becomes part of the illusion. They dance along with the performers on stage and help them forget that they are no longer the performers they once were. After the show, the fans collect memorabilia and cover themselves in the warm blanket of nostalgia in order to shield themselves from the brain-freezing reality. They use the illusion of Guns N' Roses to help them re-experience the pleasures of their childhood. They relinquish their rationality in order to get lost in the moment.

Over five million people would attend the Not In This Lifetime Tour. There was even chatter in 2017 that Guns N' Roses would perform at the Super Bowl. They did not. Perhaps it helped preserve the fantasy. All I could think of were photos from the 2011 Super Bowl, when Slash played "Sweet Child O' Mine" with Fergie, when he wore a hideously decorated top hat. I remember Fergie snake-dancing next to him in sparkling shoulder pads. It looked like a Guns N' Roses–themed cabaret. Slash had become a confirmation of Kurt Cobain's view of Guns N' Roses. "Rebellion," Kurt would say in 1992, "is standing up to people like Guns N' Roses." Slash, Saul Hudson, and Slash, the Guitar Hero avatar, had become one. He looked like a Las Vegas magician.

A year into their blockbuster reunion tour, and Guns N' Roses were like a fully operational 360 marketing agency. Aside from a relentless blitz of social media advertising and confusing brand partnerships, they were selling merchandise that had begun to defy logic. The simulation felt like it was experiencing a virus. Guns N' Roses would create a separate website to merchandise their private plane. You could preorder "GNAIR" flight pins, hoodies, T-shirts, and aviator sunglasses; Guns N' Roses were selling merchandise based entirely on the aesthetic of their private plane. They also sold toy models of the 18-wheeler trucks that would cargo their equipment from city to city. Team Brazil even produced a *Sweet Child o' Mine* children's book. In December 2018, Axl made a cameo in a rebooted *Looney Tunes* cartoon, where he would defend Earth from an incoming asteroid by singing "Rock the Rock." Guns N' Roses had become KISS.

In 2016, Axl Rose partnered with Swiss watch sponsor, HYT, who designed a skull watch made from "Damascus steel style." The "opposing elements" from Jane Boswell's classroom had been commodified into a status symbol priced at over $100,000 (which Axl wore on tour). A year after the 30th anniversary of *Appetite for Destruction*, Guns N' Roses would release a thousand-dollar box set that looked as minimalistic as the cremation urn of a Russian mobster, which was packed with things like a handmade 3D cross, custom metal guitar picks, temporary tattoos, two collectible coins, one numbered certificate of authenticity, unreleased demos, and a sterilized video for "It's So Easy." During the marketing of the *Locked N' Loaded* box set, the Guns N' Roses equivalent of a purge occurred. Around the spring of 2018, rare Guns N Roses pro-shot concert footage and bootlegs began to disappear from YouTube. The RIAA and IFPI (the Recording Industry Association of America and International Federation of the Phonographic Industry, respectively) had begun to aggressively remove copyrighted material from YouTube. Curated YouTube channels such as Gibbos, Ms. Metal, Frans N' Roses, which contained gorgeously remastered and pro-shot concert footage—a curatorial wet dream—were flagged and then removed from YouTube for copyright violations. Some fans suggested the record label, Universal Music Group (UMG), had taken action in order to increase interest in the "rarities" contained in the *Locked N' Loaded* box set. The popularity of pro-shot bootlegs from the Use Your Illusion Tour—including Saskatoon 1993, which was leaked by a Japanese bootlegger—had overshadowed the contents of the *Lock N' Loaded* box set. A large number of Guns N' Roses fans believe that Team Brazil partnered with online trolls to flag the YouTube channels, doxx, and intimidate creators into extinguishing their channels, which now operate in secrecy.

Because of Guns N' Roses' draught of rereleases, licensed footage, authorized band biographies, or new releases of any kind, the YouTube channels provided a visual (and audio) history of a band that seems to be allergic to their past, which they've been burying for the past three decades. "Axl Rose's Appetite is for Today's Guns N' Roses," wrote the *L.A. Times* in 2011.

Other than a thousand-dollar box set, Guns N' Roses basically ignored the 30th anniversary of *Appetite*—which is the best-selling debut in US history. Most attempts at merchandising their history have been disappointing. In 2014, Team Brazil orchestrated the release of a 3D concert film of a previous Guns N' Roses Las Vegas residency titled *Appetite for Democracy 3D*, which includes Axl performing "November Rain" on a gambling-themed piano, while his bandmates bathe in a waterfall of pyrotechnics. Axl does this on a levitating platform that's a mélange of Keith Emerson's flying piano and Tommy Lee's spinning drum set. The footage offers a glimpse of the band that Guns N' Roses were making fun of in 1987. The divine madness that had produced *Appetite for Destruction* had been extinguished.

Some of the YouTube accounts had been active for 15 years. It's unclear who exactly was responsible for instigating the purge, but for fans, who had relied on YouTube to connect with the history of Guns N' Roses, it felt like a book burning orchestrated by both the record label and Guns N' Roses' management. The accusation that Guns N' Roses were involved partially connected to DMCA takedown notices from 2016. *Rolling Stone* reported that Axl Rose's attorneys had issued takedown notices to remove a portly photo of the singer from Google search results and other related websites. The photo had become the basis for viral "Fat Axl" memes. Its origins are linked to a *Winnipeg Free Press* concert review dated January 14, 2010, which was taken during a Chinese Democracy Tour stop at the MTS Centre. The photo was taken by Boris Minkevich, but Axl's lawyers argued that he did not own the copyright. Every photographer who attends a Guns N' Roses show must sign an agreement that transfers all photo copyrights over to Axl's management. The "Fat Axl" photo itself looks like a funny page illustration of Axl doing a feverish back pedal. It looks like Sam Kinison riding a skateboard. The photographer captured him in the middle of the move, where his hair, wrapped tightly under a bandana, looked like it was defying gravity. The memes it generated provided gustatory amusement:

Welcome to the baker . . . we got pies and cakes

Oh, Oh, Oh . . . Sweet Pie O' Mine

Knock Knock Knockin' . . . on McDonald's Door

In the summer of 2019, it was reported that over 97 unreleased *Chinese Democracy* tracks had begun to leak across the internet. It was described by one fan as the "motherload." The source of the leak was a storage locker in Virginia. The renter of the unit was a familiar name: former Geffen A&R rep Tom Zutaut, who defaulted on the rent for the locker (thus relinquishing ownership of its contents). The Zutaut locker was filled with gold records, artwork, memorabilia, and unreleased *Chinese Democracy* demos that Zutaut would keep cloistered inside a box inside his home. The demos included the mythic track "Atlas Shrugged," a sweeping epic that fans had been obsessing over for a decade. It was not released on *Chinese Democracy* in 2008, as Axl had been planning a sequel. The sequel had now leaked. The CDs were never supposed to be in the storage unit, but during a move from Virginia to Tennessee, some of Zutaut's private collection was left behind. These were *Chinese Democracy* DAT tapes from 2001, that had now been transferred to 20 different CDs (which contained unreleased music from 1999–2001, including an extremely rare recording with Queen's Brian May). When Zutaut defaulted on the rent, he relinquished ownership of the storage locker over to the owners of the facility, who decided to auction off the locker. In the procession of an entertprising new owner, the CDs were destined for the black market. First, the CDs were sold to a collector in New York for $12,000, then, digital copies containing the files—loaded onto a thumb drive—were sold to a group of investors for $15,000. Additional copies of the CDs were made.

Superfan Rick Dunsford was part of the group of investors. Dunsford is an unusually committed fan: his body is covered in tattoos depicting the autographs of Guns N' Roses' members. Through the indefatigable drive related to his fandom, Dunsford found the individual with the "motherload" in their possession and proceeded to strike a deal. Dunsford is a bit of a micro-celebrity in the Guns N' Roses' community (he's been known to buy and share rare bootlegs in the past). After purchasing the drive (which contained all 97 songs), the CDs began to appear on eBay. Dunsford shared DIY teaser clips with members of the Guns N' Roses' community, who began leaking the audio in fan forums. What proceeded was a chaotic episode of damage control, suppression, behind-the-scenes negotiation, and high drama. Team Brazil contacted Rick Dunsford, who was paid $15,000 (a "refund check," he described it) to deliver the flash drive to Guns N' Roses and stop sharing the files. He agreed. A few days later, more files began to appear on the internet. Suddenly, all 97 tracks had been leaked (some reports suggest as much as 144 tracks leaked). Dunsford was "banned for life" from attending Guns N' Roses shows, and Universal Music Group (UMG) was threatening to sue him. Dunsford insists that he did not leak the files.

Tom Zutaut, who discovered and signed Guns N' Roses in 1986, was last seen working at a Hyundai dealership in Georgia. Axl Rose was no longer posting in fan forums, but one suspects the leaks have jeopardized any future plans of any kind of *Chinese Democracy* sequel. Axl Rose hasn't tweeted about it. In fact, he hasn't even been interviewed by a legitimate journalist in years. In 2013, he told *The Advertiser* in Australia that he was writing an autobiography. In a rare interview with the *L.A. Times* in 2011, he said that, "It was really a fight with me and Slash," after being asked about what broke-up Guns N' Roses. "Izzy was doing the same thing, but the fight with me and Slash started the day I met him. He came in, popped my tape out and put his in and wanted me in his band. And I didn't want to join his band. We've had that war since Day 1."

Axl Rose has told previous PR people and confidants that he will never do interviews with *Rolling Stone*, *Spin*, or *NME*, which he views as enemies in his three-decade "Get in the Ring" war with the media. We still don't know how Axl and Slash made up. Since the reunion tour was announced in 2016, Axl Rose has not done an interview with a mainstream media outlet.

At their peak, Guns N' Roses produced the effect of flipping through the pages of a sex magazine during Bible study. Their videos were mini-films that defined the last days of an MTV generation; their concerts produced disaster-movie levels of anxiety. There was a brief moment in the history of popular culture when witnessing Axl Rose produced the experience of having an orgasm on a roller-coaster drop (i.e., *Fear*, 1996). Over the years, they managed to produce a handful of pop songs that are omnipresent on the same classic rock radio that now plays "Smells Like Teen Spirit." Yet in terms of every micro-generation that has emerged in the past three decades, Guns N' Roses' cultural influence is undetectable beyond merchandising and hotly debated fan forum discussions. Grunge has been sewed in the threads and attitudes of Generation Z. It's a popular item filling Instagram closets across the word, from Japan to Barcelona. Hip-hop has changed the way millennials communicate on social media. Emo bands have fueled shopping mall trends and YA novels. Guns N' Roses has become a retro subculture. By the 2000s, the audience of Guns N' Roses had dwindled. The 2002 MTV VMAs may have been the last time Axl Rose captivated the attention of the nation.

"When you're old," Axl told *RIP*, "it's too hard to carry the weight of the world that you've kept trapped inside your body."

Atlas shrugged, but his back was no longer being crushed under the weight of being the torchbearer of "raw impulse and emotion" that's now buried in Paris under flowers, cassette tapes, melted candle wax, and sheets of French poetry. Axl Rose never fulfilled the doom prophecy of Jim Morrison. He became a wealthy, 60-year-old eccentric who disappeared in the bucolic hills of Malibu. He's isolated himself into a cocoon of luxury and excess. He had calmed his nerves with aristocratic indulgences. He's relinquished the madness that produced the visuals that defined him. Whatever it was that saved his life also deprived him of what Kant would have described as a *terrifying sublimity*.

In 1949's *Knock on Any Door*, actor John Derek plays a baby-faced hood accused of murdering a cop. He repeats his motto to his loyal miss: "Live fast, die young and have a good-looking corpse." The dialogue is taken from the novel the film is based on, by Willard Motley, who was said to be "recycling street talk." James Dean is said to have romanticized the motto. Lana Del Rey used it to turn her fatalism into postmodern art on "Driving in Cars with Boys," where she repeats the motto of "live fast, die young." She repeats it on "Ride." Neil Young turned it into poetry for 1979's "Hey Hey, My My (Into the Black)," singing that "It's better to burn out than to fade away." The lyric appears in Kurt Cobain's suicide note, which is the final testament of a rock star who seemed to also have the "built-in obsolescence" Jagger argued Axl had in 1989, when he was "set on self-destruct." Before taking his life, Kurt Cobain seemed like a man who could no longer bear to look at himself in the mirror. I believe Axl Rose was this person for much of the '90s, except he never pulled the trigger. His fascination with James Dean never turned him into a beautiful corpse. He never ran with the Devil. Looking back at the legacy of "Howl," Ginsburg described it as "an emotional time bomb that would continue exploding." That is my memory of Axl Rose on MTV, as I watched Kurt Loder describe the collateral damage of my generation's Jim Morrison. It's the Axl who would turn revolt into a style, which is how poet Thom Gunn described a youthful Elvis Presley. But that Elvis died when he started doing karate kicks in rhinestone jumpsuits. The Axl Rose who defined my generation died somewhere between the 1994 Rock and Roll Hall of Fame ceremony and the year 2000—somewhere in the wilderness of time. Like D.H. Lawrence, "I weep like a child for the past."

In death, Jim Morrison fulfilled the canonical rockist fantasy of Jim Morrison. Axl Rose never fulfilled his "self-immolation trip." He became the "Howard Hughes of Rock," not its James Dean. He buried the illusion, just as he had buried *Appetite*. He now occupies a discombobulated matrix in American culture, where his myth is inseparable from his biography. For Guns N' Roses fans, they are a dazzling arena-rock spectacle on par with U2 and the Rolling Stones. For others, they rot away in a gothic graveyard filled with the decomposing roses and the maggot-infested skulls of an extinct civilization. Perhaps the spiderwebs that have wrapped themselves around their tombstones will be brushed away for one final vivid moment of blue skies and rainbow arches, like Mickey Rourke's *The Wrestler* (2008), who entered the arena lifted by the billowing clouds of "Sweet Child O' Mine" and exited in a body bag filled with unanswered questions.